Postsecular Benjamin

Postsecular Benjamin

Agency and Tradition

✦

Brian Britt

NORTHWESTERN UNIVERSITY PRESS
EVANSTON, ILLINOIS

Northwestern University Press
www.nupress.northwestern.edu

Printed in the United States of America

10 9 8 7 6 5 4 3 2 1

Library of Congress Cataloging-in-Publication Data

Names: Britt, Brian M., 1964– author.
Title: Postsecular Benjamin : agency and tradition / Brian Britt.
Description: Evanston, Illinois : Northwestern University Press, 2016. | Includes bibliographical references and index.
Identifiers: LCCN 2015049030 | ISBN 9780810133198 (pbk. : alk. paper) | ISBN 9780810133204 (cloth : alk. paper) | ISBN 9780810133211 (e-book)
Subjects: LCSH: Benjamin, Walter, 1892–1940. | Benjamin, Walter, 1892–1940—Religion. | Philosophy and religion. | Philosophy, Modern. | Postsecularism.
Classification: LCC B3209.B584 B74 2016 | DDC 093—dc23
LC record available at http://lccn.loc.gov/2015049030

To Jessie, Lucy, and Anna

CONTENTS

ILLUSTRATIONS

ACKNOWLEDGMENTS

Many colleagues and friends have supported my work on this project with thoughtful suggestions, detailed comments, and challenging questions. I am especially grateful to Daniel Weidner, Lucy Britt, Alexander van der Haven, Michael Jennings, Benjamin Sax, Eli Friedlander, Gal Hertz, Sigrid Weigel, Jonathan Boyarin, Ananda Abeysekara, Eric Santner, John McCole, Antonio Vazquez Arroyo, Stephen Britt, Francois Debrix, and Ilit Ferber. I also wish to thank two anonymous reviewers for Northwestern University Press. Every part of this project developed in dialogue with colleagues and students, at conferences and in the classroom. I am particularly grateful to the students who participated in my seminar on Benjamin at Virginia Tech in the fall 2010 semester.

Generous fellowship and grant support from Virginia Tech, the German Academic Exchange Service (DAAD), and the Zentrum für Literatur- und Kulturforschung in Berlin enabled me to research and write this book. The staff of the Walter Benjamin Archiv in Berlin, Ursula Marx, Erdmut Wizisla, and Michael Schwarz, along with the wonderful librarians at Berlin's Zentrum für Literatur- und Kulturforschung, Halina Hackert and Jana Lubasch, provided patient and invaluable assistance for my research.

I wish to thank Henry Carrigan and Gianna Francesca Mosser at Northwestern University Press for their thoughtful support and careful guidance from this project's beginning to its completion.

Two chapters of this book appeared in earlier versions. An earlier version of chapter 5 appeared as "Göttliche Gewalt bei Benjamin und in der biblischen Erzählung," in *Profanes Leben: Walter Benjamins Dialektik der Säkularisierung*, ed. Daniel Weidner (Berlin: Suhrkamp, 2010), 263–86. In addition, a version of chapter 7 appeared in *Benjamin-Studien* 3 (2014): 83–104.

ABBREVIATIONS

Arcades	Walter Benjamin, *The Arcades Project.* Translated by Howard Eiland and Kevin McLaughlin. Cambridge, Mass.: Harvard University Press, 1999.
Briefe	Walter Benjamin, *Briefe.* 2 vols. Edited by Gershom Scholem and Theodor Adorno. Frankfurt: Suhrkamp, 1966.
Corr WB	Walter Benjamin, *The Correspondence of Walter Benjamin, 1910–1940.* Edited by Gershom Scholem and Theodor Adorno, translated by Manfred R. Jacobson and Evelyn M. Jacobson. Chicago: University of Chicago Press, 1994.
GS	Walter Benjamin, *Gesammelte Schriften.* 7 vols. Edited by Rolf Tiedemann and Hermann Schweppenhäuser. Frankfurt: Suhrkamp, 1989.
GTD	Walter Benjamin, *The Origin of German Tragic Drama.* Translated by John Osborne. London: New Left Books, 1977.
SW	Walter Benjamin, *Selected Writings.* Edited by Marcus Bullock and Michael W. Jennings. Cambridge, Mass.: Harvard University Press, 1996–2003.

Postsecular Benjamin

INTRODUCTION

No one would deny the place of religion in the work of Walter Benjamin (1892–1940), but no one has been able to build a scholarly consensus around it. For some a touchstone and for others an embarrassment, religion in Benjamin's work sometimes marks a boundary between scholarly camps, but it rarely faces close and sustained scrutiny. This book locates Benjamin's engagements with religious tradition in his own time and relates them to contemporary debates on secularism, tradition, and human agency. My central thesis is that Benjamin's conceptions of tradition and agency make an important contribution to modern religious thought and offer resources on current debates over secularism and religion.

Benjamin's most influential writings pertain to modern art and culture, but he consistently challenges modern secularism. Religious language and discussion appear in his early and late work, but he rejected all forms of orthodoxy and return to religion. Benjamin was, in today's terms, post-secular. There could be no simple division between religious and secular history or phenomena, according to Benjamin; instead, even the modern present belongs within the broad context of tradition. Benjamin's conception of tradition is paradoxical and nuanced: the past always informs the present, even when we deny it, but tradition is always dynamic and open to new realities. Literary and religious traditions of textual commentary provide models of tradition; without keen interpretive perception, we cannot recognize the significant of the present.[1] Institutional religion plays little role in his understanding, yet he argues forcefully and consistently that religion is central even to modernist art and culture that reject tradition. Jewish identity runs through his life and work, yet he also engages with German Christian tradition. The survival and afterlife of tradition permeate Benjamin's writings at all stages, though he contests systematic models of history. What does animate Benjamin's engagement with tradition is lively and sustained experimentation with ways of thinking, reading, and writing, practices that lead to the question of human agency.

How did he reconcile these interests in tradition and modernity? Like many thinkers, Benjamin saw analogies between premodern and modern culture, particularly in textual and creative practices of commentary, quotation, citation, and montage.[2] Through these practices and the dynamics they convey, texts and traditions survive into modernity in spite of pressures to overcome the past and secularize themselves. How these new formations relate to earlier ones is not always clear, but in Benjamin's work one can see many attempts to do so. What emerges from these attempts is a conception of tradition that includes modernity and challenges the binary division of religion and secularity. Through a wide variety of texts for a wide range of audiences, Benjamin posed questions about tradition and modernity that were rarely asked elsewhere, combining topics like religion and politics in original ways. And it was through this kind of experimentation with writing that Benjamin also engaged the question of agency.

Modern thought typically identifies agency with the free individual. In the eyes of law and custom alike, this moral agent can be held responsible for actions as their origin and cause. Freed from such pressures as the religious institutions described in Kant's "What Is Enlightenment?," this modern subject enjoys unprecedented autonomy and freedom to take actions. The modern agent is thus secular and individualistic. Recent challenges to this conception of agency from social science, history, and postmodern theory have raised doubts whether it is possible to assign full responsibility and agency to people as free individuals, raising the question how if at all agency can be conceptualized. Others, like Anthony Giddens, agree with postmodern efforts to decenter the self but affirm a social theory of agency in which individuals choose courses of action within social contexts.[3] These social contexts include the institutions and discourses of secularity and religion, which since the Enlightenment have often been aligned with freedom (secularity) and its suppression (religion). Saba Mahmood, Ananda Abeysekara, and Talal Asad have made this point in different ways.

Feminist and postcolonial debates on agency preoccupy Saba Mahmood in *Politics of Piety*. Noting the predominance of secular, liberal assumptions behind many accounts of agency, Mahmood argues that the category of agency should be understood broadly as a "modality of action."[4] Such a reframing of agency, she argues, can expand the scope of human action to include overlooked forms of behavior: "It is clear that certain virtues (such as humility, modesty, and shyness) have lost their value in the liberal imagination and are considered emblematic of passivity and inaction, especially if they don't uphold the autonomy of the individual."[5] One of the insightful implications of Mahmood's study is a criticism of a focus on "resistance" in thinking about agency. In her study of contemporary Muslims in Egypt, Mahmood suggests that traditional piety may obscure a whole range of actions and engagements from the modern secular gaze. Instead, she argues for reading these texts in their context and detached from the category of resistance in order to open up new questions about "performativity, transgression, suffering, survival, and the articulation of the body within different conceptions of the subject."[6]

In a more far-reaching way, Ananda Abeysekara argues that postcolonial and anthropological scholarship thinks and operates by exercising sovereign decision-making. The very act of separating peace from violence is, for Abeysekara, a critical decision that imposes sovereign power. Even academic studies that seek to acknowledge the agency of others engage in this powerful system of deciding:

> What I want to note here is that the recognition of native agency—as if such a thing were ever possible—also must recognize that somehow the locals, who had or have agency, lost or have lost their "agency," at some point in history! . . . . Colonialism also often claimed that natives lacked agency—either simply because they had lost it or because they simply did not embody it at all—and hence sought to give agency to them.[7]

Where Mahmood argues for a more contextualized and flexible conception of agency, less hostile to religious and cultural difference, Abeysekara pushes the question of agency further, doubting the purpose of separating agency from a consideration of life itself. Talal Asad similarly challenges secular notions of agency when he contrasts medieval Christianity to secular modernity: "Thus humility in the form of self-abasement is no longer admired in 'normal' Christianity, and modern secular thought and practice classify and treat it as one of the standard personality disorders. Rituals of humiliation and abasement are now symptoms of patients, not the discipline of agents."[8]

Benjamin's work similarly challenges secular modern conceptions of agency, placing particular emphasis on practices of reading, writing, and tradition. At a time when many considered modernity as a complete break with the past, Benjamin framed modernity as the inheritor of the past. For Benjamin, nineteenth-century culture echoes the seventeenth century as it anticipates the twentieth, but he avoids simplifying these patterns as progress, decline, or eternal recurrence. Instead, he pursues detailed description and analysis of ideas and material culture to suggest a complex understanding of tradition. In this approach to tradition, the distinction between individual and collective agency becomes blurred, as Benjamin's writings on literature, politics, and art show.

Perhaps Benjamin's most vivid text on agency and tradition is the well-known first thesis in his late work, "On the Concept of History," which describes a chess-playing automaton controlled by a dwarf hidden inside a table. Here Benjamin compares the automaton to "historical materialism" and the dwarf to "theology," which "today, as we know [*bekanntlich*], is small and ugly and has to keep out of sight" (*SW* 4:389). Both paradoxes in this image—the hidden dwarf's control of the chessboard (rather than the automaton's) and the need for theology (rather than historical materialism) to remain hidden—concern agency. Contrary to appearances, the dwarf—theology, rooted in centuries of tradition—controls the game.

Shifting from the dazzling appearance of the automaton to the hidden dwarf called theology, Benjamin's essay cuts against the grain of materialist politics. A contrasting use of puppets was made by the socialist anarchist thinker Gustav Landauer, a contemporary of Benjamin and close friend of Martin Buber, in "Puppen" (1914). Landauer's essay comments on Heinrich von Kleist's well-known story "On the Marionette Theater" (1810), in which puppets are paradoxically judged more graceful, natural, and godlike than human dancers. The self-consciousness and artificiality of human dancers renders their movement less beautiful, a fact the storyteller associates with the story of the Fall from the Garden of Eden in Genesis. First praising Kleist's story for its beauty and insight, Landauer also provokes the reader to recall that puppets are produced and sold and therefore subject to particular material conditions.[9] While Landauer offers a materialist critique of romantic aesthetics, Benjamin subordinates materialism to theology and aesthetics. Like a work of art, the automaton serves no clear practical purpose: it does no work, but it presents a striking image in its Turkish clothing. It is unclear whether Landauer's essay provided a source for Benjamin's first thesis in "On the Concept of History," but the two texts, along with Kleist's story, strikingly share the image of the puppet as a reflection on the problem of the agency and physicality of humans. As he argues in "The Critique of Violence," humanity, which includes aesthetic and religious tradition, cannot be reduced to "mere [biological] life" (*SW* 1:251).

Benjamin's chess-playing automaton relates agency directly to tradition: no action is possible for the puppet (historical materialism) without the hidden dwarf (theology). By what mechanism does the hidden dwarf of tradition enable the puppet to act? To address this question requires work with and beyond Benjamin's texts. For Benjamin, tradition cannot be swept away by modernity, nor can it be reduced to such modern categories as religion or theology, though it surely involves both. This book goes beyond familiar treatments of Benjamin's interest in Jewish messianism to explore how his work fits into the larger context of cultural and theological debates in the late nineteenth and early twentieth centuries. Against this background, Benjamin developed original and paradoxical conceptions of tradition and agency. For Benjamin, the domain of modern religious life and action is decidedly "secular": literature, mass culture, and modern cities far outweigh explicitly institutional religion in his work. Just as paradoxically, human action sometimes works against the outcomes Benjamin imagines: history typically defies human control. But Benjamin is not fatalistic; he rejects simplistic models of human history as progress, eternal recurrence, or decline. Instead, with exorbitant caution and nuance, Benjamin approaches and embodies the problem of human agency through a set of original, dialectical, and experimental writing projects. This question of agency in the face of sobering historical and political realities, along with the question of tradition, is a central focus of my book.

Benjamin's work anticipates and thus contributes to current debates about religion and secularity. After centuries as a dominant political and cultural paradigm, secularism, the idea that religion is or should be a part of life rather than a way of life, faces reconsideration, and scholars across the humanities and social sciences now take religious traditions quite seriously. Secularism fails empirically to describe much if not most of the world today, and it also fails conceptually to recognize the survival of tradition in modern life. To divide life cleanly into "secular" and "religious" domains is simply to overlook the complexity of reality. The related failure of secularization theory, the idea that religion would be replaced by secular culture, is widely recognized, but conceptual alternatives have yet to crystallize.[10]

Reframing secularity and religion is not just an exercise in conceptual housecleaning but a way to think better about human choice and agency. Whereas secularism originally aimed to expand human freedom beyond the limitations of religious institutions, as in Immanuel Kant's famous "What Is Enlightenment?" the legacy of secular institutions today is quite uneven; meanwhile, anti-secular traditionalisms, or "fundamentalisms," seem no better and only reinstate familiar understandings of religion and secularity. Asad has written suggestively about Benjamin's work as a way forward with this problem, and others, like Judith Butler, have engaged Benjamin's work along similar lines. Benjamin shifts from the problem of religion and secularity to a more nuanced discussion of *tradition* that identifies a wide range of obvious and elusive practices, dispositions, displacements, and debates that survive and change over time. These abiding and overlapping concerns in Benjamin's work can be illustrated by reference to three short texts: an essay on poems by Hölderlin, a fragment called "World and Time," and a letter on Zionism paraphrasing Martin Luther.

Three Short Texts

Benjamin's discussions of agency consistently challenge the modern paradigm of the forceful, autonomous individual, especially in the domains of language and literature. In Kantian and romantic thought, linguistic and literary expression often epitomize this paradigm of agency: the individual uses the tool of language to communicate, to express thought, or, particularly in the case of the poet, to create beautiful or sublime works of literature. Benjamin questions this paradigm directly in his essays on language and literature. In "Two Poems by Friedrich Hölderlin" (1914–15), Benjamin contrasts an earlier and a later poem in a discussion of literary quality that really concerns the problem of agency. The earlier poem, "The Poet's Courage," features "incoherence of detail" and fails to go beyond the level of myth, and its beauty remains indeterminate (*SW* 1:22–23). The second poem, "Timidity," revises the first and exhibits "a perceptual-intellectual order, the new cosmos of the poet" (*SW* 1:24). A great deal can be said about the ambitions of this text, and Peter Fenves has done much to explicate it, but one dimension of the text is particularly salient to the issue of agency, namely, how Benjamin contrasts them in terms of their shared theme of courage.[11] The first poem presents courage "only as a quality" in which "the danger of death was overcome through beauty. In the later version all beauty flows from the overcoming of danger. . . . Courage is submission to the danger that threatens the world" (*SW* 1:33). More than the overtly heroic stance of the first poem, the "timidity" of the second paradoxically represents true courage; this "complete passivity . . . is the essence of the courageous man—nothing except to surrender himself wholly to relationship" (*SW* 1:34). Here, in one of Benjamin's early works, is a form of agency characterized not by "mythic" courage but by a submission or timidity that "has now become the authentic stance of the poet" (*SW* 1:34). In "Two Poems," Benjamin derives a paradoxical model of courageous agency as submission through literary analysis. By accepting the danger of the world without imposing a forced, mythic conception of courage upon it, Benjamin attempts to solve a political as well as aesthetic problem. The search for a meaningful conception of human agency in the face of overwhelming danger is a preoccupation of Benjamin's work, and it is a goal of this study to show how his efforts may contribute to contemporary debates on agency as well.

Paradox and perspective inform most of Benjamin's reflections on agency and tradition. "World and Time," an aphoristic fragment on religion, politics, and violence from 1919–20, contrasts divine and human perspectives with respect to agency: "In the revelation of the divine, the world—the theater of history—is subjected to a great process of decomposition, while time—the life of him who represents it—is subjected to a great process of fulfillment" (*SW* 1:226). The role of the one who represents (*der Darsteller*) here is striking; to represent, in this case, brings fulfillment. Though clearly subordinated to the divine, the human work of representing time, like literary analysis, has value as action. But not all agency is so fulfilling. Describing Catholicism as a false theocracy, Benjamin links it to the ascent of anarchism, presumably because it self-destructs and creates a political vacuum:

> The problem of Catholicism is that of the (false, secular [*irdischen*]) theocracy. The guiding principle here is: authentic divine power [*echte göttliche Gewalt*] can manifest itself *other than destructively* only in the world to come (the world of fulfillment). But where divine power enters into the secular world, it breathes destruction. That is why in this world nothing constant and no organization can be based on divine power, let alone domination as its supreme principle.[12]

Anarchy, he notes, "must be defined from the locus of freedom in the philosophy of history" (*GS* 1:227).

Benjamin goes on to contrast divine and human agency in language that echoes his essay, "Toward the Critique of Violence" (written during the same period), noting the destructive potential of "pure divine violence" and its place in the world to come. Here Benjamin defines politics as the fulfillment of "an unimproved humanity" and names the Ten Commandments as "direct divine intervention" beyond profane politics (*GS* 2:226). Manifestations of divine force, on the other hand, appear not in the social realm but "in perception [*Wahrnehmung*] oriented toward revelation and, first and last, in language, sacred language above all." The fragment concludes with the striking assertion that " 'religious' is nonsense. Between religion and faith [*Konfession*] there is no essential difference, but the latter is a more narrow and mostly marginal concept" (*GS* 6:99–100).[13] Benjamin's text affirms divine power and revelation, but it marginalizes religious institutions and language. Conventional forms of agency at the social and ecclesiastical level are discounted, while the acts of perceiving revelation and representing historical redemption play a central role.

"World and Time" displays Benjamin's paradoxical interests in combining religious and political lines of thought. The claim about divine violence and the world to come has a messianic tone like that of the "Theological-Political Fragment" and the "Critique of Violence," along with Benjamin's interest to combine tradition and modernity. There is no way to read this text conclusively, since it consists mainly of notes, but its paradoxical statements and juxtapositions clearly reflect some of the same tensions and antinomies Benjamin discusses elsewhere. The rejection of institutional religion (Catholicism) as a "false theocracy" and "nonsense" on the one hand, combined with the affirmation of sacred language and revelation as a source of divine violence on the other, affirms particular notions of tradition and agency. In the case of tradition, institutions play a negative role while categories like revelation and divine violence loom large: this separation allows Benjamin to affirm religious tradition without all the manifestations of religion. As for agency, there is the paradox that active efforts in institutional religion are flawed in contrast to "divine violence" and the more subtle point that human perception and representation, normally not considered the most forceful kinds of action, constitute important forms of agency. Benjamin's fragment does not settle the questions of agency or tradition, but it suggests how Benjamin's understanding of these categories attempts to overcome the binary of secularity and religion.

Sooner or later, discussions of agency and tradition lead to the question of identity. For Benjamin, the question of German and Jewish identity often goes beyond biographical interest to focus discussions of the meaning and purpose of his writings. A third text that illustrates Benjamin's engagement with agency and tradition around the question of identity is a short passage from a 1912 letter on Zionism to Ludwig Strauss. Here explaining his "cultural" Zionism and intention to remain in Germany, Benjamin writes: "I am bound here . . . Here I will stand and, as I must believe, will you also stand" (*Ich bin hier gebunden. . . . Hier will ich stehen und wie ich glaube müssen auch Sie hier stehen*, *GS* 2:838). By itself, this statement allows Benjamin to claim Jewish and German identity on his own terms. In addition, I believe this text alludes to Martin Luther's legendary statement at Worms in 1521, "Here I stand. I cannot do otherwise. God help me, Amen!"[14]

By citing Luther in defense of his Jewish self-understanding, Benjamin effectively refuses to choose between Jewish and German identity. This orientation to German-Jewish identity, I argue, remained remarkably consistent throughout Benjamin's life, which ended in flight from German authorities in Europe after he had declined to leave for Palestine or the United States. Benjamin's 1912 letter on Zionism, along with his letters to Scholem about political developments in Palestine, suggest personal and political reasons for his decision to avoid emigration there.[15] In the case of the United States, Benjamin's comment to Hannah Arendt that he imagined the spectacle of being put on display there as the "last European" forms a kind of bookend to his Luther-like declaration of intent to remain in Europe.[16] In contrast to ethnic and nationalistic discourses that compelled a choice between the two, Benjamin's abiding German-Jewishness reflects a critical agency that insisted on the possibility of being fully Jewish and German, not as a mere "hyphenated" or hybridized mix.

Much later, in the 1936 collection of letters called *Deutsche Menschen*, Benjamin returns to this identity question when he cites Hölderlin, saying "German I will and must remain, even if spiritual and physical privation drives me to Tahiti" (*SW* 3:207). Like the letter to Strauss, *Deutsche Menschen* plays on the boundaries of German and Jewish identity (see chapter 7). The quotation introduces a letter from another German writer, Georg Büchner, a political activist and author of a play about the French Revolution, *Danton's Death*. Benjamin ranks these authors among "a long procession of German writers and thinkers who, fettered to a common chain of penury, drag themselves along at the foot of the Weimarian Parnassus on which the professors have just set off on another of their botanical rambles" (*SW* 3:207). Like his earlier letter to Strauss, this quotation alludes to Luther's legendary claim to stand his ground. Luther, the quintessential German whose Bible translation shaped the modern German language and was defended by Benjamin, may seem an odd model for Benjamin, who always affirmed his own Jewishness and embraced French culture even before he was forced to flee Germany.

Chapter Summary

The seven chapters of this book present contemporary debates on tradition and agency in dialogue with particular texts by Benjamin and his contemporaries. The topics of the chapters, in order, are culture wars, Jewish tradition, mental illness and religion, Orientalism, political violence, image culture, and German-Jewish identity. It is possible to read each of these chapters on its own, but together they aim to develop a sustained discussion of agency and tradition in Benjamin and contemporary thought. Though not ordered chronologically, the chapters follow Benjamin's growing interest in the problem of collective agency. Each chapter shifts between Benjamin's early twentieth century and our early twenty-first, seeking to credit Benjamin with insights and approaches to contemporary debates without overstating his contribution or neglecting his limitations. To suggest that Benjamin's work anticipates and fully resolves current debates would be to credit him with the kind of soothsaying mentioned in his "On the Concept of History." Yet contrary to readers who divide Benjamin's work into religious and political phases, I show how Benjamin persistently combined these interests in a way that anticipates current "postsecular" thought.

The inherent limitations of this project include not only the challenge of taking Benjamin's texts out of context, but also the particular difficulties of working with Benjamin's writing. Notably complex, allusive, unsystematic, and even evasive, Benjamin's writings do not easily yield clear interpretations. The readings I propose here attempt selectively but rigorously to engage Benjamin's work on agency and tradition, categories that preoccupied him throughout his writing career, though he discussed them in varying terms and contexts. Each chapter initially relates Benjamin's work to a contemporary debate but then goes beyond Benjamin to discuss, for example, science and the culture wars in the United States, Orientalism, or identity.

But Benjamin's work is not limited only by cultural and historical context. Despite his interests in politics and mass culture, his work falls short in dealing clearly with agency and the role of traditional practices. Benjamin criticized ideas of the morally autonomous individual on the one hand and collectivist politics on the other, particularly for their shared confidence in historical progress. But in spite of his efforts to conceptualize the mechanisms of popular culture, politics, and memory, he did not reach a clear understanding of how people act together. A related weakness of Benjamin's thought concerns practices such as recitation, reading, and writing, particularly in the context of traditions. Benjamin understood the importance of traditional practices in relation to agency, but he did not develop or conceptualize them in ways that recent thinkers like Asad, Michel de Certeau, and Pierre Hadot have done. Considering such practices in the context of traditions enhances discussions of collective agency, since traditions are inherently collective. In ways not fully explored by Benjamin, this study attempts to address the problems of collective agency and practices in relation to tradition.

The study begins with the "culture wars": passionate debates on science, religion in the public sphere, religious violence, religious and cultural diversity, and the politics of images. Benjamin's work on religion also emerged against the background of earlier "culture wars" (*Kulturkämpfe*), which staged debates on religion, politics, and group identity. My interest in each of these debates is the question of human choice and agency in the face of historical and cultural change. I begin with debates over science and religion, with "secular" scientists arguing to protect intellectual freedom, and their angry "religious" opponents arguing to protect freedom of religion and freedom from science-based government policies on climate change or school curricula. A more nuanced picture of science and religion emerges from Walter Benjamin's writings on early modernity, particularly his *Origin of German Tragic Drama*. His response to the cultural and political turmoil of early modernity was to cultivate disciplined study and perception, conditioned by melancholy. Benjamin carried these reflections on agency further in his unfinished study of nineteenth-century Paris (*The Arcades Project*) by contrasting the political and scientific interests of Auguste Blanqui to the life and work of Charles Baudelaire.

A major resource for reflection on tradition and modernity is the intellectual exchange between Benjamin and Gershom Scholem, the focus of the second chapter. Through their converging and diverging interests in Judaism, Kafka, and secular modernity, Scholem and Benjamin developed questions, methods, and perspectives on the study of tradition that anticipate current discussions of identity, tradition, and the postsecular. While both avoided theology as such, each thinker developed distinctive ways of taking religious tradition seriously. Scholem's early study of biblical lament, which influenced Benjamin's work, identifies lament as a silent and non-symbolic form of language that nevertheless belongs to tradition. Himself a declared "religious anarchist," Scholem, with Benjamin, associated tradition with modernity and conceptualized agency not simply as activity but more broadly as engagement with tradition. Yet for Scholem, tradition meant Jewish tradition in the context of Jewish identity, while Benjamin's conception of tradition questions unequivocal notions of identity.

Questions of tradition and agency coincide most vividly when individuals are detained against their will, and such was the case for Daniel Paul Schreber, whose 1903 *Memoirs of My Nervous Illness* was an attempt to gain release from a mental institution. In secular modernity, tradition can become a kind of scandal and religion a kind of madness, an insight reflected in Benjamin's discussion of the *Memoirs*, a text that has garnered many diverse critical responses not only in psychoanalytic circles but in cultural studies as well. Yet no one has given detailed attention to Benjamin's brief engagement with this text. Chapter 3 considers Benjamin's reading of Schreber's text in dialogue with readings by Sigmund Freud, Michel de Certeau, and others, as an instance of the scandalous nature of tradition in modern culture.

Having identified the problem of human agency and sketched a model of tradition beyond the binary of religion and secularity, I take up the question of cultural interaction in terms of conflicts over the Middle East, Islam, and "Orientalism," a fruitful category that Edward Said framed but did not exhaust (in his 1978 book, *Orientalism*), particularly with respect to collisions between tradition and modernity. Said characterized his groundbreaking work as "secular criticism" indebted to the model of Erich Auerbach, who wrote his influential study of comparative literature, *Mimesis* (1953), while living as an exile in Turkey. Said's abiding interests in criticism and exile come to life in Benjamin's 1936–37 correspondence with Erich Auerbach during the latter's stay in Istanbul. These letters, along with Orientalist motifs from Benjamin's writings (such as the Turkish puppet that famously begins his "Theses on the Philosophy of History"), open up a discussion of tradition, modernity, identity, and agency in the context of contemporary debates on Orientalism, colonialism, Turkey, and the Middle East.

The problem of agency and tradition is nowhere more central in Benjamin's work than in his 1921 "Critique of Violence," which has fascinated and puzzled readers with its wide-ranging discussion of law, general strikes, and "divine" and "mythic" violence. By attending to Benjamin's reading of the biblical story of Korah (Numbers 16), chapter 5 argues that Benjamin's juxtaposition of political theology and the proletarian general strike articulates a model of political action that avoids secularism and simple traditionalism.

Benjamin's evocative essays on mimesis, photography, and art address contemporary debates on the kinds of human agency and collective memory enabled by the production and reception of images after catastrophe. What are the potentials and dangers of images that depict war and other disasters? How do such images reflect and change traditions, particularly when their impact depends on claims to the novelty or uniqueness of what they depict? How does today's culture of images relate to tradition more generally? Jean Baudrillard, Slavoj Žižek, and Susan Sontag have engaged these issues in various ways, and chapter 6 engages their work as it also explicates Benjamin's often-misunderstood writings on images, particularly his reflections on aura and Paul Klee's *Angelus Novus*. The discussion shifts from images of disasters to images as such and identifies resources in Benjamin's work for reflection on agency in the reception and production of images.

The book's final chapter takes up a puzzle about Benjamin's book of annotated letters by famous German authors, *Deutsche Menschen* (1936). Though Judaism and Jewish authors play no part in this text, which Benjamin published in Switzerland under the pseudonym Detlev Holz, his handwritten dedications in copies he gave to Jewish friends and family describe the book as a Jewish ark written while the flood of fascism was beginning to rise. The question of what makes such a German and often Christian book Jewish provides the starting point for a discussion of religious and cultural identity, agency, and tradition as it suggests the possibility of survival, if not restoration, after catastrophe.

Chapter 1

✦

Benjamin's Baroque and the Culture Wars

Contemporary political debates seem to thrive on anger. Passions run especially high in the "culture wars" over science and religion, which pit "secularists" against "science deniers" and question the legitimacy of some scientific work, particularly on cosmology and climate. What is going on in these debates? This chapter engages the question through a discussion of melancholy in Walter Benjamin's writings. For Benjamin, science and melancholy share a common history emerging from the astrological tradition that linked human life to celestial objects. His studies of this tradition travel from Albrecht Dürer's *Melancholia I* (1514) to the nineteenth-century writings of Auguste Blanqui and Charles Baudelaire. In these engagements with the modern tradition of melancholy, Benjamin challenges the terms of contemporary debates on religion and science and offers a conception of melancholy as a part of political engagement.

Current debates on science and religion emerge from a modern history in which the prestige of natural science skyrocketed while religious institutions lost influence. With these shifts came increasing specialization and separation of the branches of knowledge and their supporting institutions. In response to these trends, efforts to integrate religion and science arose, including Enlightenment deism, Mary Baker Eddy's (1821–1910) Christian Science, and the theosophy of Madame Blavatsky (1831–1891). One can find "religious" tendencies in the scientific writings of Darwin and the political writings of Marx, and "scientific" aspirations in the religious works of Emanuel Swedenborg and G. W. F. Hegel.[1] For Benjamin, such cases of modern engagements with tradition challenge the division between secular science and religious belief, and they represent a neglected topic in research on his work. In place of secularization narratives that depict science as progress beyond religious belief, Benjamin finds modern hybrids of religion and science that inherit and continue broader cultural traditions.

This chapter moves from the current culture wars of religion and science to a discussion of critical reflection, aesthetic reception, and melancholy as meaningful resources for conceptualizing agency. The "ascetic apprenticeship" Benjamin cultivates as a response to the complexity of early modern culture describes his engagement with modern culture in general, and it models the sort of critical activity that, while it may not transform the world, is necessary to understand it.[2] Benjamin typically approaches agency through criticism and paradox, first showing the failure of past human efforts, and then practicing and advocating forms of action that appear to address these failures only in modest and indirect ways. In his restless explorations of modernity and tradition, Benjamin identifies several scientific thinkers who blurred the boundaries of religion and science; three whose work I discuss here are Georg Christoph Lichtenberg, Edgar Dacqué, and Auguste Blanqui.

My argument is that we can learn much about popular attacks on science in the United States from what Benjamin had to say about baroque and nineteenth-century culture. I do not attempt a critical review or detailed genealogy of early modern or contemporary debates, and I certainly do not wish to make a simple one-to-one comparison between the contemporary and baroque periods. Instead, my goal is to adopt and select a number of claims, motifs, and ideas from Benjamin's writings to engage such questions as the following: What explains why large numbers of Americans deny the validity of scientific research on biology and climate?

Recent opinion polls in the United States show that one third to two fifths of Americans deny the validity of science on both evolution and climate change.[3] Why? The first thing we might notice is that these beliefs correlate highly with political and religious affiliation—so are Republicans and conservative Christians more likely to deny science because they have a robust alternative worldview? I think not. Although the culture wars are typically framed in terms of ideological and religious conflict, I do not see a resurgence of religious and political institutions that present a compelling way of life or picture of reality that competes with contemporary mass culture. If a large part of American society had really embraced a different worldview, we would expect to see massive changes in consumer behavior and popular culture, but no such changes have taken place. Nor is it helpful to conclude simply that a large part of the population is ignorant or stupid; the ingenuity of science denial and the frequent artlessness of scientists rule out this possibility. Instead, we can read the angry denials and defenses of science (and related battles in the culture wars) as anguished performances, agonistic responses to wider crises of institutional legitimacy and human agency.[4] While this chapter does not aim to narrate or excavate the American culture wars, I wish to frame them not as debates or conflicts between parties but as expressions of broad cultural forces that resonate with early modern history and religious tradition. To take sides in the culture wars, I suggest, is to reflect and even reinforce these forces.

The anger of today's culture wars generates activity, but activity alone does not constitute political agency. When activists and politicians rage at one another, they typically follow a pattern of denouncing each other according to the binary of religious faith and secular science. The result is a predictable "broken record" of angry claims and counterclaims that seem to be objects and symptoms of the culture wars rather than meaningful political interventions. What Benjamin's analysis shows is the power of this religion-and-science binary and the potential of an unlikely form of engagement—melancholy—to challenge that binary. Such intervention is political, at least in the case of Blanqui, and therefore engages the question of political agency.

A central preoccupation in Benjamin's discussion of early and later modernity is melancholy, which represents far more than mood or affect. For Benjamin, melancholy was political and aesthetic as well as affective, particularly in the seventeenth and early twentieth centuries. In today's culture wars, angry outbursts and statements about science, religion, and morality follow predictable patterns, almost as if they are scripted. What makes melancholy relevant to the culture wars is their wearying conventions and predictable discourse. Since the separation of "religion" and "science" is a widespread axiom of modernity, efforts to unite them are frequent and yet doomed. The melancholy resulting from this cultural stalemate can lead to paralysis or rage, but it can also, I suggest, be productive. The case was similar with the melancholia of the German baroque and early twentieth century which were linked in Benjamin's thinking by Lutheran theology, particularly during the wars of the seventeenth and twentieth centuries.[5] In fact, the debates on political theology and melancholy in which Benjamin engages in his study of German tragic drama (*Trauerspiel*) relate directly to the "culture war" of Germany in the nineteenth and twentieth centuries, which, like the current "culture wars," concerns the role of the church in the modern state.[6]

For Benjamin, melancholy indicates the confrontation with a failed cultural system such as baroque art and culture, but this confrontation can lead to insight: "This is the essence of melancholy immersion: that its ultimate objects, in which it believes it can most fully secure for itself that which is vile, turn into allegories, and these allegories fill out and deny the void in which they are represented" (*GTD* 232–33). Since the allegory itself fails, the melancholy perspective on this failure provides the only chance of genuine insight into the depth of the crisis and the challenge in overcoming it. A melancholy perspective on the culture wars would shift from choosing sides to observing both sides as a failure to address a crisis. In the German baroque, Benjamin's time, and the current culture wars, melancholy characterizes the gaze of those who confront failed efforts to overcome crises. But this transformation from the inaction and despair of melancholy to action or redemption is never assured. While Warburg had an optimistic, heroic understanding of melancholy's potential, Benjamin viewed melancholy more modestly as the potential basis for critical awareness.[7]

What Benjamin's melancholy offers the "culture wars," then, is first, an insight into the experience of social conflict; second, a sober awareness of the limitations of political theology; and third, a conviction that the "immersion" in melancholy can sometimes lead to the kinds of insights necessary to political thought. While such transformation is by no means guaranteed, Benjamin's conception of an "ascetic apprenticeship" to be undertaken in the face of the cultural contradictions of modernity cultivates a notion of agency that avoids quietism on the one hand and hubris on the other (*GTD* 56). Like Benjamin's reflections on agency in general, his understanding of melancholy flies in the face of conventional ideas of action. Hannah Arendt, for example, claims that the "melancholy wisdom of *Ecclesiastes* . . . is unavoidable wherever and whenever trust in the world as a place fit for human appearance, for action and speech, is gone."[8] By relating melancholy to agency, Benjamin challenges ordinary understandings of cultural conflict and political action.[9]

Science Wars, Culture Wars

Although the culture wars do not indicate a return of traditional religion at the expense of science, they suggest something like the process of delegitimation (often called secularization) that religious institutions faced in the early modern and modern periods. Today, the legitimacy of scientific institutions is increasingly under attack. But populist culture warriors do not point to a better theory or worldview; they point at themselves and perform acts of disruption and defiance: "Look at us!" they seem to say, "We are tired of being told how to think and act by scientists, and so we reject them!" Science, which is associated with secularism and elitism, has become a tyrannical force in the world, and it must be opposed. The opposition has no single name, though its political and religious labels are familiar enough, but its real force comes from the spirit of opposition itself.

The point of science denial, I suggest, is the angry act of denial itself, the organization of group opposition to delegitimize scientific institutions. But the vigor of these attacks, like the intensity of baroque allegory, conceals a crisis of meaning that often also includes the experience of melancholy, a category that Benjamin saw as having potential for human agency.

It is tempting to cast the denial of science in terms of a kind of reversal of secularization: as secular science weakened religion, religion and its allies now "secularize" science! But it is not clear that religion has staged such a "comeback," nor even that secularization ever really took place. What I see instead are specific shifts and displacements within traditions in which science was never purely secular or unmixed with religious ideas.

An Internet search of the phrase "Al Gore Rant" (in 2015) yields not only an audio recording of the Nobel Prize winner's full-throated, profane denunciation of climate change denial, but also a number of videos attacking and ridiculing the former vice president. One such amateur production shows a person wearing a Gore mask dancing and gesturing at a globe next to a dancing bird, presumably Chicken Little, while the speech plays over a musical soundtrack. For the sponsors of such videos, such as Minnesotans for Climate Change, the point is to perform a celebration of mockery; it is a celebration because Gore was "caught" on tape "ranting." What matters is not who is right or what worldview is correct—what matters is that Gore "lost it" and thereby compromised the implicit standards of impartial, dispassionate scientific and political discourse. Gore and his critics engage in a polemic whose vehemence and theatricality suggest an anxiety and cultural crisis akin to those of the early modern period.[10]

A typical scientific response to these denials recalls the turgid tone of baroque texts. In June 2011, the American Association for the Advancement of Science (AAAS), the "world's largest scientific society," issued this statement condemning attacks on scientific work:

> We are deeply concerned by the extent and nature of personal attack on climate scientists. Reports of harassment, death threats, and legal challenges have created a hostile environment that inhibits the free exchange of scientific findings and ideas and makes it difficult for factual information and scientific analyses to reach policymakers and the public. This both impedes the progress of science and interferes with the application of science to the solution of global problems. AAAS vigorously opposes attacks on researchers that question their personal and professional integrity or threaten their safety based on displeasure with their scientific conclusions.[11]

This official statement by the AAAS bears the traces of an institution unaware of its own declining legitimacy. The document speaks of "vigorous opposition," but I seriously doubt that its appeal to "free exchange of scientific findings" and "the progress of science," couched here in the form of an institutional press release, stands much chance of changing the public debate on science. When a significant percentage of the public rejects what most scientists agree is clear, the very principles of science defended by the AAAS can no longer be taken for granted.

It is not my goal to flesh out the analogy between baroque and contemporary culture in historical terms, but rather to identify ways of thinking about the baroque and the present culture and science wars that give us novel ways of thinking about cultural conflicts. We can understand contemporary denials of science, I propose, if we look at them as performed displacements of debates on and imbrications of religion, politics, and science.[12]

History, Philosophy, and Images of Science

Science today faces internal and external challenges that lead historians and philosophers of science to reconceptualize "science" and its supposed object of study, "nature." Theories of science now recognize higher levels of uncertainty, historical variation, and pluralism. Mario Biagioli proposes "contingentism" as an alternative to the impasse between relativism and rationalism. Biagioli's contingentism proposes an approach to the history of science that attends to its own position and situation without denying the possibility that things have been, could be, and will be otherwise.[13] Similar attempts to steer between relativistic and absolutist conceptions of science can be found in the work of Bruno Latour, Ian Hacking, Arnold Davidson, Peter Galison, and Lorraine Daston. Latour has called the entire project of modernity into question, and with it the categories of nature, culture, and science as monoliths.[14] Less dramatically, Galison and Daston make an analogy between moral and scientific pluralism:

> Moral philosophers have argued for an irreducible plurality of visions of the good, which can be reasonably debated in specific cases but never eliminated in principle by reason alone. Analogously, we believe that a plurality of visions of knowledge, understood in the most capacious sense of fidelity to nature, is likely to be a permanent aspect of science.[15]

Daston and Galison appeal to pluralism in *Objectivity*, a historical study that argues that the familiar category of objectivity arose only in the nineteenth century. A heady mix of Enlightenment and romantic thought with rapidly changing human institutions generated objectivity and then fused it with an idea of the self: "Like parallel lines meeting at the vanishing point of a picture painted in perspective, objective science and subjective art converged in the dissolution of the self into its object."[16]

While history and the sociology of science have quietly been questioning and adjusting conceptions of science, objectivity, and nature, a separate and much louder set of debates has broken out in public; two of these are the "science wars" in the wake of the *Social Text* scandal of 1996 and the ongoing "science wars" or "culture wars," particularly over the science of evolution and climate change. How dangerous or serious are these attacks on science? Historian of science Steven Shapin doubts that the "science wars" amount to much at all: "Those who might be genuinely hostile to what they take to be the essence of science are probably just as ineffective as they are misguided. Who reads this stuff anyway?"[17] What Shapin has in mind may be the postmodern criticisms of science in academic journals, but his essay, first published in 2001, appeared long before public figures and opinion polls began openly to challenge the integrity and value of scientific consensus. Today the "science wars" of the Sokal affair and its aftermath have given way to broader culture wars in which postmodern and neoconservative critiques together have eroded the legitimacy of traditional scientific institutions. It may be the goal of historians like Galison and Daston to provide an alternative to the polemical all-or-nothing approach of the culture wars, but such an intervention would require a higher public profile for the history of science.

A distinctive feature of Daston's and Galison's project is a focus on the production and use of visual representations in scientific practice. Their use of images in the history of science belongs to a wider trend that recognizes the significance of images along with texts as sources for scholarly inquiry. Consideration of images not only expands the scope of inquiry to new media, however. It also opens up new questions about the distinctness of images, how they affect viewers, and how they become part of collective memory. The study of images pertains to ideas of "nature," a category like "objectivity" with roots in a confident epistemology that Bruno Latour and others argue has outgrown its usefulness.[18] This turn to images animates the present project as well, which hinges on the influence of Aby Warburg and Irwin Panofsky on Walter Benjamin's conception of the baroque.

Warburg's Pathos Formula

For Warburg and Benjamin, images can transmit tradition. The one work by Warburg that most compellingly narrates the transformation from premodern to early modern culture in science, theology, and images is "Pagan-Antique Prophecy in Words and Images."[19] Through a vastly erudite survey of Reformation-era texts, motifs, and images, Warburg demonstrates the survival and transformations of medieval notions of astrology, prophecy, and human fate in the hands of those like Luther and Dürer, who wish to affirm human liberty. But the inherited past never quite goes away: "Just as Luther still went in fear of cosmic portents and omens (not to speak of the antique *lamiae*), Dürer's Melancholy has yet to break quite free of the superstitious terrors of antiquity."[20] Warburg reformulates the problem in terms of Faust's struggle between new science and old magic: "This was the age of Faust, in which the modern scientist—caught between magic practice and cosmic mathematics—was trying to insert the *conceptual space* of rationality between himself and the object." In his self-described "exegetical grand tour," Warburg places special emphasis on the ability of images and "pictorial memory" to carry traditions of the past forward and recommends further alliances between art history and religious studies.[21]

As a counterpart to Warburg, Irwin Panofsky attends less to the survival of premodern tradition than to how it points toward something new. Far from describing "everything wildly abstruse, obscure, fanciful, and useless" or "unbridled movement," Panofsky depicts the baroque as a reaction against some Renaissance and mannerist art, sometimes reinstating classicism, but often showing a "conflict of antagonistic forces merging into a subjective unity."[22] This version of the baroque links to new kinds of consciousness, including critical (e.g., Descartes) and the humor of writers like Shakespeare and Cervantes. The baroque, in short, signals not the decline of the Renaissance but its continuation and the beginning of modernity.[23]

The struggle between novelty and tradition plays out in the contrast between Panofsky and Warburg. In his study of Panofsky and images, Georges Didi-Huberman compares Panofsky to the exorcist in the Jewish legend of the Dybbuk. What Panofsky tries to exorcise is, in effect, the power of images over historical knowledge, a power associated with the groundbreaking work of Aby Warburg.[24] Warburg's *Pathosformeln*, the "emotive formulas" handed down from antique art, do not reduce simply to superficial formal qualities; rather, they constitute expressive motifs that constitute the afterlife (*Nachleben*) of art history, the haunting survival that Didi-Huberman claims Panofsky sought to exorcise. This power has to do with how images are capable, like the Dybbuk, of returning again and again and adhering to the present as a spirit of the dead can adhere to the living. In Warburg's art history, this power is "*Nachleben*: 'afterlife' or 'survival'—precisely the powers to *adhere* and to *haunt* that inhere in all images . . . a *surviving image* is an image that, having lost its original use value and meaning, nonetheless comes back, like a ghost, at a particular historical moment: a moment of 'crisis,' a moment when it demonstrates its latency, its tenacity, its vivacity, and its 'anthropological adhesion,' so to speak."[25] But control over this power eludes Panofsky, as Didi-Huberman shows by placing Panofsky in dialogue with Kant, Heidegger, Freud, and major works of art. The uncanny image haunts history.

Benjamin's engagement with Warburg and Panofsky on melancholy, particularly Dürer's *Melancholia I*, is well documented; as Jane Newman shows, Warburg's more heroic account became a foil for Benjamin's focus on paralysis.[26] Against the context of the First World War, Warburg and Benjamin looked at the early modern period as a formative influence on modern secularism and revived interests in occultism and astrology. Both saw the afterlife of the seventeenth century in the twentieth, but where Warburg saw the flow of astrology and Lutheranism into modernity as an opportunity for liberation through heroic melancholy, Benjamin denied this political theology without completely foreclosing the possibility of agency through melancholy.

Benjamin on Science and Baroque

Depending on one's point of view, it is either a virtue or a failing of Walter Benjamin that he could not choose between a present haunted by the past and a present fully and freely engaged in something new. If this ambivalence was a failure, it is one that Benjamin would ascribe not just to the baroque but also to himself. His major study of early modernity, *The Origin of German Tragic Drama* (*Ursprung des deutschen Trauerspiels*, 1925), depicts the *Trauerspiel* as a flawed and misunderstood genre that enables sustained reflection on the problem of critical reception. The study begins with an "Epistemo-Critical Prologue" in which Benjamin insists that ideas must be understood within the parameters of representation and history (*GTD* 29, 46). The genre to which Benjamin dedicates his study poses intense resistance to critical understanding: it is complex, extravagant, and not particularly good in literary or aesthetic terms: it takes "the appearance of an incompetent [*unbeholfene*] renaissance of tragedy" (*GTD* 50).

This "incompetent renaissance" coincides with profound historical and epistemological transformations, one of which is often called the scientific revolution. But while most studies of this period focus on new knowledge, Benjamin is far more interested in its representation and reception. How did transformations in knowledge, political formations, and religious institutions find their way into the dramatic art of the day? As his prologue makes clear, Benjamin's fascination with baroque tragic drama lies beneath the aesthetic details of a literary genre and the novelties of its time. His project rather pursues a critical *via negativa* through the literary texts to what they represent, what they fail to represent, and their reception.[27]

Playing the role of advocate for this literary lost cause, Benjamin argues for the contemporary relevance of his topic and study as follows:

> In this state of disruption the present age reflects certain aspects of the spiritual constitution [*Geistesverfassung*] of the baroque, even down to the details of its artistic practice. Just as the pastoral play [*Schäferspiel*] formed a contrast to the political novel [*Staatsroman*], which then, as now, attracted the interest of respected authors, so, nowadays, do the pacifist avowals of faith in the "simple life" [English] and the natural goodness of man. (*GTD* 55; *GS* 1:236.)

To this similarity between baroque and modern writers Benjamin adds a contrast: whereas baroque writers were bound to "the ideal of an absolutist constitution" in a Christian context, modern writers are either hostile or indifferent to the state (*GTD* 56). Modern readers, then, can benefit from the idea of the baroque drama that sought "to reduce both its contemporaries and posterity [*Welt und Nachwelt*] to silence through the extravagance of its technique, the unfailing richness of its creations, and the vehemence of its claims to value" (*GTD* 56).

Benjamin warns of the "feeling of dizziness [*Schwindelgefühl*] which is induced by the spectacle of the spiritual contradictions [*Widersprüchen kreisenden Geistigkeit*] of this epoch" and advocates an "ascetic apprenticeship" for the understanding of his topic to allow a "position of strength from which it is possible to take in the whole panorama and yet remain in control of oneself" (*GTD* 56; *GS* 1:237). It is this emphasis on experience, on the reception of baroque texts, that seems to motivate Benjamin's study. Under-theorized to the point of reticence, the act and experience of careful reading nevertheless animates a project that places representation beside ideas and insists on the importance of literary form to understanding the religious, political, and aesthetic world of the baroque.[28]

A passing reference to science in the *Trauerspiel* study makes a strong claim for the beauty of science: "The geologist and the botanist can indeed do just this [awaken a feeling for beauty]. Without at least an intuitive grasp of the life of the detail in the structure, all love of beauty is no more than empty dreaming" (*GTD* 182). Benjamin continues by delineating how the material and "historical content" of art becomes "philosophical truth" and how at the same time the decay of beauty over time becomes "the basis for a rebirth, in which all ephemeral beauty is completely stripped off [*alle ephemere Schönheit vollends dahinfällt*], and the work stands as a ruin. In the allegorical construction of the baroque *Trauerspiel* such ruins have always stood out clearly as formal elements of the preserved work of art" (*GTD* 182; *GS* 1:358). In this passage, Benjamin not only affirms the link between the truth of science and the beauty of art, but also uses science as a bridge between fine details and larger claims to truth. Then, in his most original move, Benjamin adds another stage to this process, when the decay of beauty into ruins enables new forms like the *Trauerspiel* to stage a rebirth of beauty by exposing the "construction" and "formal elements" of the ruined work. In this new phase of the dialectics of beauty and truth, the baroque allegory serves a function similar to that of science, revealing fine details of structure that generate awareness of beauty and truth. The *Trauerspiel* in this sense is a kind of "new science"!

At the heart of Benjamin's *Trauerspiel* study is a polemical argument for the greatness of allegory as opposed to the regnant aesthetic concept of romanticism, the symbol. This claim paradoxically admits to the ugliness, the artificiality, and the failure of baroque literature, but in so doing finds unexpected beauty and truth in the melancholy reception of these ruined forms. The failed form of the baroque allegory corresponds to the melancholy experience of its audience: "For the only pleasure the melancholic permits himself, and it is a powerful one, is allegory" (*GTD* 185). It is crucial here to resist the uncritical urge to think of melancholy as an extension of Benjamin's personal experience—it is rather a subject of representation as well, particularly as the baroque or modern inherits the medieval theory of the humors. Here Benjamin follows Warburg and Panofsky closely in his pursuit of "sublime melancholy," particularly in Dürer's *Melancolia I* (*GTD* 151).

The influence of Warburg and Panofsky on Benjamin's *Trauerspiel* study is explicit. The related motifs of melancholy and science characterize this engagement, especially in the discussion of Dürer's *Melancholia*

I. Benjamin sees Dürer's image as a space in which "the utensils of active life are lying around unused on the floor, as objects of contemplation." As such, it represents a shift from the Renaissance, which "explores the universe," to the baroque, which "explores libraries" (*GTD* 140). The baroque inheritance of melancholia includes its development in astronomy and in the figure of the prince in the *Trauerspiel* (*GTD* 142, 148–49).[29]

The melancholy or saturnine temperament of Dürer's *Melancolia I* combines the disposition of the scientist, a "tireless investigator and thinker," with the prophet whose dreams come from "geomantic slumber in the temple of creation, and not as sublime or even sacred inspiration [*nicht als erhabene oder gar heilige Einflüsterung zu verstehen*]" (*GTD* 152; *GS* 1:330). Benjamin's melancholy "betrays [*verrät*] the world for the sake of knowledge. But in its tenacious self-absorption [*ausdauernde Versukenheit*] it embraces dead objects in its contemplation, in order to redeem them" (*GTD* 157; *GS* 1:334). The baroque period includes both the slothful melancholic of medieval thought and the "sorrowful contemplator" of the Renaissance, but Benjamin identifies only one work that combines them successfully: *Hamlet*; "Only Shakespeare was capable of striking Christian sparks from the baroque rigidity of the melancholic" (*GTD* 158).

Science, Philosophy, and Agency

Similarly "interdisciplinary" views appear in Benjamin's other writings on science. In writings on Darwin's thought and the eighteenth-century scientist and writer Georg Christoph Lichtenberg, Benjamin examines how efforts to combine science with philosophy highlight the problem of human agency. The fanciful radio play *Lichtenberg, Ein Querschnitt* (*Lichtenberg, a Cross-Section*, 1932–33) presents a debate among moon dwellers on whether Lichtenberg deserves to have a moon crater named in his honor. The text has less to do with scientific debate than human nature and agency—the committee of moon inhabitants that selects Lichtenberg for the honor of designating a moon crater with his name shares his sense of wonder at humanity. The play, written in 1932–33, contains many direct quotations from Lichtenberg (carefully noted by the editors of the *GS*), but the following passage, a remarkable reflection on agency, appears to be original to Benjamin. The play's main character, a historical figure who combines interests in the natural sciences, philosophy, and the occult, illustrates the problem of free will with an anecdote about puppet theater:

LICHTENBERG: Well, it was a puppet player who had erected his tent outside, near Covent Garden. For a few pence you could sit there for hours. But among the pieces of his repertoire one has remained unforgettable. It was, like I said, a puppet theatre. But if, normally, the puppets represented people, in this play they represented really only what they were: puppets. Five, six, seven of those puppets were hanging in front of a curtain: a merchant, a soldier, a clergyman, a housewife, a judge. They were rocking about in the wind, making conversation. And about what? You won't believe it: about the freedom of the will [*Willensfreiheit*]. It was a peaceful conversation, because there was really only one opinion among all: reason, nature, and religion combined their weight for the benefit of one free will. Only one puppet hanging a little further aside than the others—I think I forgot to mention it—was undecided. I believe this puppet was a philosopher, maybe a professor of physics. But the others paid no mind to his opinion. Suddenly, there appeared a cardboard hand from above.—But that was supposed to be a human hand.—It took away the puppets, one by one. It was very clear. The puppet player took his puppets from the rack. When one after the other was lifted up like that, the others were asked why they were leaving. And each one had an excuse. Only the hand of the puppet player was not mentioned. And finally the philosopher or professor of physics was left alone on stage.

POTTER: I don't know what you mean to say by that, dear colleague.

LICHTENBERG: Nothing, I would just like to ask something. [*Ich will nichts sagen, höchstens etwas fragen.*] Whether we, when we have a murderer drawn and quartered, make the same mistake as a child who beats the chair he ran into.[30]

How does the story of the puppet philosopher relate to Lichtenberg's abrupt conclusion about capital punishment? The case in question, the trial and execution of multiple murderer Heinrich Julius Rütgerodt, was famous in Lichtenberg's day.[31] Several reversals of expectation shape the anecdote: first, the puppets represent puppets and not people; second, the puppets discuss free will; third, the problem is apparently solved by uniting reason, nature, and religion; fourth, a cardboard hand representing a human hand removes all but one of the puppets, described as a free action. The anecdote ends with the solitary image of a puppet who is a philosopher or physics professor.

The "philosopher or professor of physics," of course, is Lichtenberg himself, and the fact that he alone remains onstage in this episode suggests that his status vis-à-vis the subject at hand is exceptional. The verdict of the court—for Rütgerodt's guilt—may have remained, but Benjamin leaves Lichtenberg's question, and the larger question of human free will, open. In the play, moon-dwelling characters with names taken from Paul Scheerbart's science fiction novel *Lesabendio* (and alluding, I believe, to the book of Job)—the Moon Committee for Earth Research—consider whether Lichtenberg is an exceptional person. After reviewing his writings and life, including his dialogue with the English actor Garrick, his letter describing his love for a girl, and the discussion of capital punishment, the committee names a moon crater in his honor. (The distinction puts him in the ranks of Thales, Helvetius, Humboldt, Condorcet, and Fourier.)

In a tradition that includes Kleist's essay on the marionette theater, Benjamin's puppet play-within-a-radio-play offers an elegantly constructed miniature on the question of human agency. Instead of lingering on its paradoxical implications, the storyteller leaps from this anecdote directly to a critical indictment of capital punishment, suggesting that to kill a murderer is like beating a chair that caused injury. The question of human freedom and agency raised by the paradoxical puppet play is thus abruptly foreclosed by an arresting analogy between juridical punishment and childish outburst. While the argument is not in any way resolved, the overall judgment on Lichtenberg, that he remains on the puppet stage and receives the highest honor of the moon committee, is clear.

Two shorter texts on the reception of Darwin's thought likewise draw attention to the problem of agency. "Crisis of Darwinism? On a Lecture by Prof. Edgar Dacqué at the Lessing-Hochschule" ("Krisis der Darwinismus? Zu einem Vortrag von Prof. Edgar Dacqué in der Lessing-Hochschule") (*GS* 4:534–36), a short text that appeared in *Die literarische Welt* in 1929, reports on a public lecture given by a biologist who linked Darwin's work to mythology, metaphysics, and philosophical anthropology. After summarizing Dacqué's presentation, Benjamin concludes that it is hard for lay people to understand, let alone criticize. Yet Benjamin places Dacqué in the company of other contemporary, groundbreaking thinkers who take an interest in the integration and unity of different domains, Husserl and Einstein in particular. He concludes: "These highly contemporary connections with the man who has thrown down the gauntlet of open confrontation with official Darwinism before a sold-out hall should secure the greatest general interest" (*GS* 4:536). Like Lichtenberg, Dacqué was interested in bridging philosophy and natural science for the general public (he "threw down a gauntlet to a sold-out hall," *GS* 4:536). (See the Fuchs essay, where Benjamin discusses the role of Darwinism in lending a deterministic drift to socialism, *GS* 2:487.) By placing Dacqué in such distinguished company, Benjamin suggests his own sympathies for a science that not only criticizes Darwin but also seeks to draw together disparate areas of research, something Benjamin himself so often sought to do. (Darwin also appears in a satirical fragment in the form of a short review of a nonexistent illustrated book: "Charles Darwin: Journey of a Naturalist" [*GS* 4:443]. Here Benjamin wittily turns the struggle for existence on the scientists: "Especially effective are the representations of the struggling naturalists themselves.")

The pursuit of any general integrative theory, particularly between the natural and human sciences, entails significant epistemological as well as political risks. How can human freedom ever reconcile with the laws of nature? The question becomes even more sensitive when religion enters the scene. In one of his most forceful and searching studies of Benjamin's work, Irving Wohlfarth probes the risks and meanings of Benjamin's last entry in *One-Way Street*: "To the Planetarium": "What *Zum Planeterium* attempts to do—and actually, rhetorically, performs—is to span the great world-historical divide that separates cosmogony from cosmology, astrology from astronomy, myth from enlightenment, *Gemeinschaft* from *Gesellschaft*, and thereby to heal the rift on which the modern world is built."[32] What worries Wohlfarth is that the eros of war technology in the First World War links for Benjamin somehow to revolutionary and messianic potential. In other words, Wohlfarth sees a rhetoric in this text that too closely resembles the ideas of thinkers such as Ludwig Klages and Ernst Jünger, who are considered to glorify war.

While Benjamin's engagement with Klages and Jünger certainly entailed the political risks that concern Wohlfarth, it also bridged his interests in early modern and modern culture. "To the Planetarium" highlights the analogy between the political aesthetics of the *Trauerspiel* study and modernist works like *One-Way Street*. No doubt the association between the "ecstatic trance" of pre-modern astrology and the "epileptic bliss" of the human body in modern war is risky, even potentially reckless in political terms. But Benjamin's main point here, which is underscored by the *Trauerspiel* study and the *Arcades Project*, is the abiding human need to relate humanity to the cosmos. It is not until Benjamin finds the work of Blanqui, however, that I believe he identifies a fitting modern expression of this problem: a political radical who sought to understand the cosmos.

Figure 1. Albrecht Dürer, *Melancholia I* (1514). Photo © bpk, Berlin / Joerg P. Anders / Art Resource, NY.

Baroque and Modern: Blanqui and Baudelaire

The link between astrology and baroque melancholy finds its modern counterpart in Benjamin's later fascination with the astronomical work of the French socialist Auguste Blanqui. Like Lichtenberg, Darwin, and Dacqué, Auguste Blanqui combined scientific and philosophical inquiry in ways that draw out the problem of human agency. Herein lies Benjamin's main concern with the natural sciences: as for Kant, the domain of nature immediately raises the question of human culture and agency. Benjamin credits Blanqui with claiming the idea of eternal recurrence years before Nietzsche: "Humanity—remaining true to [*à l'égal de*] the universe—is the enigma of the infinite and eternity; and the grain of sand remains true to humanity."[33] Like Dürer's *Melancolia I*, Blanqui's text links heavenly bodies—astronomy rather than astrology—to melancholy: "At bottom, it's melancholy—humanity's eternity according to the stars [*astres*]—and sadder still is the sequestering of these brother-worlds by the inexorable barrier of space."[34]

Deriving a concept of infinity from the astronomy of Laplace, Blanqui extends it to a discussion of human history and experience as melancholy

Figure 2. Felicien Rops, illustration for Charles Baudelaire's *Les Épaves* (1866)

and repetitive. For Benjamin, Blanqui represents a later version of the link between astronomy and melancholy, science and the saturnine, that one finds in the baroque of the *Trauerspiel* and Warburg. Benjamin finds a counterpart to Blanqui's melancholy astronomy in another nineteenth-century French writer, Charles Baudelaire. The connection becomes even clearer when Benjamin writes that "Blanqui's astronomical melancholy also corresponds to Baudelaire's 'spleen': The formula of *L'Eternité par les astres*—'The new is always old, and the old always new'—corresponds most rigorously to the experience of spleen registered by Baudelaire" (*Arcades* 362). Of course, both melancholy and spleen fall under the astrological sign of Saturn, so prominently featured in Dürer's *Melancholia I* (figure 1; compare the allegorical symbolism of the frontispiece of Baudelaire's *Les Épaves* (1866; figure 2).

Both likewise represent a kind of melancholy secularism:

> With Blanqui, the cosmos has become an abyss. Baudelaire's abyss is starless; it should not be defined as cosmic space. But even less is it the exotic space of theology. It is a secularized space: the abyss of knowledge and of meanings. What constitutes its historical index? In

> Blanqui, the abyss has the historical index of mechanistic natural science. In Baudelaire, doesn't it have the social index of *nouveauté*? Is not the arbitrariness of allegory a twin to that of fashion?" (*Arcades* 271)

What ties the genre of allegory in its baroque and modern forms to melancholy is this characteristic of arbitrariness, the recognition that "any person, any object, any relationship can mean absolutely anything else" (*GTD* 175). This arbitrariness necessarily leads to the abyss, but it is an abyss with an "index," which means that melancholy leads not just to experience but also to the kind of representation and agency one finds in the political thinker Blanqui and the poet Baudelaire.

Melancholy as Equipment for Living

What can be said for this melancholy? Melancholy suggests loss and weakness, but Benjamin finds in Dürer and Blanqui a melancholy of resilience amid the tumult of the baroque and modern periods, while in Baudelaire he sees melancholy more as a pathology without political consciousness. If it is pathological, as Freud would have it, then how can it accompany critical awareness? If it is not, what is Benjamin's argument against Freud's designation of melancholy as pathology? The two figures most deeply connected to modern melancholy for Benjamin are Baudelaire and Blanqui. In Baudelaire, melancholy plays a symptomatic role that allows Benjamin to discuss him as a kind of brooding genius: "The attraction which a few basic situations continually exerted on Baudelaire belongs to the complex of symptoms associated with melancholy. He appears to have been under the compulsion of returning at least once to each of his main motifs" (*Arcades* 328–29). Here melancholy is a disorder with symptoms, and the idea of repetition compulsion echoes Freud's thinking in *Beyond the Pleasure Principle*.[35]

But Baudelaire's symptoms result just as much from his world, particularly the domain of secularism, as from intrapsychic imbalance: Baudelaire and Blanqui are both damaged by their times, both are haunted by the saturnine tradition of melancholy and spleen: "Baudelaire's spleen is the suffering entailed by the decline of the aura. 'Adorable Spring has lost its perfume' " (*Arcades* 343). Their agency bears little resemblance to the autonomy of the Kantian subject, but it does not simply reduce to powerlessness either. Rather, it faces off against catastrophe: "Spleen is the feeling that corresponds to catastrophe in permanence" (*Arcades* 346).[36] In fact, it seems a melancholy disposition is best able to train the faculties of perception to confront the confusion and ruins of early modern and modern experience. But as his sustained attention to Baudelaire shows, melancholy alone does not guarantee political insight. To put it in terms of the *Trauerspiel* study, the "feeling of dizziness which is induced by the spectacle of the spiritual contradictions of this epoch" leads to melancholy and spleen, but without the "ascetic apprenticeship" Benjamin advocates as a response to this condition, critical insight will not be forthcoming.

Benjamin sees the case of the revolutionary socialist Blanqui differently.[37] The study of astronomy written by Blanqui in prison represents a critical consciousness that links political action to a melancholy image of science, theology, and the notion of eternal recurrence Nietzsche would develop years later. Writing to Max Horkheimer, Benjamin admits that Blanqui's book includes "the clumsy reflections of an autodidact," but he also sees it as a "speculation about the universe" which he finds surprising coming from "this great revolutionary":

> If hell is a theological subject, this speculation may be defined as theological. While deriving his data from mechanistic natural science, the worldview that Blanqui outlines is in fact an infernal view, and is at the same time, in the form of a natural view, the complement to a social order that Blanqui had to recognize as victorious over him in the last years of his life. . . . It represents unconditional submission [*vorbehaltlose Unterwerfung*], but at the same time the most terrible accusation [*die furchtbarste Anklage*] against a society that has reflected this image of the cosmos as a projection of itself onto the heavens.[38]

Beaten down by the political forces of his time, Blanqui's turn to the melancholy eternity of the stars represents for Benjamin a simultaneous submission and frightening accusation against a political order modeled on it. Blanqui reveals the "secularization of time in space" through the "worldview of the natural sciences" (*Arcades*, 472). Personal and historic catastrophes may prevent victory, but they do not eliminate personal agency. In Blanqui Benjamin had found the embodiment of the astronomical reflection, "To the Planetarium," with which he concluded *One-Way Street* ten years earlier. There, in contrast to the ancient sense of wonder for the cosmos, Benjamin sets the modern attempt to subdue it in technology, particularly military technology: "But because the lust for profit of the ruling class sought satisfaction through it [the cosmos], technology betrayed man and turned the bridal bed into a bloodbath" (*SW* 1:487).

The association between spleen and catastrophe takes us to the *Angelus Novus* of the *Theses*. Here the angel is depicted as facing the past while being blasted into the future; for Benjamin, this gaze into the past is shared by the historian and prophet alike (*GS* 4:405, 407). Historical wreckage piles up at the angel's feet while the storm called Progress blows the angel, which stares at the viewer, backward. The angel "would like to stay, awaken the dead, and make whole what has been smashed," but Progress prevents it from doing so. In the face of a catastrophe one is helpless to prevent, the plunge into melancholy is understandable. The point here is that Benjamin's angel is a witness to the catastrophe, and at the same time the angel looks out at the spectator, who becomes a witness to the witness. By meeting the gaze of the spectator, this "dialectical image" of the angel of history manifests an aura that connects melancholy to critical consciousness and even a kind of agency. It would be wrong to describe this agency as "rescue" in any direct sense, but rescue takes more than one form, particularly for a thinker whose work is steeped in theology:

> On the concept of "rescue" [*Rettung*]: the wind of the absolute in the sails of the concept. (The principle of the wind is the cyclical.) The trim of the sails is the relative. . . . [Benjamin's next note reads:] What are phenomena rescued from? Not only, and not in the main, from the discredit and neglect into which they have fallen, but from the catastrophe represented very often by a certain strain in their dissemination [*Überlieferung*], their "enshrinement as heritage [*Würdigung als Erbe*]"—They are saved through the exhibition of the fissure [*Aufweisung des Sprungs*] within them.—There is a tradition [*Überlieferung*] that is catastrophe. (*Arcades* 473)

The catastrophe of tradition of which Benjamin speaks evokes the workings of history and memory, and the kind of rescue described here requires a precise kind of critical reflection. To rescue phenomena from their "enshrinement as heritage" is to read history against the grain, to discover the catastrophe of tradition, and this is very much the kind of work Benjamin cultivates in his studies of baroque drama, Blanqui, and Baudelaire. In doing this kind of work, Benjamin participates in the tradition of melancholy reflection he recognizes in these three "texts," and in so doing articulates a kind of Marxian praxis that refuses both the grand narratives of his day: eternal recurrence and progress.

What kind of praxis this is continues to be a significant matter for debate, related closely to debates on Benjamin's political theology. In the face of catastrophe, critical consciousness—a recognition of the situation—becomes necessary to any political agency. For Benjamin, this consciousness includes a sober recognition of failed human aspirations to shape history and counteract catastrophe, along with frequent but unclear appeals to the realm of the divine. This recognition risks melancholy, but for Blanqui and others, it does not prevent continued engagement.

One pitfall of this debate is a tendency to reduce Benjamin's thought to an expression of his personality. Even Max Pensky, who insightfully analyzes the dynamics of melancholy in Benjamin's work, gives in to the tendency to explain Benjamin's study of melancholy with his personality.[39] What I hope to have shown here is that Benjamin's attention to baroque literature and images informs his political and aesthetic engagements with modernity, and that the category of melancholy emerges for him as a way to think, act, and live with the catastrophes of modernity.[40]

Back to the Culture Wars

In the context of contemporary culture wars, Benjamin's writings on melancholy and science call forth a double irony: first, political anger may not constitute political agency at all but rather a symptom or by-product of discourse based on sharp binary distinctions between religion and science or faith and reason. Second, melancholy contemplation, far from a psychological disorder characterized by inaction, may broaden the category of agency by promoting the kind of thinking and "ascetic apprenticeship" necessary to intervene meaningfully in modern debates over science, religion, and politics.[41]

Finally, a few words on how this mobilization of melancholy relates to the culture wars. The suggestion that melancholy offers anything positive or constructive seems unlikely, even preposterous. For in its modern guise, depression, melancholia is defined as a kind of psychological paralysis in which the individual can't do anything. Medications to treat depression have gained wide use precisely because they are credited with restoring agency to those who take them. The paradox of agency lost and gained runs through Michel de Certeau's study of Jean-Joseph Surin, the seventeenth-century exorcist of Loudun who went mad, condemned himself, and committed suicide, but not without a certain self-determination. Noting the associations of melancholia with genius and madness alike, Certeau observes that Surin, "existing as refuse in this way, living in a fallen state, still allows the subject to retreat into an 'interior' where knowledge of the world grows as one's own being falls into decay."[42] More vividly, Lars von Trier's 2011 film *Melancholia* suggests that melancholy, in the form of a planet of that name moving toward earth and as a beautiful but disturbed woman, will captivate but also destroy those who get in its way.

But melancholy is typically associated with medical and psychological disturbances, as in Robert Burton's *The Anatomy of Melancholy* (1621) and Freud's "Mourning and Melancholia" (1917). For Burton, the scholarly life can contribute to melancholy, but often only because of unjust treatment at the hands of patrons and others. Neglected and mistreated, scholars and even the Muses often fall prey to melancholy.[43] Melancholy can interfere with agency, but Burton's depiction of scholarly melancholy critically defends the value of scholarship as action.

One can find traces of this noble melancholy in Benjamin's work. In Baudelaire and Blanqui Benjamin sees two highly sensitive witnesses to nineteenth-century culture and science. In different ways for these two figures, the experience of modernity leads to melancholy, but melancholy also becomes a condition for and object of their experience. This dialectic of experience and representation endows the melancholy subject with an agency that is particular and even necessary to times of profound crisis and catastrophe. Against conventional understanding, including Hannah Arendt's, the *vita contemplativa* of melancholy is thus also a kind of *vita activa* in which the observer not only gazes upon the world but also engages it critically.[44] To quote a passage cited above, the melancholic "betrays the world for the sake of knowledge. But in its tenacious self-absorption it embraces dead objects in its contemplation, in order to redeem them." Further explanation of this dialectic, particularly in relation to Freud, would be necessary to develop this claim fully, but for now I suggest the possibility of a postsecular kind of agency in Benjamin, not a political theology but a political melancholy.[45] With the *Angelus Novus* of Klee and the *Melancholia I* of Dürer, Benjamin poses the melancholy of Blanqui and Baudelaire as dialectical images in their own right, capable of political agency through keen perception, representation, and embodiment of catastrophe. This agency may seem contemplative or even quietistic, but it is nevertheless critical. And insofar as it resembles the melancholy disposition of political performance in the culture wars, including the denial of science, the melancholy of the critical observer can benefit from the wisdom that "it takes one to know one." Under the saturnine influence of the baroque as it was represented by Warburg and others, Benjamin makes sense of the catastrophes of modern history. Without this kind of melancholy dialectic, there can be no hope of understanding or intervening in today's culture wars of science and religion.

Chapter 2

Secularism between Scholem and Benjamin

Benjamin's friendship with the scholar of Judaism Gershom Scholem was not only his closest but also his most intellectually productive. From their time together in Switzerland during the First World War until Benjamin's death in 1940, the two maintained a steady and lively exchange over ideas of religious tradition and modern culture. Much has been written about these two Jewish Berliners—the cultural and literary critic and the founder of modern research on Jewish mysticism—but there has been less discussion of how their work relates to contemporary discussions of tradition, secularism, and agency. Both challenged secularism and traditionalism in different but parallel ways that related tradition to agency.

To read many of the recent high-profile studies of "religion" and "secularity," one might conclude that tradition and modernity have previously been understood in only one way, and that doubts about the decline of religion or confidence about secularism have no precedent.[1] The present chapter argues otherwise by explicating Scholem's and Benjamin's thinking about tradition and modernity in the context of their intellectual friendship.[2] My claim is that Scholem's work, in dialogue with Benjamin's, makes distinct contributions to contemporary debates on tradition and secularism. In spite of their clear differences over Zionism and Jewish identity, this chapter identifies parallels between Benjamin and Scholem on questions of tradition and identity. Paradoxical and unsystematic, Scholem's writings on modernity and tradition represent not only a necessary companion to Benjamin but also an important twentieth-century criticism of secularism and a set of strategies for reading beyond it.

Scholem's work embodies conflicts of identity, between Jew and German, traditionalist and modern, participant and observer. The biographical framework for understanding these conflicts of identity is well studied and justifiable, but it is easy to assign Scholem's preoccupations with these questions entirely to temperament and historical-cultural context. Scholem's writings on the question of tradition and modernity also involve original political and religious thought. His engagements and disagreements with scholars of Judaism, Walter Benjamin, fellow Zionists, and Hannah Arendt all reveal serious engagements with questions of identity, modernity, and tradition. In contrast to Benjamin's indirectness about group identity and religious tradition, Scholem attempts to address these issues without neglecting the challenges of modernity.

If Scholem ranked identity above tradition, one could claim the opposite for Benjamin. This formulation is simplistic, but it provides a useful starting point for discussion. While Scholem challenged prevailing ideas of tradition, he tended to affirm existing notions of identity, particularly Jewish identity. His focus on mysticism, messianism, "religious anarchism," and antinomianism tends to minimize the practices, rituals, and life (*halakhah*) that make up much of traditional Jewish life. For Benjamin, on the other hand, Jewish and European (especially German) identity can hardly be separated; explicit references to Judaism and the Bible share space in his work, early and late, with European philosophy, literature, and mass culture. Yet Benjamin's concern for tradition, broadly conceived as a category that registers even little-noticed forms of religious and cultural inheritance, runs through all his work.

Scholem's career was devoted almost entirely to scholarship on Jewish mysticism, but his work was no exercise in disinterested *Wissenschaft*. His writings abound in general discussions of tradition and modernity, and it is these interests, I suggest, that motivate his scholarship. While these discussions are wide-ranging, Scholem consistently argued against the idea of secularization as the disappearance of religion, along with the simple division of the world into religion and secularity. The persistence of tradition was an abiding concern of Scholem's, one that he linked directly to his own life and scholarly work. From his early participation in Zionist youth groups, Scholem embraced Jewish identity in contrast to his nationalist father and socialist brother.[3] At the same time, Scholem, a middle-class Berlin intellectual, never practiced traditional Judaism. In his research, Scholem set out from the beginning to subvert the dominant narrative of Judaism as a progressively rationalistic tradition or a kind of "ethical monotheism." In doing so, Scholem may be understood to have devoted himself to a lifelong project of writing a counter-narrative to the view of Judaism, regnant in his youth, as ethical monotheism.[4]

Post-Assimilationism: Against Secularism

In a 1975 interview, Scholem refers to himself as a "post-Assimiliation" Jew. Like the current term "postsecular," Scholem's self-description only indicates what has passed away. The condition of the present remains unspecified, though Scholem has no interest in a wholesale restoration of tradition. Elsewhere in the interview, Scholem makes his view of secularism explicit:

> I don't consider myself a secularist. . . . My secularism is not secular. But the fact that I addressed myself to *kabbalah* not merely as a chapter of history but from a dialectical distance—from identification and distance together—certainly stems from the fact that I had the feeling that *kabbalah* had a living center; it expressed itself according to the time, and that in another form it could, perhaps, have said something else in another generation.[5]

The "dialectical distance" of which Scholem speaks signals that his work is not detached scholarship, and that one of its purposes is to explore and challenge the boundaries of "religion" and "secularity." It also leads to the point, recurrent in Scholem's writings, that Kabbalah takes different and unpredictable forms in different generations. It is important to recall here that Kabbalah literally means "tradition," that is, that which is received. For Scholem, Kabbalah operates almost as the Torah does for students of traditional Judaism: a term that refers to specific texts as well as broader practices that take multiple and changing forms. Subject to radical variation, Scholem's Judaism is Kabbalah, not Torah, theosophy rather than ritual. Tradition is a kind of "wrestling over belief," much as Alasdair MacIntyre understands tradition to be "historically extended, socially embodied argument."[6] In "Education for Judaism" (1971), Scholem defines Jewish history and tradition as a "struggle over great ideas": "Our history is a mighty struggle over these demands [of Torah] and this struggle has many worthy manifestations, not all of which are on the side of the rabbinic tradition."[7]

Scholem consistently challenges the usefulness of the sacred-secular binary:

> The simplistic attitude to the problem of religion to which we have become accustomed over the course of generations is inadequate. The secular interpretation of religious concepts is problematic. Just as we

> may not make an absolute distinction between secularism and religion, so we may not obscure the unique nature of religious problems by means of philosophical answers. . . . Clearly there is secularism which is not at all connected to religion, but one must also note the fact that sometimes secular phenomena appear in religious garb.[8]

Because its analytical categories are flawed, the "secular" standpoint of scholarship on religion is also flawed; Scholem's notion of "dialectical distance—from identification and distance together," anticipates current methodological discussions in the study of religion.[9]

One of Scholem's most trenchant statements on secularism appears in his 1926 letter to Franz Rosenzweig about the creation of modern Hebrew in Palestine:

> They think that they have turned Hebrew into a secular language and that they have removed its apocalyptic sting, but it is not so. The secularization of the language is merely empty words, a rhetorical turn of phrase. In reality, it is impossible to empty the words which are filled to bursting with meaning, save at the expense of the language itself. And indeed, this *Volapük*, this ghostly language spoken in our streets, precisely represents that expressionless linguistic universe which alone may be secularized. But if we pass on to our children the language that we have received, if we, the generation of the transition, revive the language of the old books that it may be revealed to them anew—will not the religious power latent therein one day break out against its speakers?[10]

The secularist revival of Hebrew fails to see how that "ghostly language" will undermine secularism itself. As if to illustrate the power of Hebrew to "break out" in the future, Scholem invokes the unintended potency of the language: "At times, when, in the course of a totally unimportant speech by an anonymous speaker, we hear a religious term, we shudder—even if it might have been meant to comfort us. This Hebrew language is pregnant with catastrophe; it cannot remain in its present state—nor will it remain there."[11] Initially challenging the idea that Hebrew could be secular, Scholem presents the suppressed religious character of Hebrew strikingly in terms of catastrophe and volatility (rather than more typical religious categories like edification or redemption).

It is no coincidence that one of Scholem's most pronounced reflections on secularism concerns language. For Scholem, a lifelong amateur poet, the problem of modernity was always a problem of language, particularly the written language of Jewish tradition. In a 1919 text called "How Should One Learn Hebrew?" Scholem speaks of Hebrew in a way that closely parallels Benjamin's 1916 essay on language: "The goal of learning Hebrew is not the capability to express oneself in this language; it is to understand the expression of something other than its general meaning. It is much more valuable to penetrate Hebrew so that Judaism in its spiritual being [*geisteigen Wesen*] as identical with its spiritual being can be grasped."[12]

Scholem's theory of religious history appears at first to be conventional but turns out to be a counter-narrative to secularization theory. In his 1941 *Major Trends in Jewish Mysticism*, Scholem identifies three stages of religious history: a first in which the world is "full of gods" and therefore without any room for mysticism; a second, "creative epoch," which sees the rise of institutional religion; and a third, "romantic period" in which classic forms and institutions are reinterpreted, together with the rise of mysticism.[13] In this phase, we see mysticism reviving dormant mythical features of the tradition, even in an agonistic fashion that leads to charges of heresy.[14] Elsewhere Scholem suggests a fourth phase, of modern, post-Holocaust history, a time of crisis that Scholem believes is indeterminate but which minimizes mysticism even among the Hasidim.[15]

Scholem's foregrounding of Kabbalah was polemical, as it challenged prevailing halakhic and rationalistic views of Judaism. *Major Trends*, written largely during the 1930s, stresses the role of Kabbalah in providing a new kind of agency to Jews in the aftermath of the exile from Spain of 1492. Lurianic Kabbalah, for Scholem, developed a notion of the "fragmentary character of Jewish existence" out of a "movement which originated either in the catastrophe of 1492 itself or in the Kabbalistic-apocalyptic propaganda attached to that event."[16] One could argue that contemporary events were not far from Scholem's mind when he wrote these words.[17]

For most moderns, he writes, mysticism is impossible because belief in the Torah is lost—thus producing a state of anarchism, which though linked to secularism is not reduced to it for two reasons: the religious dimensions of secular writers like Kafka and Whitman, and the possibility that the flux and uncertainty of the present could produce something new.[18] Throughout his study of Judaism, Scholem encountered and resisted the scholarly counterpart to the assimilationist ideology of his parents. Historians of Judaism like Heinrich Graetz inspired Scholem to develop counter-narratives to what he construed as the dominant rationalistic and assimilationist paradigms of Judaism.[19] The structure of this counter-narrative was the consistent return and transformation of tradition in history.

Benjamin shares Scholem's broad disagreement with ideas of secularism and secularization, but his work complicates the boundary between religion and secularity. His writings on history, tradition, and religion insist on the survival of the religious past in the present, and even though he does use terms like "profane" (*profan*) and "secular" (*säkular*), Benjamin consistently inserts religious categories and terms into discussions—of Kantian philosophy, radical politics, and modern art—that ordinarily excluded them. The survival of religious tradition in modern thought, technology, and popular culture preoccupy Benjamin, but he resists replacing one simple historical paradigm—progress toward secularization—with any other: "Overcoming the concept of 'progress' and overcoming the concept of 'period of decline' are two sides of one and the same thing" (*Arcades* 460).[20] In his critique of secularism, Benjamin affirms a dynamic model of tradition without traditionalism. The metaphor of text and commentary, common to literary and religious discourse, informs many of Benjamin's reflections on tradition (see chapters 3 and 7). But unlike Scholem, whose consistent focus is Judaism, Benjamin finds elements of tradition in unexpected places, such as surrealism, modern cities, and historical materialism. In a letter to Scholem, for example, Benjamin identifies the survival of tradition in the work of Kafka, who, he says, had no "'prophetic vision.' Kafka eavesdropped on tradition, and he who listens hard does not see."[21] The writer who eavesdrops on tradition is no prophet but an author of parables whose work has "sacrificed truth[22] for the sake of clinging to transmissibility [*Tradierbarkeit*], to its aggadic element."

Religious Anarchism

Scholem's statements about belief in God and the nature of Judaism always lead to a qualification, usually framed as "anarchism": "I myself believe in God, but I am a religious anarchist. I do not believe in the Torah of Moses from Sinai. If God really exists, then there is something sublime in the very wrestling over belief in Him."[23] What does Scholem mean by "anarchism"? The term seems to have at least two senses. The first is political and bears the influence of thinkers like Gustav Landauer: "Anarchism held many attractions for me, especially its positive utopianism. . . . To this day I would say that the only social theory that makes sense—religious sense, too—is anarchism, but it is also—practically speaking—the least possible theory."[24] A 1917 journal entry by Scholem combines religious and political uses of "anarchism": "Anarchism (not socialism) is the only conceivable ideal precursor, if one may call it that, of the state of God. This does not mean that anarchy should be sought as a condition, but that the theocratic position in opposition to every non-eternal now [*jede nicht ewige Gegenwart*] is anarchism."[25] This passage exhibits a direct path to utopian realities, while Scholem later embraces a more "dialectical" view of these matters. Scholem recollects this early "naive" period in a 1975 interview: "I was one of those who took the Biblical passage 'And you shall be unto Me a kingdom of priests, and a holy nation' as the definition of Zionism. . . . If I was capable of putting down a thought like that without a second thought, then clearly I was naive and not dialectical."[26]

The second sense of "anarchism" is a more descriptive account and affirmation of historical and religious change as contingency. Against theories of Judaism derived primarily from the Torah, Talmud, and rationalism, Scholem's notion of "anarchism" allows Kabbalah and even the "heresies" of Sabbateanism to be counted as part of the tradition, thus denying supremacy to rabbinic and rationalistic forms of Judaism. It further serves to shift Scholem's focus to experiential and theosophical forms of Judaism. This sense of anarchism is restricted largely to Scholem's understanding of Jewish history. According to Yossef Schwartz, Scholem abandoned his early interest in socialist and anarchist thought after emigrating to Palestine in 1923, though he continued to speak of "religious anarchy" in his later writings.[27] This sense of anarchism links to Scholem's engagement with secularism. Noting Scholem's reluctance to study present-day Kabbalists, Shaul Magid notes Scholem's secularist belief that ultra-orthodox practice was and would remain insignificant in the contemporary world, and that "for Scholem, secularism coupled with a diffuse but definite belief in God was the foundation of his 'religious anarchism.' "[28] Such secularism, focused as it is on religious tradition and belief in God, fits squarely in today's discussions of the "postsecular."

Both senses of "anarchism" mingle without resolution in Scholem's frequent uses of the term. Neither nihilism nor a concrete program for political action, Scholem's anarchism names a political dimension of Jewish tradition and its study. In its radical innovations on tradition and its grandiose assertions about human power, Kabbalah certainly has a political dimension. For the most part, anarchism represents a position of metaphysical and historical uncertainty or contingency on Scholem's part. "I am a religious anarchist, since I cannot judge one or another phenomenon of the past and decide who was right and who was wrong."[29] Anarchism is linked to mysticism and modernity: "Anyone attempting today to bring matters of inspiration and mystical cognition within the range of public understanding, without seeing himself, with a clear conscience, as being connected in an unqualified way with the great principle of Torah from heaven, of that selfsame Torah with those selfsame letters as it is, is a religious anarchist. . . . One who does not share the firm faith of our forebears, whether he is engaged in other paths toward faith, or whether his path has become clouded by history and historical criticism (for there are many sources of doubt regarding this matter of Torah from heaven), may be objectively considered a religious anarchist. All of us today may be considered to a great extent anarchists regarding religious matters, and it should be stated openly."[30]

The religious anarchism that characterizes modernity means that mysticism itself may no longer be possible: "It is not surprising that, within this path to anarchy, and within anarchy itself—a way that is no way, yet one nevertheless walked by thousands and tens of thousands of people, every day, every hour—we have no clear knowledge as to whether mystical experience can in our generation assume a crystallized form obligating any sort of community."[31] Noting the risks of "secular" modernity (including Zionism), Scholem repeatedly expresses such uncertainty about what the future will hold for Judaism. Scholem then moves to a discussion of secularization, "or the sanctity of the secular": "We find it difficult today to judge the possibility of secularization as a camouflage for holiness that has not yet been recognized as such. This is our secular reality here in eretz Yisra'el, into which most of the paradoxical power present in the Jewish people during this generation has entered."[32] Outside Israel, the "sanctity of the secular" takes surprising forms, even in literature: "Perhaps holiness will be revealed within the innermost sanctums of this secularity, and the traditional concepts fail to recognize mysticism in its new forms?" An example Scholem gives is the poetry of Walt Whitman, "who a hundred years ago sang the song of America with a feeling of the absolute sanctity of the absolutely secular."[33] Even more curious than his interest in Whitman is Scholem's fondness for the popular work *Cosmic Consciousness*: "the classical text of secular mysticism, as an extreme expression of what I have said here."[34]

Blurring the boundary between "religion" and "secularity," the category of "religious anarchism" not only allows Scholem to consider Kabbalah and the Sabbatean movement as legitimate parts of Jewish tradition; it actually marginalizes the dominant paradigms of Torah observance, Maimonides's Thirteen Principles, and rationalistic forms of modern Judaism by their misplaced compulsion to fix Jewish thought and practice in one form. Anarchism remains one of the irreducible paradoxes of Scholem's thought, along with of the combination of utopianism with entering history; anti-secularism with anti-halakhic Judaism; belief in God with denial of accessible revelation; and Zionism with criticism of its messianic (too-religious) and too-secular forms. Though unresolved, what remains after tallying these paradoxes is a dynamic model of tradition so flexible that it can include the antinomian heresies of a Messiah who becomes a Muslim, the hidden beliefs and practices of the Marranos and the Turkish descendants of the Sabbateans (known as Dönme, or converts), or the critical scholarship of an assimilationist Berliner in Jerusalem.

Benjamin, by contrast, never embraced anarchism, though he engaged anarchist thought seriously, most famously in his essay "Toward the Critique of Violence" (1921). During that time he read several works on political anarchism by Mikhail Bakunin, Gustav Landauer, Rudolf Stammler, and Georges Sorel (*GS* 7:446–47). Whereas Scholem's "religious anarchism" appears to focus on Jewish identity and tradition, Benjamin's engagement with anarchist thought integrates religious categories with general reflections on politics and culture. With its blend of anarchist and religious categories, Benjamin's essay could be regarded as a variation on Scholem's "religious anarchism." In fact, Benjamin's engagement with Sorel's thought, particularly the notion of the proletarian general strike, goes into greater political detail than Scholem's work, yet his essay is far from partisan or programmatic. "Toward the Critique of Violence" refuses to settle the questions it raises, highlighting instead the difficult challenge of confronting various political, juridical, and theological discourses in order to address the question of violence (see chapter 5).

Benjamin revisits anarchist thought in his 1929 essay on surrealism. The surrealists, for Benjamin, are inheritors of anarchist thought: "Since Bakunin, Europe has lacked a radical concept of freedom. The Surrealists have one. They are the first to liquidate the sclerotic liberal-moral-humanistic ideal of freedom, because they are convinced that 'freedom . . . must be enjoyed unrestrictedly in its fullness without any kind of pragmantic calculation' " (*SW* 2:215). But, asks Benjamin, how do they link this freedom to politics: "Have they bound revolt to revolution?" (*SW* 2:215). Benjamin's next paragraph proposes what it would take "to win the energies of intoxication for the revolution," though it is not clear whether the view he expresses there is an explication of surrealism or his best hope for it. In any case, Benjamin says surrealism must go beyond the "anarchic" view that "an intoxicating component lives in every revolutionary act" (*SW* 2:215). Benjamin insists rather on a dialectical approach to intoxication, aesthetics, and the occult that goes beyond "pernicious romantic prejudices" (*SW* 2:216). This move beyond intoxication and "romantic prejudices" requires what Benjamin calls the "profane illumination of reading" and thinking, which, he says, is more important for learning about "telepathic phenomena" and "the hashish trance" than their "most passionate investigation" (*SW* 2:216). Like Scholem, Benjamin engaged anarchist thought in pursuit of larger questions about tradition and agency. But unlike Scholem's "religious anarchism," Benjamin's uses of anarchism challenged the divide between religion and secularity and sought to engage the problem of political agency.

Agency within Tradition

One of the most striking features of Kabbalah for Scholem is its elevation of human action to a cosmic level:

> Man is the perfecting agent in the structure of the cosmos; like all the other created beings, only even more so, he is composed of all ten *sefirot* and "of all spiritual things," that is, of the supernal principles that constitute the attributes of the Godhead. If the forces of the *Sefirot* are reflected in him, he is also the "transformer" who through his own life and deeds amplifies these forces to their highest level of manifestation and redirects them to their original source.[35]

Because human nature has such an exalted structure, human action has far-reaching powers:

> Man on earth is obviously capable of exerting an influence upon the macrocosm and upon primordial man above. Indeed it is this which bestows on him the enormous importance and the dignity that the kabbalists went to great lengths to describe. Because he and he alone has been granted the gift of free will, it lies in his power to either advance or disrupt through his actions the unity of what takes place in the upper and lower worlds.[36]

This power is not limited to extraordinary experiences but rather resides in "the normal life of the individual within the community."[37] Such power has clear social and political implications, and it would be a source of fascination for Scholem for precisely these reasons. Taken with Scholem's principle of religious anarchism, the human power associated with Kabbalah opens up significant space for political agency in many forms.

Of course, this power remains esoteric, as Scholem insists even for the most well-known forms of Kabbalah. Unlike the Judaism of halakhah

(Torah observance), Scholem's Kabbalah and other forms of mysticism tend to be theosophical schools rather than sources of social organization. Though he couched his analysis in terms of Jewish history and even understood mysticism in political terms, Scholem preferred esoteric texts to public, collective practices.[38] Scholem spent most of his life writing counter-narratives to the grand narratives of European and Jewish history, immersing himself in the minutiae of marginalized and esoteric traditions. Apart from recommending this kind of study and public engagement about it, however, Scholem's work presents human agency as one of the great problems of modernity, and he regards most forms of collective human action in the modern world with suspicion.

Neither secularist nor traditionalist, Scholem understands the modern perspective on tradition to be inherently paradoxical. He concludes *Major Trends in Jewish Mysticism* with the famous anecdote about the great Hasidic rabbi Baal Shem Tov and the persistence of a ritual (through story) even when the ritual itself is forgotten:

> You can say if you will that this profound little anecdote symbolizes the decay of a great movement. You can also say that it reflects the transformation of all its values, a transformation so profound that in the end all that remained of the mystery was the tale. That is the position in which we find ourselves today, or in which Jewish mysticism finds itself. The story is not ended, it has not yet become history, and the secret life it holds can break out tomorrow in you or in me. Under what aspects this invisible stream of Jewish mysticism will again come to the surface we cannot tell. . . . To speak of the mystical course which, in the great cataclysm now stirring the Jewish people more deeply than in the entire history of Exile, destiny may still have in store for us—and I for one believe that there is such a course—is the task of prophets, not of professors.[39]

Scholem's final word here is partly a rhetorical flourish, but it constitutes one of Scholem's most optimistic statements on Zionism and modernity. It also raises a question that Scholem himself never fully addressed: was his stance toward Jewish tradition, as a non-practicing scholar of heretical texts and a frequent critic of Zionism, robust enough to stand on its own, or did it depend for its well-being on the stability of a majority Jewish culture? Like Benjamin, Scholem loves esoteric and indirect expressions; does this love avoid or challenge the problem of social and political agency? The understated hope in "destiny" expressed in the 1941 conclusion to *Major Trends* could be said to follow from Scholem's "religious anarchism," a conviction that anything might happen, a notion of contingency critical of grand narratives and tinged very slightly with messianic hope. But without a more fully developed sense of agency on the social level, one could ask whether Scholem's counter-narrative ever broke free from the grand narratives it criticized.

Walter Benjamin's articulations on agency remain similarly elusive and paradoxical. At the individual level, certain practices of reading, writing, and thinking suggest themselves. The "ascetic apprenticeship" he advocates in the *Trauerspiel* study thus resonates with the "profane illumination" of the surrealism essay (*GTD*, 56). At the collective level, Benjamin tends to be even more reticent about agency, often choosing to criticize existing programs of political action rather than to advocate for others. Still, as subsequent chapters of this study attempt to show, agency was an abiding concern of Benjamin's work closely connected to questions of religion, modernity, and politics.

Scholarship on Tradition, Scholarship as Tradition

It is a paradox not lost on Scholem that while modern Jewish scholars tended to eschew Kabbalah, much of the scholarly and philosophical interest in Jewish mysticism came from Christians like Franz Joseph Molitor. Molitor, whom Scholem read in 1916, was Scholem's first major encounter with Kabbalah scholarship.[40] Like Johannes Reuchlin and Pico della Mirandola before him, Molitor was a Christian for whom the Kabbalah was a source of esoteric wisdom and romantic speculation. Scholem's response to the state of research on Jewish mysticism was to surpass Jewish and Christian scholarship on Kabbalah in comprehensiveness and rigor. Given the landscape of Jewish and Christian uses of Jewish mysticism and the counter-narrative of Jewish tradition Scholem wished to write, the question remains how he thought his modern scholarly work itself related to this tradition.

Scholem's response to the question is rich and considered. Like most scholars of religion, he typically makes a sharp distinction between the scholarship and practice of religion. In a few instances, though, Scholem blurs the boundary between modern scholarship and traditional practice. Nowhere does he make this link more explicitly than in his 1958 "Unhistorical Aphorisms on the Study of Kabbalah." In his first aphorism, Scholem observes the inherent irony of a philological study of mysticism, which deals with the "veil of fog" which encloses its subject: "Does something of the law of the thing itself remain visible to the philologist, or has its essence already disappeared in this historical projection?" Scholem then turns from this familiar point about the elusiveness of mystical studies to compare this study to mysticism itself: "But doesn't this element of irony lie already in the object of this Kabbalah itself, and not only in its history?"[41]

Scholem's bold analogy between scholarship and mystical practice has been identified by Daniel Weidner, and it anticipates contemporary discussions about the standpoint of religious studies.[42] Jonathan Z. Smith, for example, emphasizes the role of religion in making meaning through narrative and reasoning, and the paradox that religious studies often overlook this dimension of religion in their search for deeper, hidden meanings within religious language and practice.[43] Smith and others have also raised the potential "religious" dimensions of religious studies.[44] In simplest terms, religion can be a bit like scholarship, and scholarship can be a bit like religion. This is not to equate religious scholarship with "religion"; rather, to consider these analogies is to question such time-honored categories as "religion," "secularity," and "tradition."

Scholem pursues the analogy between scholarship and mysticism only obliquely in the remaining aphorisms, but he begins the second with the paradox that the explicitness of Kabbalah can guarantee its secrecy, and that such secrecy in openness involves "mystical-anarchistic politics."[45] The esoteric fascination of Scholem, which has diverse resonances for Benjamin and Leo Strauss, here belongs to a challenge to exoteric theologies that would claim the immediate availability of tradition. According to David Biale, Buber and Barth are both targets of this polemic.[46] As it develops in the aphorisms, Scholem links this anti-exoteric theology to his initial analogy between scholarship and mysticism: "Totalities can only be handed down in occult fashion. The name of God can be spoken but not expressed. [*Ganzheiten sind nur okkult tradierbar. Der Name Gottes is ansprechbar, aber nicht aussprechbar.*]"[47] Biale observes:

> The absolutely concrete word of God cannot be comprehended by human beings directly, as existentialists such as Barth, Schoeps and Martin Buber thought. Instead, this word must undergo a process of mediation, of translation into human terms, which is the historical tradition. Thus the commentator on the tradition rather than the ecstatic, who claims direct communication from God, is the true *homo religiosus*. In this sense, the historian, who deals with the sources of tradition, is a secular manifestation of the religious personality.[48]

If mysticism concerns esoteric knowledge, then the scholar of mysticism inherits the tradition of seeking that knowledge. What Biale leaves unexamined, though, is Scholem's striking mention of "mystical-anarchistic politics." What could this term mean? While elsewhere anarchism refers for Scholem to the radical contingency of religious tradition and its freedom from rigid orthodoxy, here it describes the preservation of secrets even when Kabbalah becomes widespread. The mystical side of the politics, then, would be this esoteric or occult dimension of Kabbalah, while "anarchistic" refers to the contingent public expansion of Kabbalah in the work of the seventeenth-century popularizer Bacharach.

In his final aphorism, Scholem draws a different analogy, this time between the religion of Kabbalah and secular nihilism, with Kafka's writings as the main illustration. Kafka's writings, concludes Scholem, destroy something of that powerful luster of the canonical, the perfected.[49] Here as in many other places in Scholem's work, Kafka represents a modernist inheritor of mystical tradition, a modern "kabbalist."[50] According to Moshe Idel, Kafka significantly influenced Scholem's ideas of Kabbalah even though Kafka was not deeply familiar with Jewish tradition.[51] Idel credits Scholem's early reading on Kabbalah as a key influence on his own and Benjamin's ideas of language, but the parallels could also result from their common reading of Hamann, Baader, and Molitor.[52] In spite of these diverse and modern influences, Idel challenges the idea that Scholem was a secularist, arguing that his "demonic" and anarchistic orientation to traditional Judaism was still religious.[53]

For Scholem as for Benjamin, the labels "religious" and "secular" fail to capture the complexity of their engagements with tradition and modernity. Their extended correspondence on Kafka's work, which includes a long poem by Scholem, goes back and forth on the status of scripture and revelation in his work. Was scripture in Kafka's world lost (Benjamin) or simply indecipherable (Scholem)? For Benjamin, the question whether scripture is lost or indecipherable doesn't matter, because "without the key that belongs to it, the Scripture is not Scripture, but life . . . It is in the attempt to metamorphize life into Scripture that I perceive the meaning of 'reversal,' which so many of Kafka's parables endeavor to bring about."[54] Scholem disagrees, coining the phrase "nothingness of revelation" to describe "a state in which revelation appears to be without meaning, in which it still asserts itself, in which it has *validity* but *no significance*."[55] True to his religious anarchism, Scholem insists on the survival of scripture and revelation even without meaning, while Benjamin's concern is to recognize the messianic and theological dimensions of Kafka's work without pinning them down.

Commenting on this exchange between Benjamin and Scholem, Robert Alter detects an ambivalence in Scholem on whether the "nothingness of revelation" is exceptional or typical in religious tradition.[56] In either case, suggests Alter, Scholem held to the view that some path of tradition remained open, and so "to say that the pupils have simply lost their Holy Writ is to concede what Scholem the religious anarchist was unwilling to concede, that there is no working connection between human consciousness and ultimate being."[57] In other words, despite genuine commitments to anarchism and nothingness and deep suspicion of any kind of orthodoxy or orthopraxis, Scholem simultaneously insisted on the reality of tradition in the present. For Alter, this position distinguishes Scholem from Benjamin somewhat, but well before anyone coined the term "post-secular," Alter notes that, like Kafka, both of them "stood at different points, which did not remain wholly fixed for any of them, in the no-man's-land between religious tradition and modern secular culture."[58]

Scholem's work follows a historical trajectory from Bible to Kabbalah to scholarship to Kafka and literary criticism on Kafka. Far from a grand narrative, though, the lines of historical change traced by Scholem reflect his dialectical understanding of tradition as an ever-changing, contingent, and minimally coherent process. The central position Scholem assigns to the scholar or critic emerges partly from the central role of commentary in Judaism: "Over the course of generations, commentary became the first ranking form of Jewish creation. . . . By their very nature, the commentators were modest in demanding authority for themselves. Their authority underwent changes and at times even went unchallenged, but the theological demand implied in their words was fundamentally radical: the Divine Revelation was interpreted through them to the human intellect."[59]

The scholar is thus as much a part of tradition as an independent observer of it. In an earlier methodological essay (from 1944), Scholem names three contradictions within the history of Jewish studies that could very easily be translated to religious studies and area studies in general:

1. "The contradiction between the repeated declarations of being a pure and objective science, which is no more than a branch of academic studies in general and which has no purpose outside of itself—and the striking fact of the political function which this discipline was intended to fulfill . . ."
2. ". . . Contradiction between the spiritual stature of most of the great figures of this science, and those ideals which they inscribed upon their banner . . ."
3. "The conservative tendencies and destructive tendencies within this discipline are interwoven with one another."[60]

These three "contradictions" find no easy resolution for Scholem, but they indicate Scholem has parted company with the confident *Wissenschaft* of the past without abandoning the scholarly enterprise. Scholarship takes place in a context with political, institutional, and theological lineaments; to see this means to be self-critical but not self-defeating. Scholem's self-awareness as a scholar of religion echoes his self-awareness as a "post-Assimilationist" German Jew and his consistent challenge to secularism. Like his remarks on anarchism, Scholem's comments on the wider implications of scholarship remain inconclusive but suggestive of an ongoing dialectic of proximity to and distance from tradition in Jewish studies. This dialectic is reflected in his own ambivalence toward his predecessors in the *Wissenschaft des Judentums*.[61]

Scholem's reflections on Jewish studies have political as well as theological implications. Scholem's forceful rejection of the *Wissenschaft des Judentums* he inherited is matched by the equally forceful rebuilding of the field in the context of Zionism. In an essay on modern Jewish studies, Scholem observes: "This was a charged atmosphere, an atmosphere electrified by the powerful vision of a renewed discipline which would draw its power from the roots of the national renewal, from the Zionist awakening, and from the constant contact with the atmosphere of rebuilding a nation."[62] During this process, Scholem acknowledges the burden of his generation scholarship: "We came as rebels and found ourselves to be heirs," and the building of a nation was accompanied with the rebuilding of the discipline, a fact Scholem expresses in biblical terms: "The stones that were rejected by the builders will become the cornerstone."[63] The project of a Jewish state creates space for this academic field: "This change [Zionism] produced something new: it became possible for people to devote themselves fully to the Science of Judaism as a result of their Zionist commitment. These men had no theological attachments and did not approach the subject because of rabbinical interests. . . . Within the framework of the rebuilding of Palestine it led to the foundation of centers like the Hebrew University in Jerusalem where Judaic studies, although central, are pursued without any ideological coloring. Everyone is free to say and to teach whatever corresponds to his scholarly opinion without being bound to any religious (or anti-religious) tendency."[64]

On the other hand, Jewish studies after Zionism still faced obstacles in Scholem's view: "All of these ills [sentimentality, "Enlightenment ideology regarding its pre-judgment of religious phenomena," dilettantism] have now assumed a national dress. From the frying pan into the fire: following the emptiness of assimilation there comes another type, that of the contentious nationalist phrase. Instead of religious homiletics and religious rhetoric, we have developed a national homiletics and a national rhetoric in science."[65] Jewish studies was enabled but also compromised by Zionism.

Scholem often relates secularism to Zionism, but there is scholarly disagreement about his views on both. Jacqueline Rose emphasizes Scholem's work in the peace group B'rit Shalom and his warnings about the dangers of mixing messianism with Zionism.[66] Gabriel Piterberg, on the other hand, regards Scholem as a mainstream supporter of Zionism. One reason for this disagreement could be the inner tensions in Scholem's thought. According to Stéphane Mosès, there are two distinct tendencies in Scholem's writing on the subject: "One the one hand, Scholem quite quickly accepted the secularization of Judaism as a historically inevitable stage in what he was to call the 'dialectic' of Zionism."[67] At the same time, though, Scholem expresses severe doubts about the value of this secular turn and its potential to lead to a meaningful survival of Jewish tradition. Moses quotes Scholem thus: "'When you look at the secularization process, at the barbarization of the so-called new culture, you can perceive grave processes in which it is difficult to discern any seed of [the] future."[68] Scholem never resolves the tension in his thought about the dangers and promise of secularizing Zionism, but he consistently opposes the view that these modern phenomena follow a necessary historical plan, either in Hegelian or messianic terms.

It is therefore an exaggeration to suggest, as Gabriel Piterberg does, that Scholem's scholarship on Kabbalah served primarily to buttress his Zionism. Piterberg regards Scholem's scholarship as a Zionist "yearning for an ancient myth that would renew, reinvigorate, and transform" Judaism. Piterberg is correct to challenge Biale's relatively apolitical reading of Scholem, but it seems to me that Scholem's Zionism, problematic as it was, was subordinate to his scholarship, and not the other way around.[69] However flawed and unsystematic, Scholem's work challenges the binary of secular politics and religion so often imposed on his work. The related tendency to regard Scholem and Adorno as rivals in a religious-secularist tug of war over Benjamin, while not totally unjustified, is also misleading. Already in 1938, Scholem befriended Adorno and

> formed an unexpectedly close relationship at a subsequent long meeting at Adorno's home. . . . The good spirit that prevailed in the meetings between Adorno and me was due not so much to the cordiality of the reception as to my considerable surprise at Adorno's appreciation of the continuing theological element in Benjamin. I had expected a Marxist who would insist on the liquidation of what were in my opinion the most valuable furnishings in Benjamin's intellectual

> household. Instead I encountered here a man who definitely had an open mind and even a positive attitude toward these traits, although he viewed them from his own dialectical perspective.[70]

The ambivalence toward traditional *Wissenschaft des Judentums* goes back to Molitor:

> Notwithstanding the fact that everything he said about history was utterly groundless, he nevertheless did note a place in which the hidden life of Judaism had once dwelled, to which I attached myself in my meditations. I did not enter this field with the intention of writing the history of Kabbalah, but rather its metaphysics. I was struck by the impoverishment of what people were fond of designating as the philosophy of Judaism. The only three authors I knew—Saadiah Ga'on, Maimonides, and Hermann Cohen—annoyed me, in that they saw their primary function as setting up antitheses to myth and pantheism and disproving them.[71]

Like Molitor, Franz von Baader, another nineteenth-century German scholar of Kabbalah, interested Benjamin and Scholem alike.[72] Molitor was among the first writers Scholem read on the subject.[73] In 1916, the year in which Benjamin wrote his essay on language, Scholem and Benjamin read and discussed Molitor's *Philosophy of History* and Baader's *Lectures on an Emerging Theory of Sacrifice or Cult.*[74]

Jewish Identity and Zionist Modernity

Scholem frequently links his scholarly project to Jewish and Zionist identity. What this identity means for him is not completely clear, outside of the persistent but ever-changing tradition he studies. Although he denied the need to practice Judaism, he claimed to believe in God; although he quarreled with many forms of Zionism, he lived in Palestine and Israel from the time he left Germany in the 1920s. In his letter to Hannah Arendt about her *Eichmann in Jerusalem* (1963), Scholem chides her for her apparent lack of *ahavat Israel*, the "love of Israel," which entailed for him a commitment to the Jewish people: "In you, dear Hannah, as in so many intellectuals who came from the German Left, I find little trace of this."[75] In her response to Scholem, Arendt writes: "I have never in my life 'loved' any people or collective—neither the German people, nor the French, nor the American, nor the working class or anything of that sort.

I indeed love 'only' my friends and the only kind of love I know of and believe in is the love of persons."[76]

In the same paragraph with his remark about the Jewish value of *ahavat Israel* Scholem invokes the German value of *Herzenstakt* (sensibility): "In circumstances such as these, would there not have been a place for what I can only describe with that modest German word—*Herzenstakt*? You may laugh at the word; although I hope you do not, for I mean it seriously." Scholem illustrates with an example: "Your quotation (taken over without comment from a Nazi source!) about the traffic with the armbands with the Star of David in the Warsaw ghetto, or the sentence about Leo Baeck 'who in the eyes of both Jews and Gentiles was the "Jewish *Führer*."' "[77] Arendt responds to Scholem's remark about *Herzenstakt*: "Generally speaking, the role of the 'heart' in politics seems to me altogether questionable. You know as well as I how often those who merely report certain unpleasant facts are accused of lack of soul, lack of heart, or lack of what you call *Herzenstakt*."[78]

It may not be a coincidence that Arendt and Scholem also differed on the question of secularization. For Arendt, "secularization" means "the separation of religion and politics," a dramatic phase of modern history that means "nothing is less likely to have taken place than the gradual transformation of religious categories into secular concepts which the defenders of unbroken continuity try to establish."[79] Arendt's point depends on a sharp distinction between public and private:

> The fact is that the separation of church and state occurred, eliminating religion from public life, removing all religious sanctions from politics, and causing religion to lose that political element it had acquired in the centuries when the Roman Catholic Church acted as the heir of the Roman Empire. . . . . Thus the political theorists of the seventeenth century accomplished secularization by separating political thinking from theology, and by insisting that the rules of natural law provided a basis for the body politic even if God did not exist.[80]

In *The Human Condition*, Arendt extends the "Christian hostility toward the public realm" to religion in general: though religion inhabits the world, in its otherworldliness it does so negatively: "fleeing the world and hiding from its inhabitants, it negates the space the world offers to men, and most of all that public part of it where everything and everybody are seen and heard by others."[81] In her letter to Scholem, this distinction appears in her statement about love (see above) as well as in her comment on *ahavat Israel* (above).

Scholem and Arendt also differed on Zionism: Zionism, he writes, is "a utopian return of the Jews to their own history," yet he viewed the utopian and messianic strains of Zionism critically.[82] The deepest ambivalence or paradox in Scholem is the difference between historical contingency and the claim to destiny inherent to his Zionism. The term that captures or finesses both sides of this paradox is anarchism. As for Arendt, the essays collected in *The Jewish Writings* reveal several criticisms of particular forms and expressions of Zionism at different times, but they also demonstrate an abiding seriousness that would place her closer to Scholem's thinking and sympathies than the correspondence over *Eichmann in Jerusalem* would suggest.[83]

Yet the intensity of Scholem's exchange with Arendt may reveal a deeper ambivalence or sympathy toward *Eichmann in Jerusalem.* In "Jews and Germans," he writes that Jews responded to anti-Semitism with "peculiar blindness," and that Jewish assimilation rose to the level of "self-contradiction" and "self-surrender" by the 1930s.[84] But as if to suggest that assimilationist thinking from before the war continues to do damage after the war, Scholem adds that the postwar theory that Nazism was a "historical accident, was invented by *Jews*."[85] It is on such ground that Scholem, however ambivalently, criticizes Arendt.

Scholem's ambivalence exends also to Zionism in several of its pre- and post-state forms. In a 1975 interview, Scholem bluntly denounces Zionists from both periods: "The Blau-Weiss people started as romantics and ended up fascists. As you know, it isn't popular to say that Zionism has fascists, too. But I think it does, even in Israel."[86] In "Reflections on the Possibility of Jewish Mysticism in Our Time" (1963), Scholem frames state-building as a secular distraction from the "realm of holiness":

> Having entered into this productive life, is there any energy left for the creation of forms through which the connection of these forms to the realm of holiness may be recognized, yet will nevertheless have eternal significance for us beyond that? One may express some doubt as to whether there is a positive answer to this question. Or perhaps there is the possibility of a double path of holiness and secularity, toward which we are moving? . . . Perhaps holiness will be revealed within the innermost sanctums of this secularity, and the traditional concepts fail to recognize mysticism in its new forms?[87]

Arendt seems to think Scholem is a naive traditionalist, and Scholem seems to think Arendt is a naive secularist. Neither is true. Neither could deny the power of tribalism in politics. The question is what to do about it. In a striking passage in *The Life of the Mind* (1971), Arendt quotes a parable by Kafka called "HE," in which "He" is pressed from behind and from the front. Arendt interprets the text to be a struggle between past and future for the "thinking ego."[88] Between past and future, the thinking subject occupies a *nunc stans* ("standing now")which Arendt attempts to diagram as a diagonal line toward infinity, a "present which is timeless." She continues, "We call it the region of the spirit, but it is perhaps rather the path paved by thinking, the small inconspicuous track of non-time beaten by the activity of thought within the time-space given to natal and mortal men. Following that course, the thought-trains, remembrance and anticipation, save whatever they touch from the ruin of historical and biographical time." This track of thought, the capacity to think in the *nunc stans*, accounts for the "strange survival of great works," the capacity of human writings to transcend time.[89]

But Scholem's sense of Jewish identity long preceded the Holocaust. From the time his father threw him out of the house for his Zionism, Scholem embraced Jewish identity as a part of himself he believed his parents had denied themselves and him. As a self-described "post-assimilatory Jew," Scholem rejected the assimilationist orientation of his parents at the age of fifteen (1912), arguing that German middle-class Jews lived in self-deception. When he began to pursue the study of Judaism, his parents asked him, "'Do you want to return to the ghetto?'" and he replied, "'You are the ones who are living in the ghetto. Only you won't admit it. Where are the Gentiles? I've never seen a single one of them come to your homes for a social call.'"[90] Later, during the First World War, his father disowned him and kicked him out of the house over their disagreement over the war, saying, "It's all the same—socialism, Zionism—it's all antipatriotic."[91]

Putting aside any psychoanalytic explanation for Scholem's commitment to Jewish identity, Scholem's understandings of personal and group identity may be linked to his rejection of the secular-religious dichotomy insofar as he saw German identity as a secularist self-denial of Jewish tradition, even while his understandings of Zionist and Jewish identity strove against nostalgic traditionalism. Yet while Scholem was a lifelong critic of many forms and positions taken in the name of Zionism, his Zionism was, as Daniel Weidner puts it, less of a conviction than a paradoxical personal position: "Scholem does not write about Zionism, rather, he could only write as a Zionist."[92]

It may also be a matter of the ethics of group affiliation or particularism. It must be added that Scholem's Zionism included significant critical and self-critical moments. He was a harsh critic of Zionist groups that imitated German youth groups, arguing instead that Jewish youth should learn about Jewish tradition.[93] In Palestine he belonged to a group called B'rit Shalom from 1925 to 1933, which criticized the Zionist goal of a Jewish majority.[94] He steadfastly resisted any tendency to associate mystical or messianic claims with Zionism. In a 1934 review of Isaac Breuer's *New Kuzari: A Way to Judaism*, Scholem writes, "Zionism needs badly to be mindful of its religious problems; it needs historical consciousness and criticism of its activities and slogans. But just as it will not find its salvation, its *tikkun*, in the wild apocalypticism of the Revisionists, it must not give way to a politics of mysticism which uses the most profound symbols of our inner life to usurp a power which others have fought for and have sacrificed themselves to firmly establish—which uses these symbols to subjugate a way of life whose development the adherents of that politics have followed with nothing but excommunications, maledictions, and hate."[95] From his early engagement with Zionism until late in his life, Scholem insisted on this distinction between Zionism and messianism.[96]

The exchange between Scholem and Arendt on *ahavat Israel* indicates something of a political dilemma for German-born Jews after the Holocaust. One side of the dilemma is marked by Scholem's uneasy Zionism, a critical but committed attachment to the Jewish settlement of Palestine that became the state of Israel. Scholem's life there from 1923 until his death in 1982 led to many expressions of pride and self-criticism; both can be found in "A Lecture about Israel," delivered shortly after the Six Day War in 1967.[97] The other side of the dilemma is Arendt's challenge to the principle of *ahavat Israel*, a position that refuses the particularism or exceptionalism that tends to go with that principle. Taken to an extreme, Scholem's position leads to a kind of fierce nationalism that denies the dignity and rights of those who stand in the way of Zionism. What is more, Scholem's "anarchistic" understanding of Judaism suggests an atavistic group identity unmoored from its historical tradition. Arendt's rejection of *ahavat Israel*, for its part, can lead to a kind of universal humanism cleansed of cultural and historical particularity. (One could, in any case, question Arendt's lack of *ahavat Israel* solely on the grounds that her numerous writings on Jewish people and politics were anything but dispassionate statements.)[98] Arendt's claim that love applies only to one's friends, moreover, appears to inscribe a sharp boundary between a private domain (where love is possible) and a public domain (where love is impossible). Such a distinction is arguably alien to Arendt's own thought.[99]

Of course, the exchange between Arendt and Scholem is a polemic, and neither thinker affirms the extremes toward which their letters tend. Both thinkers are clear-eyed observers of the promises and failures of modernity, and neither places naive hope in atavistic attempts to revive (political or religious) tradition. It is therefore unfortunate that the polemical exchange of letters did not lead to a more sustained engagement with the problems of modernity and tradition so central to the work of both thinkers. Imposed to an extent on Arendt and Scholem by history, the debate over *ahavat Israel* highlights the confrontation of tradition and modernity, and it remains as difficult today as it did in 1963.[100]

For Benjamin, who endorsed cultural Zionism in 1912 and chose not to emigrate to Palestine from Europe, the affirmation of Jewish identity and tradition was separated from the claim to a Jewish nation-state. He thus avoided the simple tribalism and simple universalism that divided Scholem from Arendt. His interest was not to justify a particular political order but to think about the place of tradition and agency at a time of danger. The particular configuration of modern Jewish identity, which straddled the boundaries of religion and secular affiliation, particular and universal, framed Benjamin's conception of tradition as an inheritance to be studied and recognized.

Biblical Tradition and Benjamin

For Scholem, the Bible or Torah represents an eternally receding horizon of myth and revelation, and as the institutions of tradition become more distant from this horizon, myth and revelation return transformed in the form of mysticism. This pattern, which Scholem sketches at the beginning of *Major Trends in Jewish Mysticism*, represents a "revival of mythical lore" in mystical tradition: "Thus through wide and scattered provinces of Kabbalism, the revenge of myth upon its conqueror is clear for all to see, and together with it we find an abundant display of contradictory symbols."[101] This "revenge of myth" upon dominant forms of institutional Judaism has a counterpart in the "revenge" of mysticism upon rationalistic models of Judaism in Jewish studies. Mysticism recovers and transforms early forms of religious experience in reaction to the rationalizing institutional forces of rabbinic tradition. The stage for this process was the text of the Bible itself; from the *merkabah* tradition of mystical speculation named for the chariot in Ezekiel 1 to the sheer fact that the primary genre of kabbalistic literature was midrash, or biblical commentary, Scholem recognizes the central place of the Bible in Jewish mystical tradition, even though the bulk of Scholem's analysis gravitates toward theosophical doctrines more closely tied to gnostic thought and medieval history.[102]

Like Benjamin, Scholem holds the Bible at arm's length. Unlike Benjamin, though, Scholem had the linguistic training and professional standing to pursue biblical scholarship. But for both thinkers, the Bible as revelation stands far removed from modern consciousness. One way to make the point is to distinguish between the Bible itself and the idea or the "world of the Bible":

> The jump to the Bible is fictitious. The Bible is a reality that does not exist today. But there does exist an ideal which we call the world of the Bible and which we wish to promote today. That is certainly legitimate, even though I believe that this jump may cause an educational failure with regard to the continuity of the generations, which has bequeathed us strength and a powerful tradition which would be fostered, from which we would select, and which we would treat as a problem. In this sense, I am a religious anarchist, since I cannot judge one or another phenomenon of the past and decide who was right and who was wrong.[103]

Scholem also criticizes Zionist uses of the Bible:

> Ben-Gurion encouraged the Canaanites because he skipped directly to the Bible and rejected all exile. But he leapt into the moral Bible, while they turned to the pagan Bible. Ben-Gurion has today forgotten the fact that he alienated himself. He thought then that we were returning to a Biblical historical continuity. But such a continuity exists only in books, and not in history. The continuity of the biblical period existed within a religious reality and not within an historical reality. Ben-Gurion encouraged movements towards cutting off their ties with Judaism here in Israel. But it is impossible to strike roots right into the Bible.[104]

Scholem's few writings on the Bible are more philosophical than philological. "The Lament Songs" ("Die Klagelieder," 1918) is a 39-page typescript of five translated biblical lament texts and a ten-page essay, "On Lament and the Lament Song" ("Über Klage und Klagelied"), that bears special interest for Benjamin's work on language and the *Trauerspiel.* Scholem describes this study of biblical lament as a "metaphysical theory on the essence of the *kinnot,*" and he presents his commentaries on Jonah and Job as the "basis for a commentary on Jonah and Job—metaphysical reflections of mine that were suppressed."[105] The study of biblical lament echoes Benjamin's 1916 essay on language. The characterization of lament includes the following: "All language is endless, but there is one kind of language whose endlessness is deeper and different from all others (except for the language of God). . . . it reveals nothing, for the being revealed in it has no content."[106] Using the same phrase Benjamin uses to describe language, Scholem compares the "spiritual being" of lament to tragedy and mourning (*Trauer*). My interest here is to consider how Scholem's notion of lament compares with Benjamin, particularly on the categories of tradition and human agency.

For Scholem, the lament is a form of language with no content or symbolic form: "It is not symbolic, rather it only points toward the symbol."[107] Associating lament with the language of tragedy and mourning as forms of language similarly connected with being (*geistige Wesen*, a term used by Benjamin as well) and symbolic nature, Scholem focuses on the negative, self-effacing character of these forms of language. Scholem considers the language of lament to be unanswerable; the "language of silence," continues Scholem, is lament, and its tendency toward silence is the "truest anarchy."[108] But this silence and inexpressibility raises the question of tradition: lament can only be transmitted if an "entire people speaks in the language of silence." The biblical lament over the destruction of the temple, he claims, captures the "tragic paradox" and the "endless tension" of expressing the inexpressible.[109] Jewish tradition, from ancient Israel to Judah Halevy, enacts this paradox of tradition. Though it marks an interest in biblical studies he largely abandoned, Scholem's essay on lament anticipates many of his later concerns and reflects his early dialogue with Benjamin.

Noting that only God can respond to lament, Scholem explains this tradition in political terms—*Anarchie, Volk, Revolution*—that will lead him to wonder how a tradition of silent laments became possible: "Whatever incredible revolution must come upon a people to enable their lament to be passed down, that an entire people should speak in the language of silence, can only be guessed." Tracing the tradition of lament through biblical and rabbinic history, Scholem describes a process whereby "teaching laments and lament teaches."[110] With this Scholem relates his modern metaphysical interests to particular historical realities of Jewish tradition. This is where his work contrasts with Benjamin's, where the history and group identity of Israel play no serious part. At the same time, Scholem leaves the question of human agency open, focusing instead on divine revelation as the means for lament to become "tradierbar."

Benjamin wrote Scholem that his "Lament" text helped him understand law, mourning, scripture, and identity in the Jewish tradition.[111] In the passage of his language essay that most resembles Scholem's lament text (and predates it by two years), Benjamin writes that all of nature laments after the Fall: "Lament, however, is the most undifferentiated, impotent expression of language. It contains scarcely more than the sensuous breath" (*SW* 1:73). Benjamin then relates lament to mourning in what I believe is an allusion to biblical texts: "Because she is mute, nature mourns" (*GS* 2:255; the same statement appears in the *Trauerspiel* study: *GS* 1:398). Like Scholem's lament, Benajmin's relates closely to mourning and belongs to a unique form of language. By calling it powerless, Benjamin seems to deflect the question of human agency, though his general theory of language opens space for at least two kinds of efficacious human action: uses of human language that affirm the Fall, and, more obliquely, acts of critical perception or insight into this linguistic state of affairs. This move echoes his notion in the *Trauerspiel* study of the "ascetic apprenticeship" (*asketischen Schulen den Geist*) to allow a "position of strength from which it is possible to take in the whole panorama and yet remain in control of oneself" (*GTD* 56).

But whereas Scholem pursues the question of how lament could enter religious tradition in spite of its singularly silent nature, Benjamin follows lament into the world of literature, especially the seventeenth-century *Trauerspiel* of which lament is so important a part. Beyond the *Trauerspiel* study, the next location for lament and reflection on it for Benjamin is the Kraus essay of 1931, where his characterization of Kraus's project includes its status as an "endless lament" rooted in the history of creation (*GS* 2:345, see also 349). The category of lament returns in the *Arcades Project*, where it describes one of the genres in Baudelaire (*GS* 1:1149), and in the Paris essay for the *Arcades Project*, Benjamin's description of how Haussmann transformed the flaneurie and phantasmagoria of nineteenth-century urban life, he characterizes the critique of Haussmann as jeremiads that take the form of biblical lament (*GS* 5:57).

Scholem's 1919 text on the book of Jonah testifies to the intellectual exchange between him and Benjamin. It is also one of Scholem's rare close readings of a biblical text, one that operates like a teacher who "educates through questions, not answers."[112] He describes Jonah as a theory of prophecy: "Its purpose is to introduce this spiritual continuum which is its ethics—and hence its purpose is to inaugurate a problem." The problem is the idea of divine justice and history, which "designates the relation of the canonical to tradition."[113] Divine judgment, like Benjamin's notions of divine violence and language, is self-referential and self-defining: "Divine judgment is the judgment that is its own execution."[114] Scholem, like Benjamin, resolves the problem of divine judgment and history through the category of messianism, the "eternal present" that defers the last judgment. Scholem's reading of Jonah is idiosyncratic, driven more by the abstract theological and philosophical problem of theodicy and history than by an engagement with the literary features of the text. Written at the end of World War I while he and Benjamin were living and working closely together, Scholem's essay on Jonah represents a crucial stage in his lifelong attempt to relate tradition to modernity. For Scholem as well as Benjamin, the category of messiah, drawn from traditional Judaism but far from orthodox, would provide a lasting solution to the problem: deferral of divine judgment acknowledges modernity without affirming secularization.

In the 1975 memoir of his friendship with Benjamin, Scholem recalls conversations with Walter and Dora Benjamin on being Jewish without observing Torah: "For me that manner of life was connected with the concretization of the Torah in a false, premature sphere—as evidenced by the paradoxes of the tricks that become manifest in the process and that are necessarily inherent in such a false relationship. Something is wrong with the application; the orders clash. I said I had to maintain the anarchic suspension. Only later did my historical perspective change—in a direction that disposed of the problem, for my understanding of the sense in which one may speak of revelation had changed."[115] The change Scholem describes was likely the conviction that revelation lay beyond the easy reach of modern hands, but whether the problem had really been "disposed of" is doubtful, as Scholem's continued engagement with it, and with Benjamin's work on it, suggests.

Scholem wonders at the paradoxical nature of Benjamin's engagement with tradition:

> That I never heard him make an atheistic statement was surely no cause for surprise to me, . . but it did surprise me that he still could speak quite unmetaphorically of "God's words," in distinction to human words, as the foundation of all linguistic theory . . . Benjamin evidently was torn between his predilection for a mystical theory of language and the equally strongly perceived need to struggle against it in the context of a Marxist view of the world. I mentioned this to him, and he admitted this contradiction quite candidly. He said it was simply a matter of a task that he had not yet mastered but for which he had high hopes. His "Janus face" still bore the liveliest expression.[116]

With this passage late in his memoir, Scholem reiterates his frequent criticism of Benjamin's double interests in Jewish and Marxist tradition and thought, though with a tone of admiration (if not acceptance). The paradox of this view of Benjamin is that it violates Scholem's own careful criticism of the secular-religious dichotomy. For a world-renowned scholar to pay such close attention to the writings of a failed scholar who died thirty-five years earlier and who made a living writing for newspapers, radio, and small magazines, is remarkable. In so doing, perhaps Scholem acknowledged that the "task" Benjamin had "not yet mastered," the task of relating religion to politics and tradition to modernity, remained unfinished for him as well.[117]

Of the fact that Scholem wanted to give a number of strong readings of Benjamin's work in his memoir there can be little doubt. Less clear and beyond the scope of this inquiry is why Scholem felt such a need, so late, to write such a detailed intellectual memoir. Leaving aside the temptation to psychological speculation, one can say of Scholem a version of what is often said of Benjamin: that, despite differences, he remained deeply engaged with the work and preoccupations of his friend to the very end of his life.[118] One of these preoccupations was undoubtedly the question of biblical tradition and modernity.

A striking example of Benjamin's and Scholem's understanding of biblical tradition appears in Scholem's account of Benjamin's collection of annotated letters by German poets and thinkers, *German Men and Women* (*Deutsche Menschen*), a short book he published in 1936 under the pseudonym Detlef Holz (in order to hide his Jewish identity). In his inscription to Scholem's copy of the book, Benjamin wrote, "May you, Gerhard, find a chamber in this ark—which I built when the Fascist flood started to rise—for the memories of your youth," and in his sister's copy Benjamin wrote, "This ark, built after a Jewish model, for Dora—From Walter."[119] Scholem comments: "Just as the Jews took refuge from the persecutions in the Writ, the canonical book, Benjamin's own book constitutes a saving element fashioned after the Jewish prototype."[120] The paradox of this example is that Benjamin's text, a celebration of the "secular," gentile tradition of German letters, elicits one of the most explicitly biblical passages in Scholem's book on Benjamin. (Chapter 7, on *German Men and Women*, develops this point further.)

The Bible may mark a boundary for Scholem not only of inaccessible revelation but also of universalism. For while Scholem could perform an almost complete retrieval of Jewish mystical tradition against dismissive Jews and uncritical Christians, the field of biblical studies was far too crowded and diverse to make such a project possible for him. In 1918, the same year he wrote "On Lament and the Lament Song," a text on biblical lament, he expressed fear about the Bible in his journal: "I'm afraid of the Bible sitting on my desk because I have to vindicate myself before it. And I'm not able to."[121] Perhaps alluding ironically to Luther's successful self-vindication before the Bible, Scholem embarks on a path different but comparable to Benjamin's: a thorough engagement with biblical tradition that paradoxically avoids the biblical text.

Conclusion: Questions of Tradition

The unsystematic nature of Scholem's writings on religion, culture, and politics makes it difficult to assemble a univocal theory on their basis. It is clear, however, that Scholem's achievements in the study of Jewish mysticism form a counter-narrative to modern characterizations of Judaism as a progressively rationalizing tradition. It is also apparent that Scholem considered his scholarship to be part of tradition as well as a *wissenschaftliche* enterprise external to it. But in spite of his encyclopedic achievements, Scholem did not consider his scholarship to provide a grand theory of religion or to resolve the paradoxes of tradition and modernity. Nor, in spite of his abiding concerns with mysticism, esotericism, and anarchism, did he develop a theory of human agency in traditions.

Swerving between Jewish exceptionalism and humanism, theology and *Wissenschaft*, esotericism and exotericism, Scholem's writings sharpen the questions he and Benjamin pondered together in their youth. That he did not resolve them is not a consequence of his lack of theoretical ability or interest. Like Benjamin, Scholem recognized the dangers of the secular/religious distinction, especially its attendant extremes of secularism and traditionalism, and his writings on the study of religion and modernity provide resources for thinking beyond the religious-secular binary. Scholem's category of religious anarchism, though underdeveloped, gestures beyond this dichotomy by recognizing the place of politics and contingency in religious history. In spite of his personal political views, religious anarchism suggests ways of thinking about Jewish tradition without narrow essentialism or exceptionalism. Given Scholem's interest in heretical and non-halakhic forms of Judaism, the notion of "dialectical distance" anticipates and in some ways resolves the methodological conundrums of "standpoint" that afflict religious studies today.[122]

Scholem's categories of dialectical distance and religious anarchism place tradition in confrontation with historical contingency. In an essay on Melville's "Bartleby the Scrivener," Giorgio Agamben notes the risk that writing can foreclose contingency:

> On the writing tablet of the celestial scribe, the letter, the act of writing, marks the passage from potentiality to actuality, the occurrence of a contingency. But precisely for this reason, every letter also marks the nonoccurrence of something; every letter is always in this sense a "dead letter." This is the intolerable truth that Bartleby learned in the Washington office, and this is the meaning of the singular formula, "on errands of life, those letters speed to death."[123]

Scholem's work may be seen as a disciplined effort to write against this tendency toward the "dead letter." Politically and metaphysically understated (and sometimes underdeveloped), Scholem's work recognizes the place of politics and metaphysics in Jewish history and tradition. By its resistance to doctrine, messianism, and such grand narratives as secularization, and by its openness to new forms of tradition, even in "secular" literature and scholarship, Scholem's work identifies significant contours of tradition within modernity. If his work leaves questions of identity and tradition unresolved, it nevertheless informs current debates in the study of religion and culture.

"Is Walter Benjamin really a Zionist? Isn't there an immense chasm between us?" asked Scholem in a 1917 journal entry.[124] These questions go to the heart of one of the most compelling epistolary friendships of modern German-Jewish history. For Scholem, the decision to pursue political Zionism in contrast to what Benjamin had years earlier staked out as "cultural Zionism" meant that the two parted ways after 1923 when Scholem emigrated to Palestine. This decision may also help explain other intellectual differences between Scholem and Benjamin, though as with Arendt, these differences reflect deeper common engagements with questions of modernity, tradition, and agency. Whether Benjamin's reluctance to follow Scholem's approaches to Zionism and revelation reveals differences of principle, circumstance, or disposition may never be resolved. If Scholem seemed more definite at times about Zionism and revelation, I suggest that he was closer to Benjamin's (and Arendt's) thinking on these questions than he seems, and that his pursuit of these questions illuminates their common engagements and commitments. Both thinkers formed idiosyncratic ideas of Judaism that enabled broader affirmations of tradition and agency.

To create space for his scholarly and theoretical work, Scholem sided with "secular" politics (Zionism) and academic conventions. He hoped these choices would allow for the continuation of Jewish tradition in some form, though he avoided declarations of what those forms would or should be. For Piterberg, Scholem's Zionism was the cart pulling the horse of his scholarship, but this perspective overlooks the complexity of Scholem's writings on Zionism and mysticism alike. A separate concern accompanies Scholem's overwhelming influence and success: has his work contributed to the kind of vulgar popularization of mysticism he repeatedly denounced?[125] The popularized, exoteric versions of Kabbalah now practiced worldwide by such celebrities as Madonna would not be possible without Scholem. Scholem's bargains with Zionism and popularity may in the end have undercut his deepest insights into religion and "secular" modernity, but the questions and discussions he shared with Benjamin, Arendt, and Adorno remain vital today.

Chapter 3

Madness and the Scandal of Tradition

The mention of tradition can imply a secular standpoint, since it is difficult to speak about tradition from within it. But this presumed standpoint outside tradition, secularism, can become a kind of worldview in its own right, and one of its goals is to establish norms that exclude tradition and sometimes identify it with madness. In a short essay called "Books by the Mentally Ill," Benjamin relates religious tradition to madness in the context of modern secular culture. The questions he poses invite reflection on how madness exposes the complexities of tradition and agency in modernity.

"Madness" paradoxically suggests too little and too much freedom. For antireligious forms of secularism, religious tradition denies the "rights" of individual freedom and expression. Religious tradition avoids innovation and originality, favoring the stultifying sameness, even madness, of ritual practices and mindless recitations. Yet madness is also associated with creativity and artistic originality. The myth of the mad genius finds equal support in Kant's aesthetic critique and the romantic tradition that came later. So is madness the domain of secular artists or religious traditionalists? For Daniel Paul Schreber, who suffered from what today would be called paranoid schizophrenia, the answer would seem to be both. His 1903 *Memoirs of My Nervous Illness* stages a confrontation with mental illness by all the means at his disposal, a wide range of cultural and religious ideas and practices that includes the recitation of texts.[1]

Michel Foucault speaks of the scandal of religious unreason in *Madness and Civilization*: in the early modern period, "Christian unreason was relegated by Christians themselves into the margins of a reason that had become identical with the wisdom of God incarnate."[2] For Foucault, Christianity would not reclaim the scandal of its own claims until Dostoevsky and Nietzsche, and in the meantime this scandal became "secular": "It was as if scandal, driven out of that superhuman region where it related to God and where the Incarnation was manifested, reappeared, in the plenitude of its force and pregnant with a new lesson, in that region where man has a relation to nature and to his animality."[3]

Benjamin's essay concerns books about madness—what they contain, why they are published, and how to classify and interpret them. The question is not so much the phenomena of mental illness as the books about it, and what these books tell us about their religious and cultural contexts. Following Benjamin's lead, I wish to develop Foucault's notion of the scandal of madness to consider the scandal of tradition. For from a secularist standpoint, tradition itself is a scandal just as from a rationalist standpoint madness is a scandal. Religion and madness thus converge in this period and way of thinking, and together they carry on not just the particular tradition of religious madness but the religious tradition itself.

But how and in what form? We hear much about postsecularism, but it takes many forms, from robust traditionalism to the kind of faint allusions and afterlives of religious tropes and practices. Talal Asad may be the most prominent thinker currently to challenge the conceptual edifice of secularism, not by appealing to religion but rather by examining and challenging the categories themselves. In so doing, he also attends to the category of religious practices in Christian monasticism, which include the particular practice of recitation on which I focus here. Like Pierre Hadot's concept of "spiritual exercises," Asad's account of monastic practice challenges the dichotomy of religion and secularity through particular forms of life. By linking Benjamin's interest in texts about mental illness to Schreber's interest in textual recitation, I call attention to the curiously forgotten religious category of religious recitation as a case of the scandal of tradition to which Schreber points.

In his *Memoirs*, Schreber describes poetry recitation as a defense against the symptoms of his nervous disorder, which today would likely be called paranoid schizophrenia. Secular works by Schiller and Goethe, as well as children's literature, provide relief from the tormenting voices he believes to be inflicted on him by God. Yet with this secular reading goes religious writing, as the purpose of his book is not only to obtain release from the asylum but also "to further knowledge of truth in a vital field, that of religion."[4] Mental illness, insists Schreber, has unveiled metaphysical truths which it is his book's purpose to share. Schreber's madness thus associates both with (secular) artistic freedom and (religious) tradition, an apparent contradiction noticed by Walter Benjamin that challenges secularist assumptions about tradition and agency. For if Schreber does manage to combine artistic freedom with religious discipline, then his *Memoirs* constitute a scandal for secular ideas of madness and tradition alike.

The *Memoirs* combines elements of theological treatises, mystical tradition, and the scholarship of modern law and literature. The text's complexity results as much from these conflicting discourses as from Schreber's illness. As Michel de Certeau notes in "The Institution of Rot" and *The Possession at Loudun*, modern texts like Schreber's relate to tradition conceived not as a stable body of beliefs and practices but as an unstable dynamic of competing practices, beliefs, and institutions. Long after the seventeenth century, argues Certeau, "the mechanisms brought into play by the uncertainty of epistemological and social criteria . . . [are] taking place today with respect to other 'sorcerers' . . . Once the poison of the other no longer presents itself directly in religious language, social therapeutics and repression just take other forms."[5] The cultural transformations of early modernity usually described as secularization preoccupy Certeau's work and constitute what I describe as the displacement of tradition.[6] Transformed but not replaced, the dynamics of religious tradition in Schreber's case play out in terms of self and society, competing forms of authority, and the power of words, particularly recited words, against the definition, experience, and institutional treatment of mental illness.

The many commentators on Schreber's *Memoirs*, from Sigmund Freud and Jacques Lacan to Elias Canetti and Michel de Certeau, confirm the resonance of Schreber's case with modern interests in religion, mental illness, and the institutions of medicine and law. Freud's secularism unsurprisingly leads him to pathologize Schreber's religious expression, but he is too astute an observer of Schreber's text to overlook religion altogether. Walter Benjamin's reading of the *Memoirs*, published in a 1928 newspaper article on books written by mentally ill authors, concentrates on language, theology, and the disconcerting effect of Schreber's book. I wish to elaborate and build upon Benjamin's reading here by discussing Schreber's mixture of religious writing with secular reading and recitation.

It is nothing new to observe the importance of religion and theology in Schreber's account, but no one has so far addressed the significance of Schreber for Benjamin or the role of recitation in Schreber's text. My suggestion is that the recitation of secular texts, which serves as an apotropaic practice in the *Memoirs* to ward off supernatural forces, illustrates a central preoccupation of Schreber's text with the power of words across the domains of religion, medicine, and law, and that the *Memoirs* is symptomatic not just of a paranoid disorder but also of a secularist repression of religious discourse and tradition. Benjamin does not comment directly on Schreber's recitations, but I will argue that he sees Schreber's text as a scandalous affirmation of tradition that resonates with other modern engagements with tradition, particularly the public recitations of Karl Kraus and the use of quotation in critical writing.

Recitation is unfashionable today, but it formed a central part of religious traditions and educational practices until the modern period. I focus on recitation here because it is a little-noticed and much-discarded feature of religious traditions, a category of practices that runs against the principles of individual expression and creativity and comes to represent, in modern theories of education for instance, the ultimate sign of backwardness and stultification. We could find roots of this anti-recitation in Kant's "What Is Enlightenment?" and *Critique of Judgment*; in the romantic poetics of the nineteenth century, which place such heavy emphasis on individual expression and originality; and in contemporary educational theories that place a premium on student creativity and individuality. A recent article from a scholarly journal on education, for instance, laments the central role of "rote memorization" in education around the world: "Such training may be useful for those who build their lives expecting others to do what they have done; it will not be useful in developing the critical-thinking skills children will need to cope in a flexible way with a rapidly changing environment."[7] This familiar portrayal depicts memorization and recitation as obstacles to creativity, flexibility, and higher stages of intellectual development.

My interest in recitation relates to current debates on secularism and secularization.[8] In *Genealogies of Religion*, Talal Asad engages the history of medieval Christian monasticism as a set of "disciplinary practices" that include "the daily performance of liturgy, the reading aloud and the hearing and memorizing of sacred texts."[9] The language and speech of these recitations constitute for Asad "a dialogical process by which the self makes (or fails to make) itself in a disciplined way."[10] Such a process cannot be described simply as repressing certain desires, controlling subjects, or "inculcating" particular values. Because these practices contribute to the formation of particular desires and the embodiment of particular values, they complicate modern ways of thinking about freedom, coercion, and ritual. The monk is "not someone who has 'lost his own will,' as though a man's will could be truly his only when it remained opposed to another's. The obedient monk is a person for whom obedience is *his* virtue."[11] At the conclusion of his discussion, Asad notes how religious standards of practice change and vary by history and context, and he singles out secular modernity as one point of contrast: "Thus humility in the form of self-abasement is no longer admired in 'normal' Christianity, and modern secular thought and practice classify and treat it as one of the standard personality disorders. Rituals of humiliation and abasement are now symptoms of patients, not the discipline of agents."[12]

Transformations in practices of recitation, like "rituals of humiliation and abasement," call into question standard ways of understanding the self in relation to power and ritual. The place of recitation in this practice, and I would argue in a great deal of premodern religious and educational practice in the West, was absolutely central to the religious life of monotheistic traditions for centuries. Recitation spreads from particular prayers and texts in rabbinic Judaism to the crucial role of psalm recitation for Christians going back to Augustine and Benedict; and finally to the recitation of the Qur'an, which *means* recitation, in Islam, a practice whose survival today defies the secularization that has drastically curtailed the practice of recitation in Judaism and Christianity. It is vital to note, however, that Asad's purpose is not to recuperate lost practices of recitation or to promote religion at the expense of secularity. Instead, his analysis calls attention to a blind spot in secularist thought, one that takes certain categories and distinctions, like ritual, individual action, religion and secularity, for granted. In addition to echoing these goals, my purpose here is to point out how secular blindness to religious tradition enables new, sometimes powerful, uses of religious tradition.

Schreber's text, while clearly a record of mental illness, nevertheless projects enough lucidity and self-awareness to convince the authorities of his day to release him. Insofar as this is true, we can say very plainly that while he was crazy, he was also skillful if not strategic in his use of religious discourse against secular institutions. The outlandish, mystical, and obscene contents of Schreber's *Memoirs* are presented as a dispassionate record of religious truth and experience. The *Memoirs* may thus be classified loosely as a Bakhtinian novel, a heteroglot form that incorporates numerous genres, voices, and perspectives. This multiplicity also reflects particular debates and confrontations between modernity and tradition, for example, the competition for legitimacy among legal, religious, and medical discourse.

The affinity of Schreber's text to mystical and religious writings is widely recognized. Beside Certeau's sustained analysis of the concept of "rot" in Schreber and mystical tradition, one finds more matter-of-fact observations such as Zvi Lothane's question, "If Schreber's visions were not genuine, then were Saint Teresa and Swedenborg paranoiacs?"[13] The comparison to mystical writers appears already in Schreber's text: "In the cases of the Maid of Orleans, of the Crusaders in search of the Holy Lance at Antioch, or of the emperor Constantine's well-known vision *in hoc signo vinces* which was decisive for the victory of Christianity: that in all these cases a transitory communication with rays was established."[14] Schreber allows that some extraordinary experiences are hallucinations, but he denies that for his own case, because, "after all, the hallucination of being in communication with God or departed souls can logically only develop in people who bring with them into their morbidly excited nervous state an already secure faith in God and the immortality of the soul. *This, however, was not so in my case, as mentioned at the beginning of this chapter*" (*Memoirs* 83). In response to medical testimony that all his religious experiences were pathological, Schreber writes: "If I wanted to give expression to my true feelings on this point of view I could only do it with Huss' cry to the wretched peasants who were carrying wood to his funeral pyre: *Oh sancta simplicitas!*" (*Memoirs* 354). The persecution Schreber undergoes in his illness becomes his persecution at the hands of the courts and doctors, and it is a religious persecution comparable to the execution of Jan Hus.

The Schreber case and its afterlives raise the questions posed by Certeau on another fascinating case, the seventeenth-century possessions at Loudun: "What is the 'place' that will be the rendezvous of incompatible forms of reason?"[15] Certeau's essay "The Institution of Rot" relates Schreber's case closely to Christian mysticism; both are characterized by the "destruction of human dignity," "theatricalization" of the body, rotten and degraded.[16] Certeau also follows his reflections on Schreber's rot into the domain of institutions and their discourses. The institution "*lodges* rottenness at the same time as it designates it. . . . By lodging this 'rottenness' within itself, the institutions takes charge of it, limiting it to a truth that is known and pronounced on the inside, while allowing another discourse on the outside, the noble discourse of its theoretical manifestation."[17] The son of the founder of "therapeutic gymnastics" and one of the leading medical authorities on child development in his day, Schreber, a lawyer, contests the power of medical institutions by means of legal and theological ones. While his initial decision to enter a sanatorium follows his father's example of regular visits to Marienbad,[18] his respect for medical authority quickly deteriorates. His appeal for release makes this explicit: in his 1901 reply to a medical report on his condition, Schreber writes "*I do not doubt at all that his report was given in good faith*. But this cannot prevent me, where the recognition of my legal capacity is at stake, from giving expression to my conviction of the *objective error* of the report frankly and without restraint" (*Memoirs* 351).

In addition to casting the *Memoirs* in terms of the clash of religious and secular institutions, we can also see this as a case of doctors against lawyers, especially as both attempt to explain the largely religious experiences and discourses Schreber describes.[19] After all, medicine and law are two of the modern inheritors of the power and legitimacy of religious institutions.[20] No matter what their cause, Schreber's experiences, because they are extraordinary, demand explanation, whether religious, medical, psychoanalytic, or legal. In fact, Schreber's text combines all of these possibilities in its hybridic confusion. Where mysticism and demon possession might once have dominated explanations of Schreber's condition, the *Memoirs* and its reception history demonstrate a cacophony of competing authoritative discourses.

Schreber's 1901 petition for release, along with sanatorium director Weber's justification for continued institutionalization and the court's 1902 finding in favor of Schreber, brings the contest between law, religion, and medicine to light. In short, it is Schreber's command of the law and the court's admiration of this facility that wins the day. The court decision notes on the one hand that there is "no doubt that the appellant is insane" and that he "lacks insight into the pathological nature of the inspirations and ideas which move him"; but the court goes on to say that "only *one single field* of plaintiff's mental life is affected, the field of religion."[21] The court denies that pathology in this single field alone can justify continued institutionalization, citing in particular Schreber's impressive legal skills:

> The way he personally took up the fight against the tutelage under which he was placed and how he carried it through according to plan, the acuity of the logical and juristical operations developed by him, the reasonableness with which he conducted himself, and last but not least the refined measured attitude he showed when in opposition to the medical expert and the Prosecutor—all this affords indisputable proof that in *this* field plaintiff has no need of protection by a guardian; rather in conducting his case he was able to preserve his interests to the full and independently, better indeed than anybody else could have done it in his place. (*Memoirs* 429)

In other words, as outlandish and false as his religious views may be, they do not impair Schreber in other ways, including his abilities at legal reasoning. Implied here is the suggestion that legal reasoning is more salient than religion as an indicator of successful functioning in the world, along with the clear demonstration of the power of law over medicine. By appealing to the court as his own counsel, Schreber contributes to this judgment, for even though he argues that "the certainty of my knowledge of God and the absolute conviction that I am dealing with God and divine miracles towers high above all human science," this point is made in the context of a formal legal document (*Memoirs* 354). In any case, Schreber's release takes place in spite of his religious ideas; religion wins only by losing.

Benjamin on Schreber

Because Benjamin's reading of Schreber's *Memoirs* is brief, I begin with Benjamin's essay and expand the discussion by reference to Benjamin's work on German tragic drama (*Trauerspiel*). (The only other mention of Schreber in his writings, in a 1925 letter to Scholem, comes in a list of readings and additions to his library.)[22] I also make some comparative points on Freud's and Benjamin's interpretations of religious tradition.

Benjamin's treatment of Schreber appeared in *Die literarische Welt* in 1928 as part of a review of several books by mentally ill authors. As its title indicates, the topic of Benjamin's essay is books. The authors' mental illness concerns him less than the books themselves. The initial problem he poses—finding a place for books that don't fit into a clear category—leads from a de facto "library of pathology" to an active interest in books by mentally ill authors, a category he had never before recognized. The simple challenge of organizing books on the shelf, presented in loving detail as if the books were persons, leads serendipitously to fruitful discovery and reflection, as the essay's first line epigrammatically claims: "A sense of embarrassment often goes noticed as the source of a successful enterprise" (*GS* 2:123).

But what makes this enterprise successful? The conclusion of Benjamin's essay offers a clue:

> The mere existence of such works has something disconcerting [*bestürzendes*] about it. So long as we habitually regard writing [*Bereich der Schrift*] as—despite everything—part of a higher, safer realm, the appearance of insanity [*Wahnsinn*], especially when it enters less noisily than elsewhere, is all the more terrifying [*um so erschreckender*]. How could this happen? How did it manage to slip past the passport control of the city of books, this Thebes with a hundred doors? The publishing history of such works must often be as bizarre as their contents. Nowadays, one would like to think, the situation is different. Interest in the manifestations of madness is as universal as ever, but it has become more fruitful and legitimate. The writings of the insane, so we might suppose, would have no trouble obtaining a valid passport today. Yet I know of a manuscript that is

> finding it as difficult as ever to obtain the approval of a respected publishing house, even though it is at least the equal of Schreber's in both human and literary terms, and far superior in intelligibility. (*SW* 2:130; *GS* 4:618)

The success of Benjamin's enterprise, presumably, is his ability to identify books by the mentally ill in a way that informs our understanding of books in general. He concludes with the hope that his readers will take an interest in the unnamed manuscript and in the writings of the insane. Still, many questions emerge from reading this passage. What is the manuscript to which Benjamin refers? The most obvious possibilities are his *Trauerspiel* study or *One-Way Street*, but both were published several months before Benjamin's article appeared in July 1928.[23] Whatever its identity, this unpublished manuscript allows Benjamin one of his characteristic rhetorical inversions: just as books by the insane are becoming acceptable, other, more intelligible works, are becoming hard to publish. A second question is why Benjamin says insanity in the realm of writing is disconcerting, even terrifying, and what accounts for the change from the publishing history of the past to the "fruitful and legitimate" case of Benjamin's present?

Benjamin's fascination with Schreber's text includes its publishing history, theological system, theory of divine language, unusual and creative style of expression, and its capacity to mix lucid and insane elements in his writing. As with Schreber's *Memoirs*, religion and theology are recurring themes in the other works he surveys: "The Whole-Earth Universal State" is dedicated to Madame Blavatsky and "imbued" with "the spirit of vagabond Russian monks" (*SW* 2:127). And Gehrmann's *Body, Brain, Soul, God*, a work of "theological medical science," is filled with religious imagery (*SW* 2:127–30). What is "disconcerting" about these books, therefore, is precisely their unself-conscious engagement with religion (and outlandish theology).

Schreber's book and its concerns with language and religion run through Benjamin's essay from beginning to end. Benjamin finds that books by the mentally ill and writing in general do *not* belong to a "higher, safer realm" but within the changeable, often disconcerting world that produces them. What makes them disconcerting, in part, is their surprising, even scandalous, appeal to religious traditions and ideas. Books that once defied categories now tell us something about writing in general: they are not always safe or remote, even in the contemporary period when interest in madness is more "fruitful and legitimate" (*SW* 2:130). For Benjamin as for Schreber, writing has a performative power; books can be "disconcerting," even "terrifying"; the power of these books, then, constitutes a form of agency.

Schreber's book, which Benjamin reports discovering by chance, leaves him "spellbound" (*gefesselt*, *GS* 4:616). Benjamin finds Schreber's neologisms fascinating, especially for their religious content. Only a publisher known for the "quaintest spiritualist writings," notes Benjamin, would publish a "theological system in which 'only God might approach corpses without danger,' or whose author 'could be in no doubt that God is familiar with the concept of railways,' or which develops a theory to the effect that God's language, the so-called 'basic language, is a somewhat old-fashioned, but vigorous German' " (*SW* 2:124). Benjamin claims to have forgotten how he first heard of the *Memoirs* before he found it in a bookstore in 1918. Of course, it is quite unlikely that Benjamin would write or know about Schreber without Freud, and he even cites some of the same material (on the "basic language") also cited by Freud. In his memoir on Benjamin, Gershom Scholem recalls that Schreber's book appealed to Benjamin "far more than Freud's essay on it."[24] On the strength of Scholem's report and Benjamin's offhand mention of Freud, we can speculate that Benjamin did not find Freud's reading of the text definitive or exhaustive, and even that he thought Freud's neglect of religious tradition was problematic.

In his 1911 case study, based solely on Schreber's book, Freud performs a strong reading in which he replaces Schreber's self-analysis with his own. The key to Freud's reading is Schreber's homosexual desire for his father, transferred first to Doctor Flechsig and subsequently onto God. Ambivalence toward God, a "mixture of blasphemous criticism and mutinous insubordination on the one hand and of reverent devotion on the other," reflects Schreber's ambivalence toward his father and doctor.[25] The dangerous sexual impulses toward his father were thus transformed into elaborate mystical schemata: "voluptuousness became God-fearing, and . . . his father's most dreaded threat, castration, actually provided the material for his wish-phantasy . . . of being transformed into a woman."[26]

Written at the end of Freud's collaboration with Jung, Freud's essay reveals an ambition to recognize the power of mythopoeic and religious forces in the case. Even though he considers repressed homosexual feelings to be the origin of Schreber's paranoid disorder, Freud regards the case to be a manifestation of broader human religious and mythmaking tendencies.[27] Freud's satisfaction with this explanation, along with a discussion of the sun as a "sublimated 'father-symbol,' " leads him to echo Jung's belief that mythopoeic forces appear in contemporary neuroses, and to repeat his claim from "Obsessive Acts and Religious Practices"

(1907) that psychological phenomena hold the key to explaining the "formation of religions."[28] But he admits to the contest of storytelling or mythmaking between himself and Schreber with a statement that is either genuinely or falsely modest: "It remains for the future to decide whether there is more delusion in my theory than I should like to admit, or whether there is more truth in Schreber's delusion than other people are as yet prepared to believe."[29] Freud's admission may be disingenuous, but it does indicate his awareness that psychoanalysis must compete with other discourses to explain such phenomena.[30]

Freud recognizes the scandal of tradition when he notes that Schreber's transformation took place even though he was a "doubter in religious matters."[31] This surprising (if not scandalous) reversal returns in Freud's observation that Schreber had changed from a sexual ascetic and religious skeptic into a "believer in God and a devotee to sensual pleasure."[32] At the same time, Freud acknowledges that Schreber's religious ideas come from somewhere, that they have a history even if their traditional legitimacy has eroded. Arguing that Schreber's fixation on God originates with his own father, Freud notes that "the Romans used to deify their dead emperors as a matter of routine."[33] Likewise, Dr. Weber, whose observations of Schreber Freud quotes at length, notes that Schreber claimed to be a bearer of divine inspiration, "just as we are taught that the Prophets were."[34] As he so often does, Freud acknowledges the persistence of tradition even though he considers it a source of obsession and illusion.

Benjamin's preference for Schreber's text over Freud's implies a surprising answer to Freud's remark, one that may point to the comparative richness of Schreber's religious imagination, if not his sensitivity to the dynamics of agency and tradition in modern life. Benjamin's essay is really about collecting and classifying scandalous books. The category of books by mentally ill people tests boundaries; it is disconcerting and terrifying because books belong to a "higher, safer realm" than insanity. But it is not just disconcerting and terrifying; it is also spellbinding. How could such books be published, and how should they be categorized? Benjamin's answer begins with Schreber's publisher, who also produced spiritualist writings and thus would be expected to be interested in the book's theological language and claims (*SW* 2:124). Benjamin lingers on the "remarkable and succinct" phrases and "extraordinary coinages" of Schreber's book. He next takes note of Schreber's neologisms, such as the paranoid description of the "flüchtig hingemachte Männer," which leads Benjamin to consider the idiosyncratic mode of expression in the text, one that echoes his analysis of allegory, not only unusual expressions but also reversals: "Poison is called juice, food is called poison, punishment is called reward, etc. [*'Saft' heißt Gift, 'Gift' heißt Speise, 'Lohn' heißt Strafe usw*]"; this passage is also cited by Freud). Benjamin concludes the cursory survey of Schreber by noting that Schreber's attempt to record his illness is "remarkably rigorous and successful" (*strengen und glücklichen*) and that his "frequent and highly intelligent reports" (*wiederholten höchst scharfsinningen Eingaben*) secured his release from the asylum (*SW* 2: 124; *GS* 4:616).

Benjamin does not join Freud in the effort to diagnose and decode Schreber's particular disorder, nor does he attempt a close analysis of the text. His interest is how such books can be published, their extraordinary contents and modes of expression, and their abiding engagements with theology and religion. Recognizing the scandal of tradition, Benjamin turns away from the clinical analysis of Schreber's case to the broader problem of its reception. How do such books get published, and how should we classify them? What do they tell us about the present? We leave Benjamin, as we so often must, with unanswered questions, but also with a tentative conclusion: that the mere publication of Schreber and other books poses a challenge, or even creates a scandal, for modern readers, because they engage so freely and openly in religious discourse. We might even say that, whereas Freud reduced Schreber's illness and visions to a pathological version of the father complex, Benjamin preferred to take them more seriously at face value, noting the combination of intelligence and insanity, religion and secularity, in the text. The discussion of Schreber's striking language indicates more than bemused or condescending observations of insane verbiage; instead, Benjamin's comments on Schreber's lucidity and language point to their shared interests in religious tradition and human agency in modern life. I now turn to Schreber's text itself, with a particular interest in the role language and literature play in their engagement with religion and secular modernity.

Recitation

Schreber suffers from what he believes are divine rays that enter his body's nerves, and his text clearly bears the imprint of his father, Moritz Schreber, particularly with respect to the focus on the nervous system.[35] But Schreber the son takes the nervous system as the basis for a "nerve-language," which operates like a memorized and recited text,

> as for instance a child learning a poem by heart which he is going to recite [*aufsagen*] at school, or a priest a sermon he is going to deliver

> in Church. The words are *repeated silently* [*im stillen aufgesagt*] (as in a *silent prayer* to which the congregation is called from the pulpit), that is to say a human being causes his nerves to vibrate in the way which corresponds to the use of the words concerned, but the real organs of speech (lips, tongue, teeth, etc.) are either not set in motion at all or only coincidentally. (*Memoirs* 54).

While this nerve-language is normally subject to control, for Schreber it is controlled by divine rays and Dr. Flechsig (*Memoirs* 55). The nerve language and imposition of divine rays on Schreber produces a range of torments. Schreber believes that the rays to which his nerves are subject "must speak," and that they induce fear and curse his activities. When he plays the piano to drown out the "nonsensical twaddle" of the voices that torment him, they say: "'If only the cursed piano-playing would cease.'"[36] Schreber is also tormented by miraculous birds that recite "senseless phrases learnt by rote" (*gelernten Redensarten*), a phrase that appears three times in quick succession (*Memoirs* 190–92; 234 German). Nonsensical phrases "learnt by rote" are also used against him in "tiresome, monotonous repetition" by the "lower god" Ariman (*Memoirs* 167–68).

Schreber's understanding of recitation mixes secular and religious literature—memorizing a poem and the priest's sermon. It is interesting, though, that his own recitation is exclusively secular. When Schreber hears voices that overtake his thoughts, voices that sometimes slow down so much that it takes "thirty to sixty seconds" to ask a short question like "Why do you not then shit?" (*Memoirs* 202–3), he recites poetry (as well as reading books and newspapers and playing the piano):

> I usually found committing poems to memory a successful remedy. I learnt a great number of poems by heart, particularly Schiller's ballads, long sections of Schiller's and Goethe's dramas, as well as arias from operas and humorous poems, amongst others from Max and Moritz, Struwelpeter and Spekter's fables, which I then recite [*aufsage*] in silence on the quiet verbatim. Their value as poetry naturally does not matter; however insignificant the rhymes, even obscene verses are worth their weight in gold as mental nourishment compared with the terrible nonsense my nerves are otherwise forced to listen to. Even while reciting [*bei dem Aufsagen*] poems I have to combat difficulties which at times reduce their effectiveness; miracles aimed at scattering my thoughts act on my nerves and make it impossible to find the continuation of a poem learnt by heart; or when the most persistent inner voices have at last been silenced by the recital of

> longer poems and I have reached a state of great soul-voluptuousness through union of all rays, the lower God starts the bellowing-miracle until I am so breathless that I cannot continue reciting the poems even softly. (*Memoirs* 204)

The contest between external miracles and defensive recitation takes over his own voice; the divinely imposed "bellowing miracle" overtakes the recitation and culminates in a struggle to breathe. When this persists, he resorts to even simpler, cruder means of recitation: counting aloud and swearing (*Memoirs* 205).

While the recitation of poetry sometimes helps Schreber ward off divine voices and rays, other kinds of recitation overcome him. His miraculous encounters with leprosy, for instance, are accompanied by a highly ritualized recitation: "I had to recite certain strange-sounding incantations [*gewisse seltsam klingende Beschwörungsformeln*], such as 'I am the first leper corpse and I lead a leper corpse'—incantations which, as far as I could understand, were connected with the fact that lepers had to consider themselves doomed to certain death; and had to help one another so as to provide for themselves an at least tolerable death" (*Memoirs* 94; 141 German). By calling the incantations "strange-sounding," Schreber sustains a tension that runs throughout the *Memoirs*—between matter-of-fact reports of experience and the more distanced awareness that they are strange or unique (*seltsam*).

Reiteration and repetition also characterize Schreber's experience of writing. Schreber describes a system of writing that torments him in the same way as the rays and nerve-language. It works as follows: "*Books or other notes* are kept in which for years have been *written-down* all my thoughts, all my phrases, all my necessaries, all the articles in my possession or around me, all persons with whom I come into contact, etc. I cannot say with certainty who does the writing down" (*Memoirs* 123; see 234, where Schreber repeats his uncertainty on who his tormenters are). Everything he has, particularly his thoughts and words, are taken from him, even while it remains unclear who is doing so. This ultimate challenge to Schreber's sense of agency in the form of writing dismays and torments him:

> The writing-down-material, mainly *my* previous thoughts besides a few constantly recurring additions of more or less senseless and partly offensive phrases, vulgar terms of abuse, etc., serves to fill in these pauses (that is to say to give the rays something to talk about even during these pauses). . . . The offensive phrases and abusive

> words serve the particular purpose of inciting me to talk aloud and so to make sleep impossible at the proper times; for the whole policy of souls culminates in the prevention of sleep and soul-voluptuousness; but the aim of the whole policy remains totally obscure. . . . It was [also] believed that my store of thoughts could be exhausted by being written-down, so that eventually the time would come when new ideas could no longer appear in me; this of course is quite absurd, because human thinking is inexhaustible; for instance reading a book or a newspaper always stimulates new thoughts. (*Memoirs* 127)

Throughout his *Memoirs*, Schreber struggles to maintain a sense of agency on a largely verbal battleground of writing and speech, originality and repetition, creativity and recitation: "One has the boundless impudence—I can use no other expression—to demand that I should express this falsified nonsense in spoken words as if it were my own thoughts, in this fashion: 'If only the cursed piano-playing would cease' was followed by the question: 'Why don't you say it (aloud)?,' and this again was followed by the falsified answer: 'Because I am stupid, perhaps' " (*Memoirs* 126–27). When Schreber plays the piano and thinks to himself, "This is a beautiful passage," he is immediately confronted with a challenge to his agency by the writing system: "The approaching rays were sent down with the phrase 'We have already got this,' *scilicet* written-down" (*Memoirs* 128). In other words, the system tries to second-guess Schreber's thoughts and capture them (and thus him) in writing. And insofar as his thoughts are already written, they are a kind of repetition and recitation. Conversely, insofar as recitation implies the prior existence of a text to be recited, recitation falls within the cultural and conceptual orbit of writing (what Derrida calls "iterability"). Writing and recitation dominate the *Memoirs*, and in a fundamental inversion of secular ideas of the self, Schreber recites secular texts to defend his personal autonomy against the threat of losing it to divine rays that would claim to write down all his thoughts.

Religious Reading and Secular Writing

Beyond Benjamin's brief discussion of Schreber, his *Trauerspiel* study is particularly useful to understanding the text, for like allegory, the *Memoirs* contains a system of linguistic correspondences that operates like allegory; in a passage cited by Benjamin earlier, Schreber identifies a divine *Grundsprache* (basic language) spoken by God in a "somewhat antiquated but nevertheless powerful German, characterized particularly by a wealth of euphemisms (for instance reward in the reverse sense for punishment, poison for food, juice for venom, unholy for holy" (*Memoirs* 26).

This *Grundsprache* also appears in a poem Schreber claims was brought by his wife on a birthday visit to the asylum:

> And when you've done with weeping
> And weary art, so weary,
> Then comes to you a faithful guest
> God's still and silent peace [*Der stille Gottesfriede*].

Though he makes no comment on the poem's overall meaning, Schreber says it made a "powerful effect" and "singular impression" on him because the phrase "God's peace" (*Gottesfriede*) was a term in the *Grundsprache* for "sleep produced by rays" (*Memoirs* 120; 165 German). In language highly evocative of Luther's Bible, particularly the Psalms, the poem's rhymed couplets narrate a process of divinely imposed suffering that will finally be relieved by divine mercy. Among the closest biblical parallels are the following: The passage: "Daß sich nicht eine Thräne mehr / In deiner Seele finde, / Und wenn Du ausgeweint Dich hat / Und müde bist, so müde, / Da kommt zu Dir ein Treuer Gast / Der stille Gottesfriede" (And not a lonely tear be left / In your poor wretched soul. / And when you've done with weeping / And weary art, so weary, / Then comes to you a faithful guest / God's still and silent peace, *Memoirs* 120) closely parallels Lamentations 2:11: "Ich habe schier meine Augen ausgeweint, daß mir mein Leib davon wehe tut" (My eyes are spent with weeping; my stomach churns, NRSV) and Psalms 120:6–7: "Es wird meiner Seele lang, zu wohnen bei denen, die den Frieden hassen. Ich halte Frieden; aber wenn ich rede, so fangen sie Krieg an" (Too long have I had my dwelling among those who hate peace. Too long have I had my dwelling among those who hate peace, NRSV). The text also echoes Psalms 89 and 136.

Though Schreber notes only its coded reference to the divine rays, the poem's content and biblical allusions cannot be incidental. Even if he did not write it, the text comprises the longest lyrical quotation in the *Memoirs* and expresses the longing for inner peace toward which the entire book aims. The poem's close allusions to biblical texts of lament and petition, and its prayer-like genre, situate it clearly within biblical traditions of prayer and recitation. Of course, the most commonly recited biblical texts in Christian liturgy are the psalms, and Schreber certainly had access to regular Christian worship, even at the Sonnenstein asylum.[37] In this indirect but prominent way, Schreber's *Memoirs* appropriates the tradition of biblical recitation. The replacement of the poem's conventional message of divine comfort with an idiosyncratic code indicates the simultaneous robustness and decay of this tradition in the face of Schreber's modern "nervous illness."

The limits of language concern the *Memoirs* from the beginning. In terms that evoke allegory as well as mystical writing, Schreber notes: "To make myself at least somewhat comprehensible I shall have to speak much in images and similes, which may at times perhaps be only *approximately* correct; for the only way a human being can make supernatural matters, which in their essence must always remain incomprehensible, understandable to a certain degree is by comparing them with known facts of human experience" (*Memoirs* 16).

Schreber's recitations of secular literature do not affirm the power of culture and *Bildung* against the threat of the voices tormenting him. As quoted before, he says "Their value as poetry naturally does not matter; however insignificant the rhymes, even obscene verses are worth their weight in gold as mental nourishment compared with the terrible nonsense my nerves are otherwise forced to listen to." Poetic value (*Wert*) is unimportant; what matters is the practice of recitation and the verse form of the text being recited. Schiller, Goethe, Spekter's *Fables*, and obscene lyrics are all the same; in other words, the edifice of great literature, which Schiller and Goethe both built in part to replace the church, has fallen to ruins. Here we can see a connection between Schreber's recitation and Benjamin's account of the allegorical *Trauerspiel*, the baroque mourning plays that embody ruins: "Any person, any object, any relationship can mean absolutely anything else. With this possibility a destructive, but just verdict is passed on the profane world: it is characterized as a world in which the detail is of no great importance. . . . Considered in allegorical terms, then, the profane world is both elevated and devalued" (*GTD* 174–75).

What Benjamin shows us is a literary form whose content is the decay of meaning, particularly the meaning of religious discourses and institutions in early modern Europe: allegory goes "beyond beauty" and corresponds to the cult of the ruin (*GTD* 177–78). But the decay is never complete, and the *Trauerspiel* continues tradition in a new way. In so doing, the *Trauerspiel* challenges the division between religion and secularity by making them interchangeable. Almost three centuries later, Schreber documents the decay of another discourse, great literature, but the decay somehow leads to a new vitality sufficient to ward off the religious torments of his disorder. In his idiosyncratic vocabulary, as in the *Trauerspiel*, anything can mean anything else. The allegory of the *Trauerspiel* conjures images of all kinds, good and evil, but because these images are all interchangeable, they lead to an awareness that knowledge is subjective. But it is also biblical: echoing his 1916 essay on language, Benjamin associates this knowledge with nonsense (*Geschwätz*) and the Fall of Genesis 3 (*GTD* 233–34).

Benjamin's allegory and Schreber's recitation converge on the struggle between past and present in written tradition. It would be easy to label the allegory and the *Memoirs* simply as melancholy texts of decline, but such a judgment would miss the dynamics of religious and literary tradition in both. If allegory is the genre of the cult of the ruin, then it represents a new form of tradition, one in which the past becomes self-consciously present even in its decrepitude; and if Schreber's recitation of secular literature treats Goethe and children's stories alike, it elevates both to a quasi-magical status as they serve to ward off the supernatural evils of his "nervous illness."

The *Trauerspiel* and *Memoirs* also combine written text with oral recitation: just as the drama is written to be "recited," Schreber renders written texts oral in his self-defensive practice. Both forms of recitation presume antecedent written texts, and with their written analyses, Benjamin and Schreber perform commentary on these texts. Text and commentary, of course, constitute the core of biblical and literary tradition alike; as Benjamin notes in *One-Way Street*, a text written concomitantly with the *Trauerspiel* study: "Commentary and translation stand in the same relation to the text as style and mimesis to nature . . . On the tree of the sacred text both are only the eternally rustling leaves; on that of the profane, the seasonally falling fruits" (*SW* 1:449).

Beyond his essay on Schreber, the *Trauerspiel* study, and *One-Way Street*, the strongest resonances with recitation in Benjamin's work point to the influential essayist, translator, and editor Karl Kraus, whose public readings of texts were famous in the German-speaking world, and the related category of quotation, also central in Kraus's work and crucial in Benjamin's *Arcades Project*, a new kind of history writing to be composed entirely of quotations. In an essay on Karl Kraus's public reading of the operettist Offenbach, Benjamin says that Kraus does not speak Offenbach but rather "speaks out of him" (*GS* 4:516). The "double meaning" (*Zweideutigkeit*) of Kraus's reading makes him comparable to a puppeteer (*GS* 4:517). Kraus, whose journal *Die Fackel* and entire career were based on strategies of quotation, provided Benjamin with a model of critical practice that contributed directly to his theory of history writing as quotation. Quotation and recitation of traditional texts, whether "religious" or "secular," opens up important if paradoxical forms of human agency. No one would deny Karl Kraus's distinct and influential personality, though it was achieved largely through practices of quotation and recitation.[38]

This chapter has argued that Benjamin's reading of Schreber's *Memoirs*, along with Schreber's recitation, demonstrates an engagement with tradition that transcends the binary of religion and secularity and puts his text into dialogue with Benjamin's *Trauerspiel* study, writings on Kraus, and reflections on quotation. By reciting secular literature to defend against the torment of divine voices, Schreber paradoxically uses a symbol of heteronomy (recitation) to assert autonomy and agency. In the end, Schreber's recitation displays neither secularization nor the eternal recurrence of religious tradition but rather the hybridic mixture of genres and conflicts that one finds theorized in Certeau and Bakhtin, along with an affirmation of Asad's use of recitation to challenge modern ideas of autonomy and secularity. The scandal of Schreber's book is its combination of tradition and innovation. That is what makes the book, as Benjamin says, so "disconcerting."

Chapter 4

✦

Hybrid Identities: Benjamin, Auerbach, and Orientalism

> There lived in the neighbourhood a famous dervish, who was reputed to be the greatest philosopher in Turkey. They went to consult him, and chose Pangloss as their spokesman.
>
> "Master," said he, "we have come to ask a favour. Will you kindly tell us why such a strange animal as man was ever made?"
>
> "What has that got to do with you?" asked the dervish. "Is it your business?"
>
> "But surely, reverend father," said Candide, "there is a great deal of evil in the world."
>
> "And what if there is?" said the dervish. "When his Highness sends a ship to Egypt, do you suppose he worries whether the ship's mice are comfortable or not?"
>
> "What ought to be done, then?" said Pangloss.
>
> "Keep your mouth shut!" said the dervish.
>
> I had been looking forward," said Pangloss, "to a little discussion with you about cause and effect, the best of all possible worlds, the origin of evil, the nature of the soul, and pre-established harmony."
>
> At these words the dervish got up and slammed the door in their faces.
>
> —Voltaire, *Candide* (1758)[1]

The work of Benjamin's contemporary Erich Auerbach generated and continues to shape discussions in the field of comparative world literature. Edward Said, author of *Orientalism* (1978), regarded Auerbach, who emigrated to Turkey in 1936, as a central figure in literary studies and the model of an intellectual in exile.[2] Auerbach's description of the intellectual isolation of his Turkish exile has been the subject of much discussion, yet very little has been written about Oriental motifs and ideas in the work of Auerbach or Benjamin. [3] Auerbach wrote to Benjamin with detailed impressions of Turkey, and Benjamin's work includes frequent and often overlooked references to Turkey and the Orient. In contrast to the Orientalist culture critically mapped by Said, as well as the "secular criticism" he advocated, Benjamin and Auerbach blur the boundaries between Oriental tradition and Occidental modernity.

Auerbach's letters offer impressions of modern Turkey that suggest a mix of nostalgia and distance from the traditions of the Orient. While we do not have Benjamin's replies to Auerbach's reflections on Turkey, this chapter takes their correspondence as a starting point for a survey and analysis of Benjamin's references to Turkey and Oriental culture. From the Turkish merchant of *One-Way Street* to the Turkish puppet of his "Theses on the Philosophy of History," Benjamin shares Auerbach's inclination to characterize Turkey as a site of tension between East and West, religious tradition and secular modernity. The complexity and richness of Benjamin's texts, especially in their treatment of secularism, tradition, and identity, indicate productive ways of engaging contemporary debates on Orientalism, Turkey, and the West.

The work of Benjamin and Auerbach informs recent debates on Orientalism and secularism. Erich Auerbach's flight to Turkey provided him the opportunity to teach at the Turkish State University and to witness Turkey and Ottoman tradition firsthand. Grounded in the European Enlightenment, Auerbach's life and work in Turkey stand today at the center of heated debates on Orientalism. Auerbach's correspondence with Benjamin included observations and questions about the Ottoman legacy in the Turkish republic. Auerbach's assertion that Turkish reforms sought "to triumph against a hated and yet admired Europe with its own weapons" has relevance for today's debates on European integration. The correspondence also relates the reform of the Turkish language to broader cultural and literary reflections. In what follows I survey the Benjamin-Auerbach correspondence and suggest how Auerbach's and Benjamin's direct and vicarious encounters with Turkey may have influenced their work, as well as how their work might inform current debates on Enlightenment, Orientalism, and secularism. The letters, which reveal Benjamin's curiosity and Auerbach's keen skills for political and cultural observation, demonstrate a more nuanced picture of Turkey than one finds in the authors' other writings or in discussions of Auerbach's *Mimesis*. For

Benjamin and Auerbach, as well as for Said, discussion of Turkey leads automatically to discussions of religion and secularity.[4] I conclude by sketching a critical reading of their work in the context of recent debates on Turkey and secularism.

The perceived distance between Turkey and Europe has a long history that realities often belie. In Benjamin's work, Turkey and the Orient appears in descriptions of exotic material objects. Auerbach's self-presentation as an alienated exile in Turkey is perhaps as well-known as the book he wrote there, *Mimesis*, and in the hands of Edward Said it became a paradigm of intellectual life in exile. Neither Benjamin nor Auerbach incorporates Turkish voices in their work, and many of their observations could be judged one-sided or Orientalist by today's standards. Yet Auerbach and Benjamin are too astute simply to echo cultural stereotypes; their descriptions engage complex questions of language, literature, tradition, and especially secularism.

A similar sensibility informs Orhan Pamuk's memoir *Istanbul*, which expresses the cultural, religious, and economic richness of that city. A wealthy native of the city, Pamuk is a novelist who originally planned a career as a painter, and his portrait of the city could be called a study in perspective. Discussing his fascination with Western accounts of Istanbul, Pamuk cites Benjamin's observation that accounts of cities are typically written by outsiders: "If we were to divide all the existing descriptions of cities into two groups according to the birthplace of the authors, we would certainly find that those written by natives of the cities concerned are greatly in the minority." According to Benjamin, the enthusiasm for seeing a city from the outside is the exotic or the picturesque. For natives of a city, the connection is always mediated by memories.[5]

Yet Istanbul is always a hybrid: what makes Istanbul unique, says Pamuk, is "its people's ability to see the city through both Western and Eastern eyes."[6] The feeling produces a deep ambivalence in Pamuk that he claims to see in the city's inhabitants in general: "As I waver back and forth, sometimes seeing the city from within and sometimes from without, I feel as I do when I am wandering the streets, caught in a stream of slippery, contradictory thoughts, not quite belonging to this place, and not quite a stranger."[7] The delight he takes in the city's "picturesque" ruins, he admits, reflects the aesthetic tastes of Westerners like John Ruskin: "Those of us who take pleasure in the accidental beauty of poverty and historical decay, those of us who see the picturesque in ruins—invariably, we're people who come from the outside."[8] In this sense, Pamuk, the "Oriental" who seeks insight into himself and his world through Western eyes, inversely mirrors the Western character in Voltaire's anecdote.

Pamuk's discussion of East and West in Istanbul acknowledges the place of religion, particularly as a marker of economic class in which his wealthy family looked down upon Islam as the backward domain of poor people, but Pamuk also describes the mood of the city with a term that has religious roots: *hüzün*, a kind of melancholy that is "not only a spiritual state, but a state of mind that is ultimately as life affirming as it is negating."[9] Pamuk, like Benjamin, attends to the material and experiential dimensions of city life as well as the cultural and historical realities behind it. Such attention is crucial to any full discussion of the intersection of East and West, religion and secularity, in Turkey and Germany, a topic that modern Turkish migrations to Germany have made very lively.[10]

Modern Turkey: Esperanto and Tradition

What was Auerbach's experience in Turkey, and how did it affect Benjamin? Auerbach's correspondence with Benjamin, though brief and incomplete, reveals impressions more complex than the image of the European scholar living in exile would suggest. On December 12, 1936, Auerbach writes:

> The situation here is not exactly simple, but it is not without charm. They have thrown all tradition overboard here, and they want to build a thoroughly rationalized—extreme Turkish nationalist—state of the European sort. The process is going fantastically and spookily [gespenstisch] fast: already there is hardly anyone who knows Arabic or Persian, and even Turkish texts of the past century will quickly become incomprehensible since the language is being modernized and at the same time newly oriented on "Ur-Turkish," and it is being written with Latin characters.[11]

Benjamin asks Auerbach to describe his "interesting and intellectually valuable experiences" in Turkey, and in his next letter (January 3, 1937), Auerbach writes, "The house on the Bosporus is glorious; as far as research goes, my work is entirely primitive, but personally, politically, and administratively it is extremely interesting."[12] He continues with a series of complaints about his academic post:

> We teach all the European philologies here—Romance language and literature, English language and literature, classical philology, German language and literature. We try to influence the instructional life

> and the library and to Europeanize the administrative management of scholarship all the way from the instructional grid down to the card catalog. That is naturally absurd, but the Turks want it, even if they occasionally try to get in the way.[13]

Auerbach's description of Istanbul and the political situation is highly ambivalent and rich with cultural and political observations:

> A wonderfully situated but also unpleasant and rough city consisting of two different parts: the old Stambool, of Greek and Turkish origin, which still preserves much of the patina of its historic landscape, and the "new" Pera, a caricature and completion of the European colonization of the 19th century, now in complete collapse. . . . But in general, the country has become decisively and completely ruled by Atatürk and his Anatolian Turks—a naive, distrustful, honest, somewhat blunt and boorish but also emotional race of men. Because they are accustomed to slavery and hard, slow work, they are tougher and more unpolished, and also more rigid and more surly, than southern Europeans, but at the same time they are quite likable and have much vital energy. The "grand chef" is a sympathetic autocrat, smart, grand, and imaginative, completely different from his European counterparts because he has actually himself turned this country into a state and because he is absolutely without eloquence. . . . Yet he has had to accomplish everything he has done in a struggle against the European democracies on the one hand, and on the other against the old Muslim, pan-Islamist sultan economy, and the result is a fanatical, antitraditional nationalism: a renunciation of all existing Islamic cultural tradition, a fastening onto a fantasy "ur-Turkey," technical modernization in the European sense in order to strike the hated and envied Europe with its own weapons. . . . The result: Nationalism in the superlative with the simultaneous destruction of the historic national character. This configuration, which in other countries such as Germany, Italy, and indeed also in Russia is not yet a certainty for everyone, steps forth here in complete nakedness. The language reform—at once fantastical ur-Turkish ("free" from Arabic and Persian influences) and modern-technical—has made it certain that no one under 25 can any longer understand any sort of religious, literary or philosophical text more than ten years old and that, under the pressure of the Latin script, which was compulsorily introduced a few years ago, the specific properties of the language are rapidly decaying. . . . I am more and more convinced that the contemporary world

> situation is nothing other than the cunning of providence to lead us along a bloody and circuitous rout to the Internationale of Triviality and Esperanto culture. I thought this already in Germany and Italy, especially in the horrifying inauthenticity of "Bluboropaganda," but here for the first time it has become a certainty for me.[14]

Carlo Ginzburg relates Auerbach's observations about Turkey to Voltaire's letter about the London Stock Exchange, comparing Auerbach's analysis of the authoritarianism of modern Turkey and Europe to Voltaire's impression of the emerging mass culture of the market; Ginzburg then relates these insights to Horkheimer and Adorno's *Dialectic of Enlightenment*. Ginzburg's analogy between Auerbach's Turkey and the Voltaire text raises interesting questions about Auerbach's sensitivity to the politics of secularism.[15] Yet one can hardly question the widely accepted view of Auerbach as a humanist. But how does humanism relate to modernism and secularism? Auerbach, whose 1929 *Habilitation* thesis was called *Dante, Poet of the Secular World*, might be expected to welcome Esperanto or Kemalism along with the "secular" humanism of his own literary criticism. But he recognized the political dangers of religious and secular culture alike. Geoffrey Green argues:

> Auerbach could see from Istanbul that if there was one way in which the ancient literature and fascist popular announcements were related, it was that both resorted to the appeal of legend and mythology in order to make more grandiose and sublime their own cause and order . . . Auerbach realized that the crucial aspect of Christianity for him was its origin as a populist movement that had emerged from the lowly people and had made their concerns and goals important and glorious.[16]

For Green, the Dante of Auerbach, who elevates ordinary humanity to sublime expression, exemplifies a political and cultural humanism that avoids the excessive grandiosity of religious or secularist ideology.

The trivial "Esperanto culture" of Turkey evokes the politics of Germany and Italy in the 1930s—in fact, it represents a more certain and advanced case of it. In a reversal of standard Orientalism, Auerbach paints a picture of Turkey as more advanced than western Europe. The "fantastic, ghostly" rapidity of the linguistic modernization in Turkey combines an atavistic, "*urtürkisch*" past with a technical modernization. This hybrid of primitive and modernist change yields an "anti-traditional nationalism" that seeks "to strike the hated and envied Europe with its own weapons."[17] A more astute and timely portrait of contemporary Turkey would be difficult to find.

Esperanto is also a motif of Gershom Scholem's well-known 1926 letter to Franz Rosenzweig about the modernization of Hebrew:

> The phantasmagoric [*gespenstische*] Volapük spoken in our streets precisely defines the expressionless linguistic space which alone has permitted the "secularization of language." But if we transmit the language to our children as it was transmitted to us, if we, a generation of transition, revive the language of the ancient books for them, that it may reveal itself anew through them, shall not the religious power of that language explode one day? . . . The initiators of the Hebrew language renaissance believed blindly, almost fanatically, in the miraculous power of language, and that was their good fortune. Because if they had been clairvoyant, they never would have had the demonic courage to resuscitate a language destined to become an Esperanto.[18]

It can only be a coincidence that Scholem and Auerbach both describe modern linguistic change as "gespenstisch" (ghostly, phantasmagoric), but it does underline a recognition that modernity is not pure novelty. Auerbach's defense of tradition can thus be compared to Scholem's, in spite of their different frames of reference. For Thomas R. Hart, "Auerbach's firsthand experience of Atatürk's attempt to transform his country into a modern secular state may have contributed to his pessimism about the rapidly increasing uniformity of twentieth-century civilization reflected more than a dozen years later in his essay 'Philologie der Weltliteratur.' "[19] The same goes for Perry Anderson, who cites Auerbach's description of Atatürk's campaign as a "cultural revolution without a social revolution" that brought about a form of secularism that became "something like an ersatz religion in its own right."[20]

It was not long after this that Benjamin mockingly described Esperanto in connection with the disaster of contemporary history in "On the Concept of History": "The completeness of history is like the completeness of languages. Universal history in today's sense can only exist through a kind of Esperanto. The idea of universal history is a messianic one" (*GS* 1:3, 1238). Auerbach, Scholem, and Benjamin all recognize the complex blend of tradition and modernity in the dream of a universal language, and they all mock Esperanto as its hopeless expression. The dream of a universal language that overcomes the fragmentation and trivialization of historical languages is shared by the modern projects of Turkish nationalism, Zionism, and universal history. For Benjamin, this striving can be expressed in the biblical story of linguistic fragmentation at Babel. The hope to overcome this fragmentation by no means disappears in the modern period, though it masquerades as secular progress. For all three, Esperanto embodies the paradoxical aspiration of a modernity rooted in the traditional striving for linguistic unity.

Turk, Moor, Arab: Orientalist Figures in Benjamin's Work

The most significant Orientalist passage in Benjamin is the first of his "Theses on the Philosophy of History":

> There was once, we know [*bekanntlich*], an automaton constructed in such a way that it could respond to every move by a chess player with a countermove that would ensure the winning of the game. A puppet wearing Turkish attire [*türkischer Tracht*] and with a hookah in its mouth sat before a chessboard placed on a large table. A system of mirrors created the illusion that this table was transparent on all sides. Actually, a hunchbacked dwarf [*ein buckliger Zwerg*]—a master at chess—sat inside and guided the puppet's hand by means of strings. One can imagine a philosophic counterpart to this apparatus. The puppet, called "historical materialism," is to win all the time. It can easily be a match for anyone if it enlists the services of theology, which today, as we know [*bekanntlich*], is small and ugly and has to keep out of sight. (*SW* 4:389)[21]

A conversational style, more like Benjamin's journalism than his scholarly articles, characterizes this text, which begins and ends with "bekanntlich" (translated here as "we know"): just as "we know" about the chess-playing automaton, so we also know about the need to keep theology out of sight. Outlandish description and astonishing comparisons appear in nonchalant prose. The "puppet in Turkish attire, a hookah in its mouth" represents the philosophical system of "historical materialism." The paradox is the choice of an Orientalist motif for a secularizing principle! It should be noted that a puppet in Turkish attire is not the same as a Turkish puppet—it is only *dressed* as a Turkish puppet, though it takes this artifice to the extreme point of putting a hookah in its mouth.[22]

The famous *Angelus Novus* of Paul Klee, the piece owned by Benjamin and made famous in his "Theses," also has a Turkish valence for Benjamin. In a 1921 letter to Scholem, Benjamin playfully invents a scholarly article that describes the picture as the "heavenly Klee-leaf" that has "added three new leaves" "under the influence of the Turkish climate." Scholem explains: "The heavenly Klee-leaf was, naturally, the picture by Klee hanging in the Türkenstrasse, and the three new leaves referred to me, Elsa Burchardt, and his friend Ernst Schoen, who was then visiting with us in the Türkenstrasse."[23]

Benjamin describes the tractate as an "Arabic form" in a section of *One-Way Street* called "Innenarchitektur": "The tractatus is an Arabic form. Its exterior is undifferentiated and unobtrusive, like the facades of Arabian buildings, whose articulation begins only in the courtyard. . . . The surface of its deliberations is not enlivened with pictures, but covered with unbroken, proliferating arabesques" (*SW* 1:462; *GS* 4:1, 111). Another entry in *One-Way Street*, "Stamp Shop," presents a Turkish merchant: "Script on Turkish piaster-stamps is like the slanted, altogether too dandyish, too gleaming breast-pin in the tie of a sly, only half-Europeanized merchant from Constantinople" (*SW* 1:479; *GS* 4:136).

An autobiographical image of the Orient comes from Benjamin's *Berlin Chronicle*, which describes his father's connection to the Lepke art auction house:

> The real token of my father's profession in our apartment was a Moor, almost life-size, who stood on a gondola reduced to one-thirtieth of its size, holding with one hand an oar that could be taken out, and lifting on the other a golden bowl. This work of art was made of wood, the Moor black, the gondola and oar glowing in many colors beneath the varnish. The whole, however was so urgently oriented toward its companion piece that I cannot tell today whether a second Moor, whom I imagine with it, really stood there originally or is a figment of my imagination. (*SW* 2:2, 619)

All of these cases—the puppet, the angel, the "Arabic" tractate, the Turkish merchant, and the Moor—represent a vivid use of Orientalist stereotypes. It would be a mistake to ascribe too much to these sometimes incidental references. Yet it is striking that all of these cases are predominantly aesthetic, emphasizing the fine visual detail for which Benjamin is well known. Benjamin's concern is the often-essentializing *representation* of the Orient rather than direct encounters with it. Another feature common to these cases is the juxtaposition of Orient and Occident: the Moor in the German apartment, the Klee painting in the "Turkish climate," the "half-Europeanized merchant from Constantinople," the tractate (a Western genre) as an "Arabic" form, and of course the European puppet "dressed in Turkish attire" and representing, paradoxically, secularism.

This case, the latest and most prominent in Benjamin's work, may justifiably be considered salient to the discussion of Turkey, secularism, and the problem of religious tradition. Like Pamuk's Istanbul, Benjamin's use of Oriental images is hybridic and resistant to the polarization of East and West.

Oriental topoi also illustrate Benjamin's literary studies. The earliest known reference to the Orient in his work appears in the 1915 essay, "Two Poems of Friedrich Hölderlin," in which Benjamin uses the term "oriental" to describe the poetic quality that exceeds the unity of mythic or Apollonian expression: "This is the oriental, mystical principle, the one that overcomes limits, which in this poem again and again so clearly supersedes the Greek formative principle, a principle that creates a spiritual cosmos from pure relations of intuitions" (*GS* 2:126). According to Peter Fenves, who discusses this essay at length, Benjamin's use of "oriental" here resonates not only with Nietzsche's category of the Dionysian but possibly with Judaism as well. The term may in fact come directly from Hölderlin himself, who spoke positively about "oriental" as opposed to "Greek" art.[24] Not only was the category of the Oriental already native to German culture in Hölderlin's time, but it also held positive associations for the exotic other and for German culture as well.

Benjamin does not develop the term here or elsewhere in his discussion of poetry, though it would return much later in his 1936 essay, "The Storyteller." There, in a discussion of memory, Benjamin cites the case of Scheherazade in *The Thousand and One Nights*. Memory (*Erinnerung*), "the muse-derived element of the epic art," allows storytellers, writes Benjamin, "especially the oriental ones," to link one story to another: "In each of them [storytellers], there is a Scheherazade who thinks of a fresh story whenever her tale comes to a stop" (*SW* 3:154).[25] In his discussion of the centrality of the sovereign or tyrant in baroque drama, Benjamin observes that "the favourite source of subject matter was the history of the Orient, where absolute imperial power was to be encountered to a degree unknown in the West. Thus in *Catharina* Gryphius takes the Shah of Persia, while Lohenstein, in his first and last dramas, uses the Sultanate" (*GTD* 68). With the storyteller Scheherazade, the sovereign shah and sultans provide Oriental paradigms for European categories, serving further to cross the boundary between East and West.

While never sustained, Benjamin's interest in European perspectives on the Orient was thus abiding. References to the Orient are entirely aesthetic in Benjamin and typically focused on European representations of this other world. Yet the case of Scheherazade suggests a form of agency that goes beyond the image of the Orient as mere object of representation.

Another hint of this concern for agency appears in an analogy between Nietzsche's account of India and Baudelaire's description of the oriental courtesans of the painter Constantin Guys: "The great physiognomic similarity between Guys and Nietzsche is worth emphasizing. Nietzsche ascribes to the pessimism of India 'that tremendous, yearning rigidity of expression in which the Nothing is reflected' . . . Compare this to the way Baudelaire describes the gaze of the oriental courtesan in Guys: it is a gaze directed toward the horizon, one in which rigid attentiveness and profound distraction are united" (*Arcades* 369). Like all his other examples, the Oriental figures of Scheherazade, India, and the courtesan come from European representations, but in these three examples the Oriental object becomes a subject, and in a way that evokes Benjamin's concept of aura, capable of returning the European gaze.

To illustrate how distinctive and supple Benjamin's engagement with Orientalism was, let me draw a contrast with Martin Buber's essay on Judaism and the Orient, which articulates what today could be called a highly essentialist, binary account of Oriental and Occidental characters and cultures. In "The Spirit of the Orient and Judaism" (1916), Buber claims that "the great complex of Oriental nations can be shown to be one entity," and that there is a definite "Oriental type of human being" characterized by "pronounced motor faculties, in contrast to the Occidental type . . . whose sensory faculties are greater than his motor."[26] Though he does admit to simplifying things, Buber sustains the Oriental-Occidental distinction as a reliable description of character types, nations, regions, and religions.

Buber's essay situates Judaism as an exceptional Oriental religion that, by its compelling ideas, "won the Occident for the teaching of the Orient."[27] As the carrier of the Orient to the Occident, Judaism provides a bridge between the two domains whose historical role affords it a key destiny in the modern world: "Europe has at its disposal a mediating people that has acquired all the wisdom and all the skills of the Occident without losing its original Oriental character, a people called to link Orient and Occident in fruitful reciprocity."[28] To establish that link, Buber invokes the Zionist settlement of "building a model community on the scanty Canaanite soil."[29]

Buber's treatment of Judaism blurs the boundaries of Orient and Occident very differently from Benjamin, whose vivid images undermine the categories themselves. Yet Buber's focus on a people who mediate between Orient and Occident, one whose religious ideas had already served to mediate these two worlds, also addresses the divide between secularism and tradition that preoccupies Benjamin. And though they disagreed sharply over politics, as the July 1916 letter from Benjamin to Buber, along with his essay on language of the same year attest, there is a broader agreement that the categories of Orient and Occident involve the categories of religion, modernity, and politics (*Briefe* 1:125–26).

Auerbach and Said: Secularism and Orientalism

Oriental and Turkish references in Benjamin and Auerbach are not simply a motif of their work; they concern directly the problem of secularism and tradition. The question extends to the reception of Auerbach, particularly in Edward Said's book *Orientalism* and essay "Secular Criticism." In what has become a common understanding among readers of Auerbach, Said regards Auerbach's exile in Istanbul as a crucial dimension of his work, specifically of *Mimesis* and its role in the study of world literature.[30] In *Orientalism* Said links this work to "the humanistic tradition of involvement in a national culture or literature not one's own. . . . The more one is able to leave one's cultural home, the more easily is one able to judge it, and the whole world as well, with the spiritual detachment *and* generosity necessary for true vision."[31]

Said takes these reflections further in "Secular Criticism," affirming the image of Auerbach's experience as exile: "In Istanbul he was hopelessly out of touch with the literary, cultural, and political bases of that formidable tradition."[32] Auerbach's achievement, according to Said, was to produce *Mimesis* in exile from a place defined as the opposite of the culture it celebrates: "To any European trained principally, as Auerbach was, in medieval and renaissance Roman literatures, Istanbul does not simply connote a place outside Europe. Istanbul represents the terrible Turk, as well as Islam, the scourge of Christendom, the great Oriental apostasy incarnate. Throughout the classical period of European culture Turkey was the Orient, Islam its most redoubtable and aggressive representative."[33] Said thus does not exempt Auerbach from Orientalism. In fact, the notion of secular criticism depends in a certain way on this principle: "We cannot fail to be convinced that the dialectic of self-fortification and self-confirmation by which culture achieves its hegemony over society and the State is based on a constantly practiced differentiation of itself from what it believes to be not itself. And this differentiation is frequently performed by setting the valorized culture over the Other."[34] Culture always combines a hegemonic norm and resistance to that norm. Criticism, for Said, is characterized by the individual's distance from and awareness of the workings of culture. Auerbach typifies this kind of criticism: "We have in

Auerbach an instance both of filiation with his natal culture and, because of exile, *affiliation* with it through critical consciousness and scholarly work."[35]

Read together, *Orientalism* and "Secular Criticism" reveal a tension within Said's thought between a negative appraisal of Orientalist projections by the West and their central place in the cosmopolitan criticism of Auerbach. I suggest this tension reveals an unexamined side of Said's conception of secularism itself. In an essay on Auerbach and Said, Aamir R. Mufti argues that Said's concept of secularism has little to do with antireligious elitism: "*Secular* implies for Said a critique of nationalism as an ideology of hearth and home, of collective *Gemütlichkeit*; a critique of the 'assurance,' 'confidence,' and 'majority sense' that claims on behalf of national culture always imply; a critique of 'the entire matrix of meanings we associate with "home," belonging and community.' "[36] "Secular criticism," says Mufti, "seeks continually to make it perceptible that the experience of being at home can only be produced by rendering some other homeless."[37] Elsewhere Mufti claims that Said's secularism refers to the stance of unbelief toward "secular" as well as "religious" claims.

Gil Anidjar boldly suggests that Said's secular criticism and conceptions of Orientalism are in fact criticisms of Christianity:

> In participating in the opposition to religion carried by the terms *secular* and *secularism* . . . Said appears simply to have forgotten the lesson taught by this most important of books, namely, *Orientalism*. For if *Orientalism* teaches us anything, it is that Orientalism *is* secularism. Why? Because *Orientalism* is a critique of Christianity, secularized or not. . . . And Christianity—which is to say, Orientalism—invented both religion *and* secularism.[38]

A passage from *Orientalism* demonstrates the possibilities and limits of Anidjar's claim: "My thesis is that the essential aspects of modern Orientalist theory and praxis (from which present-day Orientalism derives) can be understood, not as a sudden access of objective knowledge about the Orient, but as a set of structures inherited from the past, secularized, redisposed, and re-formed by such disciplines as philology, which in turn were naturalized, modernized, and laicized substitutes for (or versions of) Christian supernaturalism."[39] Modern Orientalism "secularized" earlier "knowledge" about the Orient, using the methods of secular disciplines that descended from Christianity. While this affirms Anidjar's point that Christianity and Orientalism are related, here Said follows a standard secularization narrative in which modern, secular knowledge replaces religion. Anidjar, by contrast, appears to set up a mass equivalence among Orientalism, secularism, Christianity, and religion.[40]

Mufti forcefully rejects Anidjar's reading of Said's essay as "postsecularist," arguing instead that secular criticism is "opposed in concrete and detailed ways to metaphysical grounding and authorization of culture, both secular and religious, constantly unearthing its social filiations and affiliations and identifying the 'human' costs of failing to subject to such criticism the process of critical thinking itself."[41] A different, more nuanced view is proposed by Emily Apter, who argues that Said's secular criticism remains open to religion: "Said's attentiveness to theological exegesis in the preface to *Mimesis* attests to an intellectual curiosity toward cultures of belief, a willingness to engage 'religiously' with the matter of how philosophies of transcendence have shaped revolutionary ethical militance and subjective freedom."[42]

Apter takes up the question of Said's use of Auerbach by discussing the role of Istanbul in the work of Auerbach, Spitzer, and other creators of comparative literature. Against the image of Istanbul, taken from Auerbach, as a lonely place for a European intellectual, Apter adduces evidence that the city was a lively cultural crossroads frequented by many émigré intellectuals.[43] Apter's larger point is that the origins of comparative literature were always global.[44] In the course of making this argument, Apter challenges Said's reading of Auerbach as the source of comparative humanism, along with what she calls the "fetish of 'exile' since the record shows that Auerbach was in pretty good cosmopolitian company during his Istanbul sojourn."[45]

Kader Konuk also stresses the historical complexity of Istanbul in the early twentieth century and goes further, directly challenging Said's notion of exile.[46] In *East West Mimesis: Auerbach in Turkey*, Konuk demonstrates conclusively that the Istanbul to which Auerbach traveled was diverse and intellectually vibrant, and that the Kemalist project of modernizing Turkey placed European intellectuals like Auerbach and his predecessor Leo Spitzer in positions of privilege. Through this analysis, Konuk challenges the prevailing sense of Auerbach, largely promoted by Said, as a lonely exile whose isolation bore the fruit of *Mimesis*. Konuk also challenges Said's related claim that Auerbach's Turkey was a simplistic extension of European Orientalism, showing instead how Auerbach's life in the "Hellenistic" city enabled and conditioned his work on *Mimesis*.[47] Konuk and Apter represent a crucial new turn in the discussion of Turkey and western Europe, one that takes full account of Turkish culture and perspectives. Their work brings the era of one-sided accounts of Turkey and secularism to an end.

Conclusion: Tradition, Modernity, Politics

At least since Voltaire, European thinkers have associated Turkey with religion and secularity. Auerbach, Benjamin, and Said continue this tradition in light of twentieth-century history and criticism. Auerbach and Benjamin represent naive but fascinating engagements with Turkey around their interests in language, tradition, and modernity. The image of Auerbach stranded in a cultural wilderness appeals to the sympathetic reader of *Mimesis* even though it contains a submerged Orientalist trope. Said's valorization of Auerbach's Turkish exile depends on an Orientalist motif undercut by Auerbach's own letters; it bespeaks a notion of secularism that reifies cultural difference along with the difference between tradition and modernity. If Said underestimated the richness of Turkish intellectual life in his reading of Auerbach, his error represents the risks of depending too much on Western, aesthetic terms of analysis. But along with these risks come rewards, as Benjamin's and Pamuk's suggestive descriptions show—they show that aesthetic criticism is necessary to any full discussion of Turkey, Orientalism, and modernity.

Auerbach and Benjamin wrote at a time when the divide between Turkey and Europe looked different than it does today. Then one could write "authoritatively" about Turkey without citing Turkish people or sources. Today such liberties cannot be taken without including the voices of Turkish scholars, yet the divide between Europe and Turkey, over politics, religion, and culture, may be more sharply defined than ever. Anti-Turkish sentiments in Europe, directed toward recent immigrants and to the Turkish republic, have become so intense that they have led leaders on both sides to embrace religious difference (Christianity, Islam) in place of the secularist ideologies of the twentieth century. Auerbach and Benjamin could hardly have been more innocent of these contemporary developments, but in attending to the linguistic and aesthetic lineaments of the Turkish-European divide, and particularly in seeing how it relates to the categories of secularity and religion, their writings engage Orientalist discourse with curiosity, creativity, and a reluctance to reinscribe binary distinctions.

Without overstating their capacity to understand modern Turkey, I suggest that Auerbach's and Benjamin's interests in language, tradition, and secularity are salient to contemporary discussions and that their writings resist the simplicity of the binary oppositions of religion-secularity and Orient-Occident.[48] Indeed, Auerbach's descriptions of Turkey, like Benjamin's Turkish merchant and "puppet in Turkish attire," bring these two binaries together: Orient and Occident intertwine closely with religion and secularity. As Pamuk shows, these categories combine in Turkish culture, particularly in the city of Istanbul, whose hybridity is attested by its dual names (Constantinople/Istanbul) and its European/Asian geography.

Aesthetics, language, and *perceptions* of cultural difference are crucial to the analysis of secularism and Orientalism, as the literary and humanistic writings of Pamuk, Benjamin, and Auerbach demonstrate. As Said argues, perspective and power are deeply intertwined; but as Benjamin and Auerbach imply, secularism and tradition are also intertwined. The discourses of Orientalism are not just political and economic; they are aesthetic, religious, and linguistic as well.

Chapter 5

✦

Violence and Biblical Tradition

What does divine punishment in the Bible have to do with modern discussions of political revolution? For Walter Benjamin but few others, the connection was vital and offered a way to think about the problem of political agency. This chapter argues that the notion of divine violence articulated in Benjamin's "Critique of Violence" (1921) is inscrutable. By this I mean that divine violence defies human control, and that it is difficult to distinguish from mythical violence. This argument rests on Benjamin's use of two stories to distinguish divine violence from mythic violence: the story of Korah's rebellion in the Bible (Numbers 16), and the Greek myth of Niobe (most familiar to Benjamin and his readers through Ovid's *Metamorphoses*). In the Korah episode, rebellious priests and their families are spontaneously engulfed by an earthquake and burned by the God of Israel, though we learn later that Korah's sons survive (Num. 16, 26). In the Greek and Roman myth, the gods punish a boastful Niobe by killing her children and turning her to marble.

These two ancient texts were widely available to Benjamin's readers, just as they are today. Yet for all the many insightful studies of Benjamin's essay, few have addressed how these two familiar stories relate to the central point of the essay. By taking a careful look at these texts, I show that the two stories have much in common, and that this commonality informs the essay's key distinction between divine and mythic violence: "Mythic violence is bloody power over mere life [*bloße Leben*] for its own sake; divine violence is pure power over all life for the sake of the living."[1] The distinction seems absolute, but if Korah and Niobe cannot be distinguished in a fundamental way, then neither can divine and mythic violence.

My reading raises questions and issues beyond the place of Korah and Niobe in Benjamin's essay. First, it reminds readers that Benjamin interpretation will always demand an engagement with literary and religious studies. In the case of literary methods, one must not only read *what*

Benjamin says but also *how* he says it. In the case of religious studies, understanding Benjamin's essay requires not just a catalog of religious themes and references, much less claims about the theological biography of the author, but rather a careful engagement with the categories of scripture and tradition in his thought. Benjamin's use of Numbers illustrates his notion that the sacredness of texts involves not just their meaning but also their "afterlife" (*Fortleben*) in commentary and translation (*SW* 1:254–55). This articulation of religious tradition in the context of political thought challenges the secular-religious divide and places Benjamin's work in dialogue with current discussions of the postsecular.

In making the distinction between divine and mythic violence and yet insisting that we can neither observe nor manipulate it, Benjamin identifies a deeper dilemma: religious tradition cannot be overlooked, but neither can it be mastered. Taking such a position exposes Benjamin to accusations of mystification or downright fideism, but such accusations misrepresent his project. Instead, throughout his diverse writings, he struggles with the persistence of traditions in spite of modern attempts to deny or overcome them. Simply to demonstrate this struggle, against secularist master narratives of progress and decline, is one of the achievements of "Critique of Violence," but the essay also goes one step further, to locate ancient stories at the heart of a contemporary philosophical and political problem. One cannot face political violence, or its philosophical critique, claims Benjamin, without first addressing literary and biblical traditions. And like hermeneutical theorists, Benjamin shows how addressing these traditions does not leave us unchanged. In "Critique of Violence," the dialectical struggle between past and present, tradition and modernity, takes on a compositional shape in which Benjamin experiments with form, staging a collision of disparate discourses, all of which are necessary to critique. Syndicalism, Kantianism, humanism, and biblical tradition must all participate in this critique, argues Benjamin, and if he fails to bring this critique to resolution, so has everybody else, though no one else has shown it so forcefully.

Few essays by Benjamin have drawn more attention. As Giorgio Agamben notes in *Homo Sacer*, Benjamin's notion of divine violence remains obscure even to careful readers like Derrida.[2] Derrida's long essay, "Force of Law," attempts a deconstruction of "Critique of Violence" that links Benjamin's thought to fascism. In his only reference to the biblical text, Derrida associates the divine violence of Numbers 16 with the Holocaust.[3] For Agamben, Benjamin's essay provides a starting point for a theory of sovereignty characterized by "bare life" and the state of exception of Carl Schmitt's political theology.[4] But neither Agamben nor Derrida addresses how the biblical narrative illustrates divine violence. In her *Critique of Violence*, Beatrice Hanssen expresses a similar discomfort with Benjamin's use of biblical narrative, asking "Didn't the essay rather reintroduce a theological foundationalism, that is, a decisive, authoritative ground, which was to sustain secular forms of violence?"[5] For Hanssen, terms like "theological foundationalism" and "decidedly Judaic" seem to suffice as arguments about the flawed nature of Benjamin's essay, as if the very mention of religious categories could tarnish the essay's cogency.

What follows are readings of Benjamin's essay, Numbers 16, and the Niobe myth, followed by discussion of what the essay suggests about biblical tradition and Benjamin's messianism. I do not wish to claim that any homology or structural resemblance between Numbers 16 and Benjamin's essay is in itself significant. What I argue instead is that Benjamin selects this biblical narrative in order to illustrate his concept of divine violence, and that the thematic and structural comparisons between the biblical episode and Benjamin's essay—the Korah rebellion and general strike as the kind of "Gewalt" that Benjamin considers "pure means" (*bloße Mittel*), and the nonlinear structure of the essay and biblical text as compositions—demonstrate the general importance of biblical narrative and tradition to Benjamin's work.

"Toward the Critique of Violence"

Benjamin wrote "Critique of Violence" around the same time as the "Theological-Political Fragment," a text that affords such profane endeavors as politics an indirect role in bringing about messianic reality (*GS* 2:203). The essay has roots in earlier work on questions of language, justice, and Judaism, written especially in dialogue with Gershom Scholem. Having expressed his disillusionment with Martin Buber's politics and philosophy of language in 1916, Benjamin, along with Scholem, began to articulate a religiously charged ideal of justice separate from any particular system of law, and he seemed eager to explore the relationship of such political models as nihilism, anarchism, and syndicalism to religious thought and tradition.[6] At the same time, "Critique of Violence," like "On the Program of the Coming Philosophy," bears the neo-Kantian influence of Hermann Cohen as an exercise in critical philosophy.

How are politics and religion related? Benjamin's essay stages a confrontation between several distinct theoretical models of violence and law. While the essay's affirmative stance is inconclusive even in its title ("Toward [*Zur*] the Critique of Violence"), it offers a clear polemic against theories of law and associated justifications for state-sponsored violence. The link between violence and law is established early in the essay, and it remains clear throughout that Benjamin regards positive law, natural law, and mythic violence as political means to justify the ends of state power. But the various models of violence and law Benjamin takes up in the essay, from the general strike to police, peace conferences, and education, have puzzled readers for decades. Several critics have referred to Benjamin's essay as a naive or flawed attempt to offer a political alternative to the state's near-monopoly on violence, sometimes citing his affinities to Carl Schmitt and sometimes dismissing the category of "divine violence" as a mystification.[7]

The essay appears to present an argument subject to formal standards of logic, evidence, and focus, but there is ample evidence from the essay and other works by Benjamin that other standards and qualities are in play. Benjamin was a literary critic and thinker interested in experimental forms of writing. Five years after writing this essay, Benjamin published *One-Way Street*, a collection of aphoristic meditations on modern urban life. He studied the formal experiments of the surrealists, wrote about their work, and carried out a number of writing experiments based on their ideas. Even his early philosophical essays, such as "On Language as Such and on the Language of Humanity" (1916) and "On the Program of the Coming Philosophy" (1918), as well as "The Task of the Translator," written in the same year as "The Critique of Violence," offer wide-ranging maps of particular problems rather than systematic solutions. Like "On the Program of the Coming Philosophy," "Critique of Violence" deploys Kantian terminology in a philosophical task: "The critique of violence is the philosophy of its history—the 'philosophy' of this history because only the idea of its development makes possible a critical, discriminating, and decisive approach to its temporal data" (*SW* 1:251). In these and, I would argue, most of his works, Benjamin was concerned primarily with the need to draw together the fields of literary criticism, history, philosophy, politics, and religion to articulate the task of addressing a particular question.

Hanssen's observation that the essay "fell short of providing an incisive differentiation between just and unjust uses of violence, and therefore, in the final analysis, of offering a credible critique of violence," is thus consistent with Benjamin's project of working "toward" the critique.[8] What may appear to take the form of a resolution of the critique—the opposition between mythical and divine violence as manifested in the contrast between the myths of Niobe and Korah—is in fact a rhetorical and literary strategy to illustrate what such a resolution would require.[9]

A full account of these two stories would be a primary condition of such a critique. Another such requirement, consistent with Benjamin's other writings, is an awareness that the literary form of an essay itself is inseparable from its argument. Many of Benjamin's essays display a "rhetoric of the task" whose chief accomplishment is often to argue the risks of overlooking multiple perspectives on a problem.[10] The essay begins, in fact, with the phrase "The task of a critique of violence" (*GS* 2:179).

What I propose, then, is to approach Benjamin's essay as a *composition*, one that communicates not only by reasons and evidence but also by its formal and literary qualities. Among these qualities are structure, transitions, repetitions, juxtapositions, and references to narrative. Perhaps the best way to understand the essay is in terms of a compositional technique that would preoccupy his later work on art and the Paris arcades: montage. Benjamin combines at least three *very* disparate discourses in the essay: neo-Kantian philosophy of law, the radical socialist-syndicalism of Georges Sorel, and a political theology informed by his conversations with Scholem and others. More specifically, we can mark some rather abrupt transitions in the essay, from neo-Kantian discourse to socialism (*SW* 1:239), to the case of war and the military (240), then to the police (242), until Benjamin articulates his own position on law and violence, which leads to a discussion of nonviolence and Sorel's theory of strikes (243–47), and the distinct categories of mythic violence and divine violence (247–51), concluding finally with one of Benjamin's famously suggestive concluding paragraphs (251–52). The reader, like a viewer of artistic montage, must attempt to make sense of the text by integrating disparate elements. If that kind of integration is possible, then Benjamin's ambition to combine religious tradition, politics, and aesthetics survives his own fragmentary efforts.

A complete and rigorous analysis of the essay would easily require a monograph. I attempt the more modest project of discussing selected qualities in the essay as they relate to the problem of understanding "divine violence." My main proposal is that Benjamin's reference to the biblical narrative of rebellion in Numbers 16 holds a key to this notion of divine violence, and that the biblical text offers significant resources to illuminating the essay as a whole. To emphasize the compositional nature of the essay and its use of the Bible is already a significant departure from previous readings. Merely to observe that Benjamin illustrates the most crucial idea of the essay with a biblical narrative is to call attention to a subject on which embarrassingly little has been said. But it is also important to determine *what kind* of narrative this is. How sensitive Benjamin was to the text's nuances is unclear, but there is no reason to believe that a critic and scholar famous for his attention to texts and details of culture was uncharacteristically oblivious to the text he placed at the center of his essay. Unlike many other biblical narratives, the Korah episode is not more widely available in popularized form than it is in the original text itself. At a minimum, we can assume Benjamin had read this text and knew the story. The fact that he did not attempt a careful commentary on the text does not mean he was ignorant of its details.

In his opening paragraph, Benjamin establishes that "violence can first be sought only in the realm of means, not in the realm of ends" (*SW* 1:236). By saying this, Benjamin invokes Kant's ideal of a realm of "ends," a "union of different rational beings through common laws" based on the categorical imperative.[11] At the most modest level, this observation sets parameters for the essay, but given that Benjamin's title is also Kantian, it also suggests something much bolder: because violence lies beyond the domain of ends, the question of whether violence is just also lies beyond the reach of Kantian ethics. Reference to Kant thus provides boundaries for the essay while indicating its ambitions are Kantian in scale. Like the earlier essay "On the Program of the Coming Philosophy," "Critique of Violence" attempts to carry on the Kantian project despite sharp disagreements with Kant. When Benjamin returns to Kantian terminology at the end of the essay, after introducing the concept of divine violence, the implications of his essay for Kantian thought become clearer. Benjamin quotes the pacifist Kurt Hiller, who argues for the sanctity of life against killing in the name of creating a just world (i.e., the kingdom of ends). In so doing, Benjamin attacks the notion of the sanctity of life on the grounds that it seems to defend mere (biological) life in the struggle against injustice.

While he doesn't openly acknowledge the return of Kantian goals at this point in the essay, Benjamin here appears to shift from the realm of means to the realm of ends. Benjamin describes history as the process of a "rising and falling in the law-making and law-preserving [*rechtsetzender und rechtserhaltender*] forms of violence" (*SW* 1:251; *GS* 2:202). Given that all such arrangements are designed to give a monopoly on violence to an unjust state, what hope for action does Benjamin offer? He is characteristically (and strategically) cautious: if this cycle is broken, law and state power are abolished and a "new historical epoch is founded" (*SW* 1:251–52). How? "If the rule of myth is broken occasionally in the present age, the coming age is not so unimaginably remote that an attack on law is altogether futile" (*SW* 1:252). Benjamin thus invokes "pure immediate violence," which is "violence outside the law," as an indicator that a new epoch, brought about by divine violence, is possible. The mechanism for this transformation, however, is not at all clear or even knowable: "for only mythic violence, not divine, will be recognizable as such with certainty, unless it be in incomparable effects, because the expiatory power [*entsühnende Kraft*] of violence is invisible to men" (*SW* 1:252; *GS* 2:203). Divine violence, "which myth bastardized with law," can take any form, he argues, and it resists human detection, much less manipulation (*SW* 1:252).

Direct observation and direct action guarantee no access to divine violence. Divine violence is thus messianic, and the model of change Benjamin proposes is messianic as well.[12] Yet since "the rule of myth is broken occasionally in the present age," he writes, "the coming age is not so unimaginably remote that an attack on law is altogether futile" (*SW* 1:252). The problem Benjamin faces is the failure to break out of the vicious cycle of law-making and law-breaking violence, in which rulers claim a monopoly on violence that is legitimated by mythic violence. Even when new rulers replace existing rulers, they seem necessarily to resort to the same dynamic of law-making and law-breaking. How, then, can the reference to messianism provide grounds for meaningful political action? The answer is that the kind of immediate or pure violence he identifies in Sorel's model of the general strike indicates, however faintly, the possibility of epoch-changing divine violence. Such actions can sometimes break the "rule of myth," making a complete transformation seem possible (if not fully subject to human agency). With something like the "*weak* messianic power" of which Benjamin would write almost twenty years later (*SW* 4:390), practices such as the general strike, and even the critique of violence itself, indicate the possibility of change.

Near the beginning of the essay, Benjamin introduces the strike as a possible exception to the rule that the state has a monopoly on violence. Later, after he surveys other forms and problems of violence (war, police, nonviolent resolution of conflict), Benjamin returns to the subject of the proletarian general strike as sometimes qualifying as a "pure means": "Against this deep, moral, and genuinely revolutionary conception, no objection can stand that seeks, on grounds of its possibly catastrophic consequences, to brand such a general strike as violent" (*SW* 1:245).

In structural terms, the essay is framed at beginning and end with highly abstract discussions of the relationship between violence and law. Then, in the body of the essay, the subject of strikes frames a discussion of several models and forms of violence. Finally, in a conclusion that Derrida rightly observes is powerful, Benjamin alludes to the proletarian strike as the sort of human endeavor that indicates the possibility of a divine violence that can break the cycle of successive forms of mythic violence and law.

At the heart of the essay's argument lies a distinction between mythic violence and divine violence; Benjamin illustrates the distinction with the stories of Niobe and Korah. But what is the difference between the Niobe story and Numbers 16? Close readers will observe that there is, in fact, very little difference between them: both relate a horrible punishment by the gods against rebellious mortals. Not until the end of the essay, when we read that divine violence is inscrutable and that mythic violence is a bastardized version of divine violence, does it become clear that the two narratives do not represent formal or thematic types for divine and mythic violence. Despite Benjamin's contrast between the stories ("bloody power over mere life" *versus* "pure [bloodless] power over all life for the sake of the living"), which has been read by Derrida and others as a contrast in terms of their *contents*, no such distinction is possible under Benjamin's idea of the inscrutability of divine violence.

The contrast between Niobe and Korah lies not in the stories themselves, but in what they become or represent, through tradition, to Benjamin. Here we must combine what Benjamin says with some inference on what he meant. I suggest that Benjamin's reading of the Korah story reflects the dynamic of divine violence and human agency described in "Critique of Violence," according to which cycles of human, mythic violence can only be broken by divine violence. As such, what matters in Numbers 16 is not whether Moses or Korah is "right" but rather that the manifestation of divine violence leads to tradition in which questions of authority and holiness remain vital issues. By ongoing practices of text and commentary (a recurring motif in Benjamin),[13] biblical tradition produces the context and the possibility of a messianic ideal. Benjamin's essay reads Korah as a case of divine violence "for the sake of the living."

Is Korah's rebellion a kind of general strike? Perhaps not, since divine violence stamps it out. In this case Korah's revolt would be less revolutionary strike than mythic violence designed to impose the human law of an elite group of priests. On the other hand, the Korahites turn out to survive this punishment (Num. 26), and their challenges to Moses and Aaron, insofar as they prevail on the question of holiness and help establish God and not these human leaders as sovereign, could be judged a success. But Benjamin's reading need not decide whether Korah or Moses was right; what matters is that divine violence yields divine sovereignty and a tradition that sustains human life. Benjamin would find resources for this reading in the biblical narrative and in traditions that read it in light of a messianic (and thus also narrative) orientation to history. In order to make sense of this claim, I turn to the Korah and Niobe texts.

Numbers 16 and Niobe

The story of a human rebellion and its suppression in Numbers 16 interweaves two narrative strands generally agreed to come from distinct documentary sources; the passage opens with a section from JE, shifts to P, and alternates between the two four more times.[14] In the earlier, JE version of the story (16:1–2, 12–15, and 25–34), Reubenites who rebel against Moses's leadership are swallowed up by the earth. In the later, P version of the story, a group of Levites challenge Moses and Aaron on the question of who is holy, and their punishment, in a kind of poetic justice for priests who burn incense, is to be consumed by fire. The JE version of the story is considered to be more ancient than P, and P may also have woven JE and P together.

Despite the obvious fragmentation and differences between the two versions of the story, the text includes some striking echoes, repetitions, and moments of drama. When the insurgents accuse Moses and Aaron of wanting too much, Moses replies "It is you who seek too much, you Levites!" (verses 3, 7). When he hears the charges from the faction, Moses falls on his face; later, when the God of Israel announces his plan to annihilate the faction, they fall on their faces (verses 4, 22). Their plea for mercy appears to employ a kind of double standard: whereas they had originally claimed that everyone in the congregation is holy, now they ask why the group must be punished for the guilt of a few. The punishment of fire against the rebellious Levites likewise takes on a tone of poetic justice, since fire is basic to their priestly office. In the climax of their confrontation, Moses commands the Levites to light their censers (16–22). Later, after they have been consumed by fire (and the earth), the censers are hammered onto the altar to be signs and reminders to future generations of the rebellion (17:1–3/16:36-38). In a remarkable reversal, these firepans/censers are considered to be holy. The burnt remnants of the priests' paraphernalia—firepans—have become holy despite or because of their rebellion and punishment, a rebellion which consisted of the demand that all the congregation of Israel were holy. Later, in Numbers 26, we learn that some of the Korahites survived, despite the impression of annihilation given here (verses 9–11). Thus in two ways at least, the Korahites return to the narrative after they are extinguished. They remain, despite their violent destruction, part of the tradition, not only in written memory but also in physical form.

The story of Niobe bears a striking resemblance to Numbers 16. In Ovid's version, which Benjamin is likely to have read as a student at the Kaiser Friedrich School, where he studied Latin, the myth of Niobe represents a challenge to institutional religion.[15] Boasting that her fortunes exceed those of Latona, Niobe defies the prophetess's call to worship her: "'What lunacy makes you prefer a fabled god,' she said, 'to gods you see?' "[16] Niobe claims superiority in parentage, political power, beauty, and her seven sons and daughters. When the women of Thebes end the ritual at Niobe's request, Latona complains to her children Phoebus (Apollo) and Phoebe (Diana), Apollo kills her sons one by one, and after an unrepentant speech from Niobe, the daughters as well. Niobe has, in Ovid's words, "taken no warning from the punishment / Of her compatriot to give the gods / Their proper place and moderate her tongue," so she is turned to stone, and "upon a mountain peak she pines away, / And tears drip from that marble to this day."[17] The fear and worship of Latona are thereby intensified.

Contemporary sources may have influenced Benjamin's choice of the Korah and Niobe stories. The 1919 novel *The Horde of Korah* (*Die Rotte Korahs*, by Hermann Bahr) is a philo-Semitic novel in which the main character discovers his Jewish identity upon receiving an inheritance.[18] Bahr was a prominent Austrian playwright and essayist whose work Benjamin cites in his 1931 essay on Willy Haas.[19] The novel depicts and refutes anti-Semitism along with Zionism, and what is more, the words of its title appear in the novel as an anti-Semitic slur.[20] In the likely event that Benjamin was familiar with Bahr's novel, its use of the biblical Korah casts Korah in a sympathetic light: the "divine violence" against Korah, though revelatory, is no more palatable or justified than anti-Semitism!

An intriguing detail from Benjamin's letters may help explain why Benjamin chose the Niobe myth. In a 1920 letter to Gershom Scholem, Benjamin thanks his friend for beautiful gifts (likely for his birthday) that included a work called "Niobe": "I have not been able to read *Niobe* yet. But any mythological work from you fills me with the greatest sense of expectation. The subject is significant too."[21] What this work called *Niobe* may be is uncertain. One possibility is the novel *Niobe* by Norwegian author Jonas Lie (1893), which appeared in German in 1895, but it would be difficult to establish why Benjamin would call it a "mythological work." Another, more likely case is *Niobe und die Niobiden*, an 1863 scholarly illustrated treatise that was still available in 1920.[22]

Judith Butler offers a nuanced reading of Benjamin's use of the myth: Niobe's metamorphosis into rock indicates that "law thus petrifies the subject, arresting life in the moment of guilt . . . The punishment produces the subject bound by law—accountable, punishable, and punished. She would be fully deadened by guilt if it were not for that sorrow, those tears, and so it is with some significance that it is those tears to which Benjamin returns when he considers what is released through the expiation of guilt."[23] For Butler, the mythic violence of the story is Niobe's acceptance of responsibility for her children's deaths, an act that represents the violent transition from fate to law. Butler then comes closer than any other commentator to noticing the inscrutability of the distinction between mythic and divine violence. Given the mythic violence of Niobe's condition under fate, Butler follows Benjamin's point that "one must move from fate to God, or from myth, the sphere to which fate belongs, to the divine, the sphere to which a certain nonviolent destruction belongs."[24] Butler's discussion moves to the domain of divine commandment and Benjamin's paradoxical discussion of the commandment not to kill:

> Divine power does not safeguard life itself, however, but life only for the sake of "the living." Who constitutes "the living" in this notion? It cannot be everyone who merely lives, since the soul of the living is different, and what is done "for the sake of the living" may well involve taking away mere life. This seems clear when Benjamin refers, for instance, to the blight of Korah—a biblical scene in which an entire community is annihilated by the wrath of god for not having kept faith with his word—as an example of divine violence.[25]

Butler then attempts to distinguish the case of Korah from Niobe as biblical commandment, performative speech act, rather than the imposition of guilt and fear. The Niobe myth establishes a kind of law, while the Korah episode simply imposes divine fiat without imposing judgment. The difficulty of this contrast is that the biblical text does not bear it out. By missing the striking analogy between the Niobe and Korah stories, Butler's analysis misses the central inscrutability of divine violence.[26] Nevertheless, by comparing divine violence to the category of the messianic in the "Theologico-Political Fragment," Butler acknowledges that divine violence is elusive, if not inscrutable: "There is something speculative here when Benjamin claims that expiatory violence is not visible to men and that it is linked to eternal forms: the life in man that is identically present in earthly life, death, and afterlife. Reading 'Critique of Violence' together with the 'Theologico-Political Fragment,' written at about the same time, we can discern claims worth careful consideration: first, that nothing historical can relate itself to the messianic; second, that this expiatory violence can be manifest in a true war or divine judgment of the multitude against a criminal."[27]

The parallel between Niobe and Korah is thus quite strong: a mortal initiates a revolt against religious hierarchy, one that challenges the status quo and leads to a backlash that includes death (to the party of Korah and Niobe's children). Korah and Niobe both contest the authority of the religious leadership and the hierarchy itself. Their reasons seem a bit different: Korah claims that all members of the congregation are holy and challenges the authority of Moses over them; Niobe boasts that she has more children than Latona, is also a child of a god, and therefore deserves even greater honor than she. But Korah and Niobe both challenge the cult (and its leaders) by claiming a level of dignity reserved for the gods. Both undergo severe punishment and leave behind some remnant that recalls their crime, and with that memory, the basis for tradition.

Numbers 16 and Biblical Tradition

What is the relationship between the strike and the Korah rebellion? The strike is a political action, and the rebellion is religious, but on the other hand Benjamin links the general strike to divine violence, and the Korah rebellion is certainly political. The strike is the only lawful violence not performed by the government, and the divine violence that follows the rebellion of the Korah story neither creates nor preserves law at all.

What does Benjamin's use of the biblical story of Korah assume? The closest analogy to his use of Numbers 16 comes from the essay on language (1916) in which the Genesis creation story is presented neither as "biblical interpretation" nor as "objective consideration as revealed truth, but the discovery of what emerges of itself from the biblical text with regard to the nature of language" (*SW* 1:67). Benjamin claims, remarkably, that he follows the Bible's understanding of "language as an ultimate reality, perceptible only in its manifestation, inexplicable and mystical." "The Bible," he writes, "must necessarily evolve the fundamental linguistic facts" (*SW* 1:67).

Benjamin thus treats the Bible and biblical tradition as a kind of immanent reality within which he operates. Biblical texts and traditions set the terms for his essay, not because he is mystical or irrational, but because the Bible infuses Western thought and culture in general. We know that Benjamin's understanding of the Bible works directly against Martin

Buber's project of promoting a religious revival based on direct encounters of a newly translated Bible.[28] Such a philosophy of direct personal "experience" of tradition contradicted Benjamin's notion of tradition as a mediated, layered, and paradoxical phenomenon. Like Sigfried Kracauer, Benjamin believed the artistic experiments and phenomena of modernism were more likely than a new Bible translation to convey religious tradition. Here in the essay on language, the biblical text receives several pages of Benjamin's attention, and he clearly explains how the biblical narrative presents an idealized language against which contemporary, fallen language can be evaluated. The case is much different in "Critique of Violence": Benjamin chooses a difficult text and says little about it.

Benjamin cannot read Numbers 16 as a story in which Korah has simply broken a law, since that would contradict the notion of divine violence the story illustrates. Nor can Benjamin understand this to be a narrative about the sovereignty of Moses and Aaron, since that too would suggest something much more like the mythic law he denounces. Such a reading would also overlook the apparent humility of Moses and arrogance of Korah. In the narrative, Korah and his Levitical allies represent an elite (16:1–2), and when they challenge Moses, he falls on his face, as if to underscore the sense in which the power is not his own. Divine sovereignty is central not just to Benjamin but to the biblical narrative as well.

The analogy of religious violence extends, in part, to Georges Sorel's *Reflections on Violence*, despite its overtly secular purpose. Both Numbers 16 and Sorel's text offer disjointed accounts of violence in the form of an uprising or strike; both engage debates on the nature and advisability of collective violence. According to Sorel, the proletarian general strike is not only the way to challenge demagogues; it is also a transformative, almost messianic event: "It awakens in the depths of the soul a sentiment of the sublime proportionate to the conditions of a gigantic struggle; it forces the desire to satisfy jealousy by malice into the background; it brings to the fore the pride of free men, and thus protects the worker from the quackery of ambitious leaders, hungering for the fleshpots."[29] The sublime feelings produced by the general strike evoke such religious language as "soul" and an allusion to Israelite longings for Egypt ("fleshpots," Exod. 16:3) and the complaint narratives of Numbers.

If Numbers 16 describes a general strike that was put down violently and led, indirectly, to divine violence, then does the analogy of the revolt of Numbers 16 with a general strike indicate a kind of counterrevolutionary politics? I believe Benjamin suggests, much more aporetically, that only a formidable kind of power such as the general strike of Korah could produce the divine violence of the narrative, and that Korah's "strike" deserves credit for its role in a dialectical process of triggering divine violence and the world transformation that comes in its wake. The essay's conclusion, which draws an indirect link between human political action and the messianic domain of divine violence, suggests that is exactly Benjamin's claim (*SW* 1:252). But by placing divine violence beyond human power and even knowledge, Benjamin's essay refuses conclusive answers to the question.

Reading Numbers 16, then, Benjamin would no doubt recognize the discontinuities of the narrative (fire, falling into the earth). He also must have believed this is not a story about human liberation or justice in any conventional sense. If Benjamin wished to invoke a biblical example of conventional social justice, he would almost certainly have resorted to the Exodus from Egypt, a story of slaves coming to freedom which he knew was commemorated annually by Jews at Passover. On the contrary, Numbers 16 appears to be about the suppression of an uprising, one in which a claim is made for a broader understanding of religious power: "You seek too much! The community in its entirety is sanctified, for Yahweh is present in their midst. Why, then, do you exalt yourselves over Yahweh's congregation?" (16:2). Most of all, Benjamin would recognize that Numbers 16 preserves debates on law, human agency, and divine sovereignty in an aporetic text of biblical tradition.

Benjamin's use of Numbers 16 does not offer any straightforward vision of justice, humanism, or liberation; despite his commentary, it does not differ significantly from the myth of Niobe. And as I mentioned above, the use of the narrative could not indicate the enforcement of any preexisting law. Instead, the uprising of the story looks like the sort of general strike he considers to approach violence as a pure means. Against the prevailing power structure, the Levite and Reubenite rebels claim that everyone in the congregation is holy, not just Moses and Aaron. Religious power, they insist, is shared equally by all of Israel. The force of this claim sends Moses face down to the ground. The obliteration of the rebels, while obviously a form of retaliatory punishment, is inscrutable to Benjamin as it is for many readers of the Bible. After all, the Holiness Code of Leviticus (most of Lev. 17–26, from the preceding book of the Bible, also associated with Priestly sources) assumes exactly what the rebels have said: that everyone in the congregation *is* holy.

The inscrutable, divine violence that confronts Korah gives Benjamin the chance to consider how epochal change can take place: the rebels are destroyed en masse in not one but two apocalyptic scenarios: falling into the earth and being burned alive. No lesson is taught here, no law enforced. The key point is divine sovereignty in its purest form. Unlike the chapters of Exodus on the Passover, this text initiates no ritual or law other than the assertion of divine sovereignty, always conveyed through a layered and authoritative text and a tradition Benjamin considered constitutive and yet transcendent of modernity.

The punishment in Numbers 16 thus helps bring about a state of affairs, including scriptural tradition itself—that expiates for the sake of the living. To say so is to build on the fact that Korah's descendents *do* survive, that their view that all members of the congregation are holy *is* adopted, and most of all, that the notion of divine sovereignty posited in this story makes possible the kind of messianic narrative according to which mythic, state violence can be opposed. To put it more clearly in Benjamin's terms, biblical tradition provides the messianic horizon and doctrine of divine sovereignty that, along with philosophy and politics, allows a critique of violence (and law) to take place. However closely Benjamin read the details of Numbers 16, his use of the narrative observes keenly its paradoxical affirmation, through biblical tradition itself, of resistance to state authority.

The distinction between Korah and Niobe is not any internal difference between the stories but a distinction between biblical and classical tradition: biblical (and not classical) tradition offers the messianic and life-sustaining dimension needed for Benjamin's critical project. Yet unexamined contrasts between the stories themselves play a decisive part in criticisms of the essay. According to Beatrice Hanssen, Benjamin's use of Korah represents "an attempt to reinstate a more primordial justice."[30] This conclusion depends not only on Hanssen's reading of the distinction between Korah and Niobe as self-evident, but also on the assumption that Benjamin is engaged in retrieving a lost past, the kind of project that this essay, along with the essays on translation and language, warns against. Hanssen's exposition of Benjamin's distinction goes as follows:

> The mythical force of profane law was like the immediate, nonmediated violence exemplified in the story of Niobe, for her punishment at the hands of the gods served to establish their pure presence and power—in other words, the pure instating of right . . . The crux of Benjamin's argument thus was directed at the distinction that needed to be made between the primitive violence of Greek mythology, on the one hand, and the divine, pure violence of biblical Judaism, on the other. The biblical account of the company of Korah demonstrated that divine, just violence was bloodless and expiatory as distinct from inauthentic justice, which had been incorporated into profane law.[31]

By the end of her discussion of the essay, Hanssen concludes that Benjamin's contrast between Niobe and Korah constitutes a master binary: "That the confrontation between these two forms of history—the history of continuity and of a divine discontinuity—should take the form of an encounter between the myth of Niobe and the parable of the company of Korah, or between the Greek and the Judaic, should not be cause for surprise."[32]

The criticism I raise against Hanssen's reading of Benjamin, along with Derrida's and others', could be called a literary criticism. By this I mean that Benjamin's essay must itself be recognized as a literary text written by the author of a doctoral dissertation on German romantic criticism as well as (later) experimental essays on baroque allegory, Brecht, and the surrealists. For such a thinker as Benjamin, it would be a mistake to overlook the details of any literary texts that lie at the heart of his argument. Overlooking the literary dimensions of Benjamin's analysis and of his text can, I argue, miss the point of his analysis entirely.

This literary criticism goes further to suggest not only the need to recognize literary references and the purposes of the essay, but also that there can be distinctively literary ways of *arguing* and *knowing*. Such arguments claim not only that one cannot paraphrase a text without losing its meaning, but also that traditional boundaries between literature and philosophy misunderstand the texts and traditions they claim to represent.[33] In Benjamin's essay, such literary ways of arguing can be found in the paradoxical use of two stories that actually mirror each other. And the incorporation of these two stories in the context of a Kantian discourse or critique on violence, a discourse that is presented only in provisional terms, makes use of the literary technique of mixing genres and subverting expectations in order to advance an argument much like that of "On the Program of the Coming Philosophy," that only such a combination of discourses or genres can achieve, or at least identify, the goals of this philosophical project.

Tradition, Sovereignty, and Messianism

"Critique of Violence" represents and anticipates a strand of critical thought that takes religious tradition seriously, or conversely, a strand of religious thought that takes the politics of modernity seriously. In this way, Benjamin anticipates a trend among current theorists, from William Connolly and Slavoj Žižek to Giorgio Agamben and Talal Asad, to regard religious tradition as an important dimension of culture.[34] For Benjamin, the use of religion challenges the types of Kantian thought (recall his title and such references as "kingdom of ends") that promise and fail to deliver ethical and political systems of justice. It also argues against any appropriation of tradition—mythic violence—that legitimates the state monopoly on violence in the name of law and divine fiat. And finally, it challenges ideologies that legitimate half-measures, state terror, and the atavistic longing for sacred wholeness as the best that can be hoped for. In a set of moves that Hanssen and Derrida analyze as a turn to Judaism and, ironically, as a foreshadowing of Nazism, Benjamin makes a radical claim for what it would take to carry out a proper critique of violence.[35] But there is nothing here to suggest or justify the anachronistic affiliation of Benjamin with the Nazis who would cause his own demise. What is more, similar claims appear in Derrida's own work. In his essay "On Forgiveness," for instance, Derrida invokes a messianic notion of forgiveness, one that is "unconditional without sovereignty."[36]

While it is difficult to extract a theory of sovereignty from Benjamin's essay, my analysis suggests that Benjamin harbors a deep suspicion of most or all systems of human sovereignty, grounded as they are in the mythical structures of law-making and law-breaking violence. By contrast, Benjamin is willing to invoke a category of sovereignty in the form of divine violence, but he is quite clear that divine violence is inscrutable.

Agamben makes use of Benjamin's essay and terminology, but his notion of sovereignty differs significantly from Benjamin's. Taking Benjamin's notion of "mere life" from the essay's denunciation of the "sanctity of life," Agamben reworks these terms in an argument (influenced by Carl Schmitt) that the state of exception defines sovereign power. Agamben argues that Schmitt's notion of sovereign violence, the power that blurs boundaries between state and nature and decides the state of exception, closely approximates Benjamin's notion of divine violence.[37] While Benjamin concludes his essay with an aporetic gesture toward a divine violence that is inscrutable yet sovereign, Agamben turns his attention away from the category of divine violence to the link between "mere life" and the notion of sovereignty. In *Homo Sacer* and other works, Agamben defines the contemporary state of exception as the concentration camp, in which humanity is reduced to "bare life." "Sovereignty, therefore, is the guardian who prevents the undecidable threshold between violence and right, nature and language, from coming to light."[38]

From this it is clear that Agamben's use of Benjamin is partial: he shares almost completely Benjamin's criticism of state law as justified by violence. He also incorporates religious categories into his analysis, but in a way quite different from Benjamin. While the notion of divine violence forms a kind of inscrutable horizon for Benjamin whose possibility gives some hope to such tangible projects as strikes, Agamben undertakes an analysis of Schmittian sovereignty in which camps and other exceptional states legitimate modern forms of sovereignty.

Unlike Derrida, who appears to dismiss Benjamin's essay as proto-fascist, Agamben seeks to recuperate it, using Schmitt, in the analysis of sovereign power's connection to bare life and the state of exception. Neither Agamben nor Derrida pays close attention to the use of biblical narrative in Benjamin, however, and since it is precisely the use of Korah that enables Benjamin's claim to the efficacy of political action, one could argue that Benjamin's robust use of biblical narrative provides a correspondingly robust model for political engagement. A glance at the category of "messianism" in Benjamin, Derrida, and Agamben will illustrate the point.

For Benjamin, the stories of Korah and Niobe are similar in content but different because of biblical tradition. Divine violence is inscrutable, but its reality makes possible and meaningful the claim of human actions to be revolutionary, of which Sorel's proletarian general strike provides the illustration. In other words, human action can make some difference, albeit incomplete, in taking on the rule of myth, the legitimated state monopoly on violence (*SW* 1:252). Here is a form of the "*weak* messianic power" cited by Benjamin in "On the Concept of History": "Like every generation that preceded us, we have been endowed with a *weak* Messianic power, a power to which the past has a claim" (*SW* 4:390). This late expression of critical thought as a kind of political power runs through Benjamin's corpus: in "Trauerspiel and Tragedy" ("Trauerspiel und Tragödie," 1916), the "Theological-Politcal Fragment" (contemporary with "Critique of Violence," 1921), and the *Trauerspiel* study (1925, pub. 1928). In a more indirect fashion, we can see the restorative or messianic "power" in the work of Benjamin's philosophers, storytellers, translators, and modernists. This political messianism thus runs through Benjamin's work, and it is thoroughly intertwined with scripture and biblical tradition.

In Derrida's "On Forgiveness," by contrast, messianism represents a truncated horizon against which actual human forms of forgiveness are measured. Criticizing such liberalist projects as the South African Truth and Reconciliation Commission, Derrida appeals to a distinction between "pure" and pragmatic forms of forgiveness. Observing, in a very Benjaminian fashion, that all sovereign power entails violence, Derrida expresses the aporetic hope for a "democracy to come."[39] Lamenting the danger of associating sovereignty with forgiveness, Derrida appeals to the possibility of forgiveness as a divine gift, to a notion of "forgiveness without power," unconditional and without sovereignty.[40] If this appeal resembles or depends on the work of Benjamin, then it may undercut Derrida's criticism of "Critique of Violence." But unlike so many of his works, "On Forgiveness" does not develop from close and sustained reading of particular texts. Except for brief references, Derrida's essay does not relate biblical tradition and texts to such a messianic political project.

While *Homo Sacer* and "On Forgiveness" do not incorporate biblical tradition, Abamben's essay "The Messiah and the Sovereign" does. For Agamben, Benjamin is the best example of the following observation: "The Messiah is, in other words, the figure through which religion confronts the problem of the Law, decisively reckoning with it."[41] For Agamben, the praxis of reading, the dynamic of text and commentary that so animates Benjamin's work in a political way, emerges as a primary way of knowing in his reading of Kafka's "Before the Law." Invoking the traditional rabbinic idea of two messianic figures, one who dies and one who triumphs, Agamben proposes (against Derrida) that Kafka's parable relates how "something has really happened in seeming not to happen." Only through this reading, Agamben argues, "can the event of the Messiah coincide with historical time yet at the same time not be identified with it, effecting in the *eskhaton* that 'small adjustment' in which, according to the rabbi's saying told by Benjamin, the messianic kingdom consists."[42] With this, Agamben fully embraces Benjamin's recognition of the importance of biblical tradition to critical thought. A reading of Kafka's parable that leads to Scholem, Benjamin, and to rabbinic and biblical sources produces a well-articulated idea of the political significance of messianism.

Scripture, Narrative, and Violence

To reinterpret Benjamin's critical use of the Bible as I do here is not just to make the claim that somehow all expression comes down to a gently humanistic kind of narrative. I wish instead to claim that Benjamin's essay requires attention to biblical tradition itself. The category of narrative becomes explicit not only in the use of Niobe and Korah in reference to divine and mythic violence, but also at the end of the essay where Benjamin says that "the critique of violence is the philosophy of its history" (*SW* 1:251). With this claim Benjamin begins his final paragraph, in which the present epoch in history represents only a series of alternating systems of law-making and law-breaking violence, allowing for an indirect link between human pure violence (i.e., the general strike) and the only thing that can bring in a new historical epoch: divine violence.

An apparent hodgepodge of Kantian philosophy, radical politics, and theology, Benjamin's essay claims not to complete the critique but only to identify its terms. As a text woven from different strands, Numbers 16 also combines divergent perspectives: Korah could be a rebel or an elitist, trying either to impose mythic violence or to resist its stranglehold; the rebels are Levites and Reubenites; the means of divine punishment are falling into the earth and fire. But while biblical tradition depicts the cycles of violence decried by Benjamin, it also points beyond them to the messianic hope of divine violence that breaks these cycles.

The historical turn of the essay that equates critique with the philosophy of history, then, is really an apocalyptic or messianic one. Ordinary history is nothing other than a series of human systems of law supported by mythic violence. Only critique of violence, the "philosophy of its history," provides the insight into how anti-mythical and divine violence can rupture this pattern. As is often the case for Benjamin, the work of criticism goes hand in hand with political analysis. In fact, the general strike has no meaning on its own without the critique that locates it within this messianic context.

What then is the role of biblical tradition in the critique of violence? We begin to answer by returning to Derrida's criticism of Benjamin's essay, which associates Benjamin with an extreme political program akin to Carl Schmitt and the Nazis. At no point does Derrida consider that Benjamin's position, his juxtaposition of competing models of action, or his use of biblical tradition, could signal a nuanced account of violence. Despite his reputation for meticulous analysis (Gil Anidjar calls it a "scrupulous reading"),[43] Derrida fails to account for the *compositional* nature of the essay. The essay is not any kind of political program: Benjamin's reference to the general strike is a text on which he performs commentary: he is really interested in the *idea* of violence as pure means, and Sorel's general strike (imbued as it is with language of transcendence) provides a convenient and well-theorized example.

How, then, could we consider the essay as a composition without giving up its claim to engage ideas in a serious way? As a composition, the essay follows no clear plan, and makes a number of abrupt transitions, transitions of topic (from war to police, for example) but also shifts from topics to questions (from police to unmediated violence, for example). Like montage, the essay is nonlinear, like the essays of Montaigne as well as the biblical text itself. It names a problem (the link between law and violence and the need to theorize the latter) and then explores the problem in a variety of ways.

Given that all human law seems tainted by its dependence on violence, and that violence, since it is always a means, lies beyond the domain of ends, how can human thought and action break out of this cycle? The problem is addressed by lengthy discussions of the types and sources of law, the types of violence (especially Sorel's proletarian strike, which frames the discussion), and a very hasty resolution in which human attacks on mythical violence and law gesture toward the possibility of a more complete messianic kind of violence. The solution of divine violence is anticipated in the middle of the essay: "For it is never reason that decides on the justification of means and the justness of ends: fate-imposed violence decides on the former, and God on the latter" (*SW* 1:247).

Benjamin's use of the Genesis 2–3 creation story in his essay on language makes it clear that biblical narrative and its traditional reception convey normative models of language. The same dynamic appears to operate in "Critique of Violence": a narrative that is fully accessible in contemporary human language also, as *scripture*, exercises a normative and transcendent authority, a messianic dimension, to which Benjamin's critique attends. In the language essay and in "Critique of Violence" both, then, there are two kinds of narrative: the narrative on the surface of the text, and within it, a more messianic narrative, a narrative of loss and hope for restoration, toward which the accessible, visible narrative points. With the narrative of Numbers 16 and the messianic narrative toward which tradition gestures, "Critique of Violence" reaffirms Benjamin's suggestion that "the Bible, in regarding itself as revelation, must evolve the fundamental linguistic facts."

In his essay on violence, Benjamin only sketches the kind of engagement with biblical tradition that I argue his work implies. Yet as I have shown, he places the difficult, uncanny text of Numbers 16 at the center of his argument on law and violence in a way that requires attention to the narrative and to the messianic history toward which biblical tradition points. Numbers illustrates Benjamin's notion of scripture, which identifies the sacredness of texts not with their meaning but with their tradition or *Fortleben*. Far from any demythologization that would avoid difficult texts like this or the "theological foundationalism" of which he is accused, Benjamin insists on making a difficult text central to his political philosophy. Such a move affords a robust role for narrative and biblical tradition in critical thought, one that only now has begun to come to light.

Chapter 6

✦

Critical Vision, from Simulacra to Creaturely Agency

If the horrors of recent history are unprecedented, they cannot be understood apart from their representation, dissemination, and reception in visual images. How do pictures respond to disasters, particularly in a world that blurs the boundaries of image and reality? Susan Sontag distinguishes (in her late work) between image and reality, while Jean Baudrillard and Slavoj Žižek have insisted that such a distinction has become increasingly difficult to make. Žižek's "Welcome to the Desert of the Real" associates the attacks on the World Trade Center in 2001 with cinematic fantasies, and Baudrillard makes even more provocative claims in *The Gulf War Did Not Take Place*.[1] In a world where people spend more time than ever viewing photographs, television, and film, where widespread publicity is scarcely possible without mass media, one can justifiably ask what terms like "reality" mean today. What are the political potentials and dangers of such images? What kinds of human agency are enabled by the production and reception of images?

Most treatments of Benjamin's aesthetics and politics understandably focus on his "Work of Art" essay, which narrates the decline of aura in reproducible art and concludes aphoristically by contrasting fascism, which aestheticizes politics, against communism, which politicizes art (*SW* 4:251–70). It is easy to read this essay simplistically as a secularization narrative (marked by the decline of aura) and a schematic bridge between particular forms of art and politics. A careful reading of the essay, though, makes such simplicity difficult to support. But instead of focusing only on this essay, here I pursue contemporary debates on agency, image, and disaster through several of Benjamin's writings on images. Though he died too soon to witness the full horror of World War II, Benjamin considered himself to be living, writing, and thinking in a time of emergency to which his studies of images and their reception were meaningful responses.

This chapter asks how we can think about questions of disaster, tradition, and agency by engaging Walter Benjamin's work on images. By suggesting how modernity relates to memory and tradition, Benjamin's notions of mimesis, quotation, aura, creatureliness, and "dialectical image" lead to meaningful forms of agency in response to images of disaster. My argument is that Benjamin's work addresses the question of agency in image culture through models of critical reception in the traditions of aesthetic reception and textual commentary. Today, representations of disaster, whether of wars, the Holocaust, 9/11, or Abu Ghraib, are widely distributed and hotly contested as objects of moral and political meaning. Concerned with images in relation to history, Benjamin's approach avoids difficulties faced by Sontag, Žižek, and Baudrillard, who focus on images of disaster. His writings leave open important questions on exactly how images lead to critical awareness and engagement with history, but they point restlessly toward training in thought and perception in times of danger.

Baudrillard and Žižek

Baudrillard's *Simulations* (1983) announces the replacement of reality by simulacra, an endless play of images. He makes this point in a criticism of Pierre Bourdieu's appeal to the categories of truth and morality in a discussion of the Watergate scandal: "He therefore occupies the same deterministic and moralistic position as the *Washington Post* journalists. He does the same job of purging and reviving moral order, an order of truth wherein the genuine symbolic violence of the social order is engendered, well beyond all relations of force, which are only its indifferent and shifting configuration in the moral and political consciousness of men."[2]

For Baudrillard, simulacra and symbolic systems are uniquely constitutive of political and moral reality. One of Baudrillard's key examples is the World Trade Center:

> Why are there *two* towers at New York's World Trade Center? All of Manhattan's great buildings were always happy enough to affront each other in a competitive verticality, the result of which is an architectural panorama in the image of the capitalist system: a pyramidal jungle, all the buildings attacking each other. . . . [now a model of monopoly capitalism]: the two W.T.C. towers, perfect parallelepipeds a ¼-mile high on a square base, perfectly balanced and blind communicating vessels. The fact that there are two of them *signifies* the end of all competition, the end of all original reference . . . For the sign

> to be pure, it has to duplicate itself: it is the duplication of the sign which destroys its meaning.[3]

In the hindsight of the attacks of September 11, 2001, we can acknowledge Baudrillard's analysis of the World Trade Center as a capitalist simulacrum. At the same time, we can also challenge the author of *The Gulf War Did Not Take Place* to think through the implications of his work. Yes, we might say, analysis of capitalism has surely shifted from unmediated materiality to the domain of the image, and the multiplication and dissemination of these images shapes consciousness and experience in profound ways. And Baudrillard belongs to a generation of thinkers who rule out any simple claims to universal justice, rights, and nature, human or otherwise: "The principle of simulation wins out over the reality principle just as over the principle of pleasure."[4] But what Baudrillard does not provide, and what often animates severe criticism of him and other "postmodern" thinkers, is some way of thinking through the hall of mirrors he conjures, some way of understanding his own critical standpoint, some way of making his theory of simulacra convincing at a descriptive or even evaluative level. He is, after all, very quick to criticize Bourdieu's analysis of Watergate as ideology: "But this is still only the formula of ideology, and when Bourdieu enunciates it, he takes 'relation of force' to mean the *truth* of capitalist domination, and he *denounces* this relation of force as itself a *scandal*."[5] To criticize Watergate as a scandal only strengthens and legitimates capitalism, says Baudrillard, which is fundamentally indifferent to morality, a "sorcery of the social relation."[6] Is there any way to acknowledge Baudrillard's insight into the culture of imagery without falling prey to the political quietism the hall of mirrors implies?

A clue is Baudrillard's rhetoric, for example in describing the blurring of art and production in "the prestigious, hyperbolic signs that are the great industrial combines, the ¼-mile-high tower or the number mysteries of the GNP."[7] What conditions make this kind of discourse possible? What is the history of this discourse? Baudrillard's dire declarations are not just an attempt to observe phenomena—they rather seek to elicit a response that says, "That's terrible!" But Baudrillard is not interested in presenting a bland, empirical account of "facts." Without a systematic presentation of "evidence," his descriptions carry a latent prescription; his discourse is more apodictic and performative than propositional and descriptive. The same can be said of much modern political writing, traditional sermonizing, and biblical prophecy. Insofar as this history makes Baudrillard's writing *legible*, I would speculate here that Baudrillard's text inherits a tradition of hortatory writing that would be incoherent without "religious" writing.

To Baudrillard's reading of the World Trade Center we can reply with a contrasting analysis that finds the towers' duplication to be not the destruction of meaning but a melancholy sign of the failure of meaning. We can, in other words, deconstruct Baudrillard's lament as an indication that meaning remains possible. Long before it was destroyed, the World Trade Center indicated a kind of ruin of meaning, but as Benjamin shows in his study of the German tragic drama, ruins carry meaning. What is more, Benjamin isolates mimicry as fundamental to human life: "There is perhaps not a single one of his higher functions in which his mimetic faculty does not play a decisive role."[8] The most significant of these functions, of course, is language, especially writing, "into which the earlier powers of mimetic production and comprehension have passed without residue" (*SW* 2:722).

In "Welcome to the Desert of the Real," which takes its title from a quotation of Baudrillard in the film *The Matrix*, Slavoj Žižek identifies a core American fantasy at the heart of the September 11, 2001 attacks:

> The ultimate American paranoiac fantasy is that of an individual living in a small idyllic Californian city, a consumerist paradise, who suddenly starts to suspect that the world he lives in is a fake, a spectacle staged to convince him that he lives in a real world, while all people around him are effectively actors and extras in a gigantic show. The most recent example of this is Peter Weir's *The Truman Show* (1998), with Jim Carrey playing the small town clerk who gradually discovers the truth that he is the hero of a 24-hours permanent TV show: his hometown is constructed on a gigantic studio set, with cameras following him permanently. . . . The underlying experience of *Time Out of Joint* and of *The Truman Show* is that the late capitalist consumerist Californian paradise is, in its very hyper-reality, in a way IRREAL, substanceless, deprived of the material inertia.[9]

Žižek is certainly right about all this, but like Baudrillard he overlooks a significant scene in the film that links agency to doubling. After Truman discovers the artificiality of his life, he "doubles" himself by running away while the camera films what appears to be him sleeping. This ploy, familiar from *Ferris Bueller's Day Off* and many sitcoms before it, turns the artificial world of the "Truman Show" on its head, and it leads directly to Truman's successful escape into "reality." Truman seizes meaning and agency from the very mechanism—artificial doubling—that deprives his life of those things. By copying himself with a three-dimensional image, Truman becomes an agent like the producers of *The Truman Show* and thus secures his chance to escape their artificial world. Far from direct opposition or defiance, the use of doubling and image-making represents a potent but easily overlooked form of agency. I will develop this idea of doubling and its textual counterpart, quotation, in my discussion of Benjamin's work.

Sontag

In *Regarding the Pain of Others* (2003), Susan Sontag relates moral and political agency to the act of viewing images: "What to do with such knowledge as photographs bring of faraway suffering?"[10] Her response is to suggest "reflective engagement," careful looking, and serious thinking in response to images of human suffering.[11] Sontag does not elaborate how this kind of thinking might be cultivated, but her proposal is consistent with a lifelong aesthetic approach to morality and politics. In pursuit of her question of agency, Sontag reserves her sharpest criticism for Baudrillard and others, along with her own earlier thinking (*On Photography*, 1977):

> It is common to say that war, like everything else that appears to be real, is *médiatique* . . . . To speak of reality becoming a spectacle is a breathtaking provincialism. It universalizes the viewing habits of a small, educated population living in the rich part of the world, where news has been converted into entertainment—that mature style of viewing which is a prime acquisition of "the modern," . . . It assumes that everyone is a spectator. It suggests, perversely, unseriously, that there is no real suffering in the world.[12]

Sontag's criticism of Baudrillard and others as cynical and resigned focuses on the question of reality, a topic on which theorists perennially disagree. But her mention of "the modern" raises a critical issue she does not develop: the limitations of modernism and the possibilities of tradition as a resource for reflecting on agency. Despite her critique of modernism, Sontag does not identify the category of tradition (which I develop here through engagement with Benjamin's work), perhaps because her own interests aligned closely with modern art and thought.

When we face the realities of war by photographs or other images, Sontag notes the dangers of responding with apathy, sentimentality, and even sympathy, for,

> as far as we feel sympathy, we feel we are not accomplices to what caused the suffering. Our sympathy proclaims our innocence as well

> as our impotence . . . To set aside the sympathy we extend to others beset by war and murderous politics for a reflection on how our privileges are located on the same map as their suffering, and may—in ways we might prefer to imagine—be linked to their suffering, as the wealth of some may imply the destitutions of others, is a task for which the painful, stirring images supply only an initial spark.[13]

Sontag's appeals to careful thinking and imagining as ways to address images of disaster and suffering do not go very far in articulating how this might work. Judith Butler attempts to develop Sontag's reflections in more unequivocally moral and political ways, arguing that all photographs are not only a kind of evidence but also a kind of interpretation presented within certain cultural and visual conventions or "frames." Butler pursues this line of thinking through compelling interpretations of the Abu Ghraib photographs of American torture victims, but without a broader account of these frames, one that takes account of the history and tradition of pictorial representation, the problem of agency, how photographs of human suffering relate to human action, remains.[14]

The terms of Sontag's clash with Baudrillard and others pit images against "real suffering," and in so doing beg the question, not at all obvious, what "real suffering" is. In spite of what Sontag, Butler, Elaine Scarry, and others may suggest, there can be disagreement on what constitutes suffering, particularly when the influence of cultural and psychological factors, beginning with language, is added to the analysis.[15] A richer account of this kind of thinking and imagining needs to be tied to looking and a broader conception of agency, grounded in tradition, which is one feature of Benjamin's account of the problem and the one to which I now turn.

Images of Agency and Tradition

What kinds of human agency are enabled by the production and reception of images today? After catastrophe, what role can images play for collective memory and understanding? What are the political potentials and dangers of images? These questions lead to Benjamin's works on the *Trauerspiel*, mimesis, photography, art, and history.

Agency does not come easily to Benjamin's conceptions of language and literature. In German tragic drama, the monarch is often unable to make a decision, while the martyr, the other type of main character, must submit stoically to circumstance (*GTD* 69–73). The *Trauerspiel* is a genre of melancholy, fragments, and ruins (*GTD* 145–48, 178, 235). Nevertheless, this "crude theater" draws "intense life" from the world of such emblems as "Dürer's genius of winged melancholy" (*GTD* 158, 151, 155, 216–18). In order to make sense of the contradictions of baroque literature and culture, says Benjamin, one must undertake an "ascetic apprenticeship" of reading and study (*GTD* 56). Somehow, even through failed attempts to preserve systems of meaning and representation, baroque allegory offers a dialectical synthesis of theology and art (*GTD* 177). In this way, the ruin of the *Trauerspiel* paradoxically outlives and outshines the complete structures to which it is unfavorably compared: "In the spirit of allegory it [*Trauerspiel*] is conceived from the outset as a ruin, a fragment. Others may shine resplendently as on the first day; this form preserves the image of beauty to the very last" (*GTD* 235).

Benjamin's conception of allegory initially resembles Baudrillard's account of simulacra—both detail a proliferation and subsequent collapse in systems of signification. In allegory, says Benjamin, "any person, any object, any relationship can mean absolutely anything else" (*GTD* 175). This sounds like a version of the familiar argument that our media-saturated world has desensitized us to the point of indifference to even the most horrible images of suffering. But while Baudrillard's "precession of simulacra" produces a seemingly endless hall of mirrors with little hope of escape, Benjamin's dialectical account of allegory and modernism appeals to a notion of tradition in which agency somehow survives. How? There is agency first of all in critical awareness, which Benjamin cultivated through a variety of philosophical and aesthetic categories, and which he eventually related to a politicized conception of the Messiah. This Messiah is not subject to human control, but awareness of the Messiah is not possible without awareness of tradition, which survives in modern culture.

An important aesthetic category for Benjamin, a modern counterpart to baroque allegory, is the "dialectical image." The manuscript texts collected in the notes to "On the Concept of History" include the following excerpt under the heading "The Dialectical Image" ("Das dialektische Bild"):

> The completeness of history is like the completeness of languages. Universal history in today's sense can only exist through a kind of Esperanto. The idea of universal history is a messianic one. The messianic world is the world of universal and integrated actuality . . . . This festival [of universal history] is distinguished from all other celebrations. It includes no festival hymns. Its language is integrated prose sprung from the chains of Scripture and to be understood by everyone (like the language of the birds for "Sunday children"). The

> idea of prose coincides with the messianic idea of universal history. (*GS* 1:3, 1238)

What this aphoristic text has to do with the concept of dialectical image is not immediately clear, but the idea of overcoming ordinary history also appears in the *Arcades Project*:

> Where thinking comes to a standstill in a constellation saturated with tensions—there the dialectical image appears. It is the caesura in the movement of thought . . . It is to be found, in a word, where the tension between dialectical opposites is greatest. Hence, the object constructed in the materialist presentation of history is itself the dialectical image. The latter is identical with the historical object; it justifies its violent expulsion from the continuum of historical process. (*Arcades* 475)

Elsewhere (in "Central Park"), he says the "dialectical image is an image that flashes up. The image of what has been—in this case, the image of Baudelaire—must be caught in this way, flashing up in the now of its recognizability" (*SW* 4:183).

The associations of the dialectical image with the Messiah and scripture are not accidental. The ultimate case of the dialectical image will be *Angelus Novus*, a painting by Paul Klee owned by Benjamin that featured prominently in his work from the time he acquired it in 1921 until his final work, "On the Concept of History" (see figure 3.) There are many dimensions to the dialectical image and *Angelus Novus*, but the one on which I wish to focus is the possibility of human agency in the face of images of horror and suffering. The angel of Klee's painting gazes out at the viewer, and though he never speaks of its aura, Benjamin lingers on this gaze: "His eyes are wide, his mouth is open, his wings are spread. . . . Where a chain of events appears before *us, he* sees one single catastrophe, which keeps piling wreckage upon wreckage and hurls it at his feet" (*SW* 4:392).

Before returning to *Angelus Novus*, I wish to discuss Benjamin's idea of mimesis in language and images. In "Doctrine of the Similar" ("Lehre vom Ähnlichen"), Benjamin argues that language is the archive of "nonsensuous similarity [*unsinnliche Ähnlichkeit*]": "Everything mimetic in language is an intention which can appear at all only in connection with something alien as its basis: precisely the semiotic or communicative element of language. Thus the literal text of writing [*Schrift*, which connotes scripture] is the sole basis on which the picture puzzle can form itself."[16] Speech and writing, he claims, are "the most perfect archive of

Figure 3. Paul Klee, *Angelus Novus* (1920). Photo © the Israel Museum, Jerusalem, by Elie Posner.

nonsensuous similarity . . . No longer directly, as they once did in the mind of the augur or priest, but in their essences, in their most transient and delicate substances, even in their aromas."[17] In a later version of this essay, "On the Mimetic Capability," Benjamin characterizes language as the displaced locus of magical practices: language is a "medium into which the earlier powers of mimetic production and comprehension have passed [*hineingewandert sind*] without residue, to the point where they have liquidated those of magic" (*GS* 2:213; *SW* 2:722).

Human language in its spoken and written forms is not straightforwardly mimetic, but it has become the archive of "nonsensuous similarity," that is, of the human mimetic capacity itself. A similar narrative of displacement informs Benjamin's 1916 essay on language, in which a "bourgeois language" of judgment and chatter has replaced the primordial language of naming associated with Eden. The post-lapsarian account of human language allows Benjamin to appeal to an idealized conception of language while placing it beyond the historical and epistemological reach of contemporary "prattle." What matters here is the mimetic dimension of language in Adam's naming: language, though fallen, remains fundamentally mimetic.

Benjamin denies simple histories of mimesis based on continuity and progress, yet he insists that mimesis is crucial to tradition and modernity alike. Anthropologist Michael Taussig adopts Benjamin's view to criticize colonial (and postcolonial) anthropology, not only on familiar political grounds of power and exploitation, but also on the fundamental level of mimesis: "From the mid-nineteenth century onwards, mimetically capacious machines reinvigorated the mimetic faculty such that the mythic foundational moment of colonial 'first contact' (as with Darwin on the beach in Tierra del Fuego) passed into the mechanically reproduced image as a new sort of sympathetic magic of imitation and contact."[18] The modern and the traditional have become thoroughly intertwined by the production of and encounter with images. Taussig's postsecular reading of the power and complexity of mimesis in Benjamin leads to a wholesale destabilization of the ethnographic enterprise. Like Talal Asad, Taussig turns to Benjamin for an analysis of mimesis that enables him to turn the ethnographic gaze not on the "Other" but on anthropology itself, and in so doing he adopts a critically self-aware stance that, by recasting tradition, poses the question of agency in a new way.

From Mimesis to Quotation

It is a paradox that Benjamin's engagement with modern culture, especially Baudelaire, is rooted in religious tradition, but this is what sets his modernism apart. Because of this link to tradition, there is a dialectic in Benjamin between agency and passivity when it comes to film, photography, and art in general. What this means for the problem of agency generally is first that one must abandon the Enlightenment notion of the individual as controlling agent in an absolute sense. Nietzsche, Freud, and Proust serve Benjamin's purpose here by articulating conceptions of the self based less on individual agency than on indebtedness to the past and tradition. This means that any recuperation of agency in Benjamin will be a new kind of agency, one that accounts for false consciousness and the tragic shape of history. The openness to historical and aesthetic transformations modeled by Benjamin cannot be seen either as apolitical or revolutionary in any conventional sense. Benjamin's essays on the work of art, Eduard Fuchs, photography, and Karl Kraus bear this out.

For Benjamin, engagement with modernity is like engagement with tradition: agency in both cases takes the form of highly alert reading, observation, commentary, and quotation, at least as a precondition to further forms of action. His approach thus resembles Sontag's with one important exception: an awareness of tradition. From the *Trauerspiel* to modernism, Benjamin identifies a dialectic of collapsing and continuing tradition, along with a parallel dialectic of agency and non-agency in the face of tradition. (This link between tradition and agency lies at the heart of the debate on Benjamin's use of Carl Schmitt's notion of sovereignty.)[19] Aside from criticism and translation, one of Benjamin's main techniques of exercising agency is through quotation, a practice rarely associated with agency but clearly linked to tradition: "Method of this project: literary montage. I needn't *say* anything. Merely show [*zeigen*]" (*Arcades* 460).

The individual who most personifies Benjamin's conceptions of mimesis and quotation is Karl Kraus. Through quotation and citation, Kraus carries newspaper writing "to his own sphere, and the empty phrase is suddenly forced to recognize that even in the deepest dregs of the journals it is not safe from the voice that swoops on the wings of the word to drag it from its darkness" (*SW* 2:453). Benjamin begins his essay with the image of a wild messenger, identified with Kraus and demonic forces, who brings news of danger and disaster. Kraus, who attacked and satirized his contemporaries in his journal *Die Fackel* and also staged public readings of Shakespeare and Nestroy, possessed what Benjamin calls a "mimetic genius, imitating while it glosses, pulling faces in the midst of polemics. . . . He imitates his subjects in order to insert the crowbar of his hate into the finest joints of their posture. . . . The larvae of venality and garrulity, ignominy and bonhomie, childishness and covetousness, gluttony and dishonesty" (*SW* 2:442). The mockery and satire of Kraus's quotation rise for Benjamin to a cosmic level of origin and destruction: "In it [quotation] is mirrored the angelic tongue in which all words, startled from the idyllic context of meaning, have become mottoes in the book of Creation" (*SW* 2:454).

Benjamin concludes the essay by returning to the image of the demonic messenger, Kraus. But in one of his characteristic reversals, Benjamin transforms this messenger, this demon, into an ephemeral angel from the Talmud, the *Angelus Novus*: "Not a new man—a monster, a new angel. . . . Lamenting, chastising, or rejoicing? No matter—on this evanescent vice the ephemeral work of Kraus is modeled. Angelus—that is the messenger in the old engravings" (*SW* 2:457). This reversal calls to mind other reversals in Benjamin, such as the claim in the "Theological-Political Fragment" that the "secular order . . . promotes the coming of the Messianic Kingdom" (*SW* 3:305). For Benjamin, mimetic practices such as quotation indicate a kind of agency and contribute somehow to messianic or apocalyptic reality. (The appeal to agency through quotation and mimicry has counterparts in the feminist theories of Luce Irigaray and Judith Butler.)[20]

Photography, Aura, and Mortality

Benjamin's "Short History of Photography" (1931) combines his interests in mimesis and aura with his broader investigation of modern culture. Looking back over the first ninety years of photography, Benjamin touches on photography as art, document of reality, and evolving technology in a culture that mixed nostalgia with novelty. The essay includes a discussion of aura, but unlike the better-known decay of aura described in the later essay on the work of art (1934), the photographs described by Benjamin are able to preserve, or attempt to preserve, aura, "a strange weave of space and time: the unique appearance or semblance of distance, however close it may be" (*SW* 2:518). The photos of Atget and those who follow him strip objects of their aura, but the demand for copies and imitations becomes greater and greater: "Every day the need to possess the object in close-up in the form of a picture, or rather a copy, becomes more imperative." This effect, influenced by surrealism, allows a "salutary estrangement between man and his surroundings. It gives free play to the politically educated eye, under whose gaze all intimacies are sacrificed to the illumination of detail" (*SW* 2:519). Though no longer auratic, reproduced images afford freedom and insight to the educated viewer.

Aura is defined variously in Benjamin's work, both as distance and as a returned gaze. One source for both ideas of aura is Kraus himself, whom Benjamin quotes as follows: "'The more closely you look at a word, the more distantly it looks back'"; Benjamin relates the aura of language to quotation (*SW* 2:453–454). The idea of aura as distance appears in Benjamin's writings about photography and art; this is famously the quality of images that diminishes with modern, technically reproducible forms. In the essay on photography, Atget's photos "suck the aura out of reality like water from a sinking ship.—What is aura, actually? A strange weave of space and time: the unique appearance or semblance of distance, no matter how close it may be" (*SW* 2:518). This definition is repeated in the artwork essay, but here Benjamin adds that early photos "simulate the aura which had been banished from the picture" (*SW* 2:517).

The idea of aura as a returned gaze appears in "On Some Motifs in Baudelaire" (1939): "Experience of the aura thus arises from the fact that a response characteristic of human relationships is transposed [*Übertragung*] to the relationship between humans and inanimate or natural objects. The person we look at, or who feels he is being looked at, looks at us in turn. To experience the aura of an object we look at means to invest it with the ability to look back at us" (*SW* 4:339). Like other forms of tradition, aura somehow survives into modernity: it even lingers in childhood photos of Kafka and Benjamin in the essay on photography and the autobiographical work, *Berlin Childhood around 1900* (*SW* 2:515, 3:344–13).

In the conclusion to the essay on photography, Benjamin ponders the paradox that written captions are necessary to link photographs to reality, along with the more general paradoxes that photographs are specific and general, descriptive and moralizing, secular and somehow supernatural, at the same time: "Isn't it the task of the photographer—descendant of the augurs and haruspices—to reveal guilt and to point out the guilty in his pictures?" (*SW* 2:527). These paradoxes of photography refuse any clear narrative of secularization or eternal recurrence; instead, they appropriately name this new technology as the focus of dialectical tensions between past and present. The questions and paradoxes of photography, concludes Benjamin, also serve to link past to present: "It is in the illumination of these sparks [i.e., questions] that the first photographs emerge, beautiful and unapproachable, from the darkness of our grandfathers' day" (*SW* 2:527). One could just as well say "beautiful *but* unapproachable," since beauty typically suggests closeness and approachability, while the unapproachable is traditionally associated with the more forbidding category of the sublime, a suitable domain for the elusive quality of "aura."

What these "beautiful and unapproachable" old photographs depict, of course, are people who have died; their auratic images survive them. The link between photographs and mortality also appears in Roland Barthes's *Camera Lucida* (1980). Though he never cites Benjamin, Barthes echoes Benjamin's concern with the reception and power of photographs, especially in relation to the debates on catastrophe and death that appear in Sontag and Baudrillard. Barthes proposes a twofold process for the experience of photographs: the *studium*, which entails a "general, enthusiastic commitment" or interest, but "without special acuity," and the *punctum*, which "rises from the scene, shoots out of it like an arrow, and pierces me."[21] Through highly personal and keenly observed discussions of photographs, Barthes's study extends to the general subjects of death and catastrophe. Commenting on a photograph of Lewis Payne, an assassin condemned to die, Barthes discovers a new *punctum* in the death of the subject: "He is dead and he is going to die."[22] The simple but powerful recognition that photography preserves images of the living who seem to look out at the viewer long after they die represents a catastrophe: "I shudder, like Winnicott's psychotic patient, *over a catastrophe which has already occurred*. Whether or not the subject is already dead, every photograph is this catastrophe."[23] This catastrophe, for Barthes, arouses deep feelings of love, pity, and ecstasy.[24]

For Benjamin and Barthes alike, the subject's gaze toward the camera generates reflections on death (*SW* 2:507–30).[25] For them, it is not just certain images that concern us but images and photographs *as such*. This is where Sontag, Butler, and others differ from Benjamin and Barthes. While Sontag and Butler are concerned with how images can contribute to overcoming political violence, Benjamin and Barthes reflect on photographs generally as documents of mortality that survive the moments they depict. The medium of photography, rather than particular images and subjects, leads to critical reflection, but this requires the cultivation of skills in perception and reception.

Like the discipline of reading Benjamin promotes in the *Trauerspiel* study, the discipline of looking constitutes the focus of the essay on photography and becomes, with the articulation of the "dialectical image," a primary critical practice in the Arcades project: "The dialectical image is an image that emerges suddenly, in a flash. What has been is to be held fast—as an image flashing up in the now of its recognizability. The rescue that is carried out by these means—and only by these—can operate solely for the sake of what in the next moment is already irretrievably lost" (*Arcades* 473). As with the "ascetic apprenticeship" appropriate to *Trauerspiel* texts, so with images, this discipline requires training: "Pedagogic side of this undertaking: 'To educate the image-making medium within us, raising it to a stereoscopic and dimensional seeing into the depths of historical shadows' " (*Arcades* 458). This visual education forms a central concern of Benjamin's late writings.

Agency in the "Work of Art" Essay

Benjamin's goal in "The Work of Art in the Age of Its Technical Reproducibility" (1935–39) is to develop concepts of art "that are completely useless for the purposes of fascism" (*SW* 4: 252). The first step, of foreclosing the politically volatile cult value of art, sets the stage for a second, in which new forms of mass reception can lead to political agency. All this comes at the cost, however, of the artwork's aura and tradition in general:

"The technology of reproduction detaches the reproduced object from the sphere of tradition" (*SW* 4:254).

Many of the editorial changes made by Benjamin between the second and third versions of the "Work of Art" essay (between 1936 and 1939) pertain to the question of agency. Earlier emphasis on the activity of film actors gave way to later concerns with the audience. In the second version of his essay from 1936, the basis for its first published form, Benjamin wavers between attending to individual and collective agency. Film, he claims, can "train human beings in the apperceptions and reactions needed to deal with a vast apparatus whose role in their lives is expanding almost daily" (*SW* 3:108). But Benjamin develops this point most fully in his discussion of the film actor, whose performance in front of an apparatus (rather than an audience) vindicates his or her humanity for the sake of the audience:

> For the majority of city-dwellers, throughout the workday in offices and factories, have to relinquish their humanity in the face of an apparatus. In the evening these same masses fill the cinemas, to witness the film actor taking revenge on their behalf not only by asserting *his* humanity (or what appears to them as such) against the apparatus, but by placing that apparatus in the service of his triumph. (*SW* 3:111)

In the essay's later, 1939 version, from which this passage was deleted, Benjamin shifts attention to the audience, which must "take the position of a critic" without falling prey to the "cult value" of art (*SW* 4:260). Film and other mass forms engage audience members as experts, participants, and creators, ultimately dissolving the boundary between artist and audience (*SW* 4:262). In this new reality, which enables heightened forms of perception and attention, "the extremely backward attitude toward a Picasso painting changes into a highly progressive reaction to a Chaplin film" (*SW* 4:264).

Benjamin's shift to audience reception foregrounds his interest in political agency, replacing fascist aesthetics with his version of Marxian mass aesthetics. In contrast to Adorno, who generally disagreed with this approach, Benjamin struggled to articulate a notion of politically meaningful reception. Although film viewing is characterized by distraction, "even the distracted person can form habits" based on new kinds of perception. Film "makes cult value recede into the background, not only because it encourages an evaluating attitude in the audience but also because, at the movies, the evaluating attitude requires no attention."

Comparing film to architecture, Benjamin insists that mass reception can be valuable even when it takes place through habit and "casual noticing" rather than "attentive observation" (*SW* 4:268–69). The audience gains agency in spite of its distraction.

The essay's well-known narrative of declining aura could suggest a kind of secularization, but it does not eliminate tradition altogether. The technically reproduced work's detachment from tradition may guard against fascist appropriation, but tradition still remains "alive and extremely changeable," even capable of morphing into such dangerous forms as the cult of the movie actor or worse, the Führer (*SW* 4:269). Traditions of aesthetic reception and commentary also survive in modernity, and though they differ radically from the individual contemplation and observation that characterize solitary aesthetic and scholarly reception, Benjamin mobilizes them in the search for political agency to counteract fascism.

It is not clear in the essay what Benjamin thinks of the loss of aura that attends the proliferation of mechanical reproducibility; is it a good thing or a bad thing?[26] The issue is much clearer in an essay he published around the same time, "On Some Motifs in Baudelaire" (1939). There Benjamin makes it clear that the loss of aura is a kind of necessary sacrifice. Speaking of Baudelaire as a formative poet of modernity, he writes: "He named the price for which the sensation of modernity could be had: the disintegration of the aura in immediate shock experience. He paid dearly for consenting to this disintegration—but it is the law of his poetry" (*SW* 4:343). The shock effects of modernism, which fascinate Benjamin in his late work, demand the loss or displacement of aura onto new forms. Mimesis and technical reproduction are a kind of liberation of form and of experience that yield politically significant (though volatile) forms of thought and action.[27]

Disaster, Agency, Tradition

The *Angelus Novus* returns most famously in Benjamin's last work, the unpublished "On the Concept of History." Here the angel is depicted as facing the past while being blasted into the future; this gaze into the past is shared by the historian and prophet alike, for Benjamin (*SW* 4:405, 407). Historical wreckage piles up at the angel's feet while the storm called Progress blows the angel, which stares at the viewer, backward. The angel "would like to stay, awaken the dead, and make whole what has been smashed," but Progress prevents it from doing so.

This *Angelus Novus* is the angel of history, and it also fits the description of the dialectical image, which brings thought "to a standstill" and disrupts the continuum of history. We could also ask whether the angel, who "seems about to move away from something he stares at," who comes from a modern but original work of art, manifests the quality of aura that Benjamin seems elsewhere to disavow. The *Angelus Novus* is an image that appears to have very little power, but two details of the image and Benjamin's discussion of it open up the category of agency. First, the angel *sees* the catastrophe of history, and second, we the spectators, the viewers of this image, see the angel. The angel looks out at us, just as Kafka and Benjamin do in their childhood portraits, and also perhaps with a similar kind of sadness. In spite of the decline of aura so famously cited in Benjamin's artwork essay, there is an unmistakable aura associated with *Angelus Novus*, both in its mix of distance and proximity, a point emphasized by the angel's backward motion away from the viewer, and in Benjamin's other sense of aura, whereby the angel, though a mere object painted in a fairly simple, even primitivist style, seems to return our gaze.

Creaturely Angel

I wish to ask a question that regular readers of Benjamin may find naive: why an angel, and why this angel? There are many good direct answers to the question pointing in many directions within Benjamin's work as well as to the cultural context surrounding him (Rilke, for example). Without doubting the validity and value of these answers, I wish to focus simply on the nonhuman, creaturely nature of this angel. For a "new" angel (*Angelus Novus*), the picture, like many of Klee's works, projects the air of antiquity because of the distressed colors and textures of its background as well as the "primitive" simplicity of its form. This tension inheres in the picture's form as well as its name, since angels are typically considered to be ancient or timeless. What is more, it is the angel's gaze at the viewer that I think captures and enables a discussion of the category of agency. And what makes this discussion particularly significant is the picture's creaturely qualities. Paradoxically, this nonhuman face serves to enable a kind of self-awareness in the viewer.

In her study of Benjamin's notion of "creature," Sigrid Weigel shows how the modern inheritance of theological tradition and secularity account for the central place of the "creature" in his writings on the *Trauerspiel* and Karl Kraus. Commenting on a *Trauerspiel* passage on "creature," Weigel identifies elements in the creaturely "constellation" that evoke both the biblical tradition of creation and secularization.[28] For Benjamin, argues Weigel, the issue is how elements of secularized religious traditions are inherited by modernity, a question he addresses through images and a "dialectic of secularization."[29] But these modern formations, notes Weigel, are not so much captured by the one-to-one changes from such categories as "righteousness" into "ethics" but rather as elusive touchstones.[30] Such a dialectical and reflexive model of secularization, argues Weigel, comes from the double or Janus-faced orientation that lends itself to the kinds of thought images and figures, like the creature, so central to Benjamin's work. The doubleness of the creature, whose creation evokes the Creator as well as physical reality, illustrates Benjamin's complex understanding of tradition and modernity.

In order to develop this reflection on agency and the creaturely gaze, I wish to take a detour to two other modern texts that describe a creature's gaze at a viewer: Freud's drawing from his Wolf-man study and a frightening childhood memory of Virginia Woolf.[31] As with Benjamin's *Angelus Novus*, each of these creaturely figures, gazing out at the viewer, ties directly to insight and self-awareness. Virginia Woolf's encounter with an animal's gaze appears in her late autobiographical work, "A Sketch of the Past": "I dreamt that I was looking in a glass when a horrible face—the face of an animal—suddenly showed over my shoulder. I cannot be sure if this was a dream, or if it happened. Was I looking in the glass one day when something in the background moved, and seemed to me alive? I cannot be sure. But I have always remembered the other face in the glass, whether it was a dream or a fact, and that it frightened me."[32] Woolf introduces this memory by reflecting on two other memories: the first of habitually looking at herself in a hallway mirror in secret from the age of six or seven, accompanied by feelings of guilt and shame; and the second, also very early, recounting in detail how her half-brother Gerald Duckworth sexually molested her in the same hall where the mirror was (*Moments of Being* 67–69). This incident took place when she was "very small," yet Woolf emphasizes its vividness: "I remember resenting, disliking it—what is the word for so dumb and mixed a feeling? It must have been strong, since I still recall it" (69). This feeling, she continues, must be instinctive and common to "thousands of ancestresses in the past" (69). These three elements—the persistent sense of guilt and shame associated with mirrors, the early childhood molestation, and the dream of the horrible animal face—combine for Woolf to show the complexity and elusiveness of human memory.[33]

Figure 4. "Wolves in Tree," drawing from Sigmund Freud's "Wolf-man" case study (1918).

Freud's case study of Sergei Pankejeff, the so-called Wolf-man ("From the History of an Infantile Neurosis," 1914–15, pub. 1918), takes its name from a childhood dream in which the patient saw several white wolves in a tree looking into his bedroom. A sketch of the wolves by the patient, reproduced here, appeared in the case study. (See figure 4.) Horrified by the wolves, which Freud took to symbolize the child's traumatic witnessing of his parents having sex, the Wolf-man lived long after Freud and wrote autobiographical works that contributed to the ongoing fascination of scholars with the case.[34] The image of the wolves staring at the patient, which Peter Brooks points out may have roots in fairy tales, appears to account for much of this fascination. Because Freud reproduced this image, readers of his case study can imagine themselves in the patient's position, facing the wolves that gaze out from the printed page.

What kind of agency follows from responding to these images of the creaturely gaze? For Woolf and the Wolf-man, the self stages a confrontation with itself through the projection, reflection, and encounter with the creature's gaze. The scenario resonates not only with the psychology of Freud and Lacan but also with the ethics of Emmanuel Levinas, the field of animal studies, and postcolonial theory. For Benjamin, all three domains—politics, psychology, and aesthetics—converge in the *Angelus Novus* and his "On the Concept of History."[35] Truly dialectical, the encounter of receiving the gaze, returning it, and reflecting upon this interaction derives from traditions of representation and seeing, just as traditions of quotation, literary representation, religion, and politics circumscribe models of agency.

The claim that there is something compelling about creaturely faces is vague, though it is clear that Benjamin, Woolf, Freud, and his patient did find them compelling. My more modest claim is that the creaturely gaze of Klee's angel enabled Benjamin to express ideas of agency and tradition rich with possibility at a time of danger. As a model of the dialectical image, *Angelus Novus* enables the kind of "caesura" in thought and "shock experience" Benjamin associates with modernism while also capturing both senses of aura, as distance and as the returned gaze. The angel thus occupies the space where the "tension between dialectical opposites is greatest" (*Arcades* 475). As its name suggests, the angel embodies the contradiction between tradition and modernity; it also merges power and powerlessness, human and divine agency.

What can we say about this kind of agency? First of all, its focus is primarily reception rather than production. There is no doubt that creating images involves agency, as Horst Bredekamp's *Theorie des Bildakts*, which draws on speech act theory to demonstrate how ancient to contemporary image productions constitute actions of different kinds, shows.[36] But Benjamin's interest in reception and perception indicates a more elusive kind of agency. The acts of seeing, on the part of the viewer and on the part of the angel, correspond to the kind of thinking and mimetic capacity Benjamin associates with language and images. To see the kinds of links Benjamin urgently makes—between human language and divine names, between auratic and non-auratic art, between text and quotation, between historical materialism and theology—is to see in the way that the angel and the spectator see. In the Klee painting, the spectator mimetically resembles the angel by seeing as the angel sees, gazing at the distant image as it appears to gaze back.

Seeing the returned gaze of Klee's angel endows it with aura just as the subject who looks at the camera expects to return another's gaze with an "attentiveness" that gives rise to auratic experience: "Experience of the aura thus arises from the fact that a response characteristic of human relationships is transposed to the relationship between humans and inanimate or natural objects" (*SW* 4:338). This later idea of aura expands the scope of aura from the "Short History of Photography" toward a dynamic interaction with the image as a returned gaze.[37] Consistent with the earlier notion of aura as the impression of distance, this shifting (*Übertragung*) of the gaze between humans to the photographic realm comes from a disciplined, attentive behavior whose decline Benjamin associates with the poetry of Baudelaire, who "paid dearly for consenting to this disintegration" (*SW* 4:343). For Benjamin, Baudelaire is a kind of modern prophet of decline who inherits the melancholy of early modernity in the form of "spleen" (see chapter 1).

To see as the angel does is to engage one of the only kinds of agency Benjamin thinks is available in a world of catastrophe, a world damaged by narratives of human progress and nostalgia that collaborate with each other (like Stalin and Hitler, whose infamous pact engenders catastrophe). This agency is messianic in the sense outlined in the "Theological-Political Fragment": it combines human vision and action with realities beyond human control, and it enables the kind of dialectical insights Benjamin uncompromisingly worked to show. This kind of agency cannot be described as nihilism, relativism, nor as mysticism. It is rather the kind of agency that combines the most sober vision of history imaginable with a redemptive conception of tradition that made use of all the resources of modern and traditional thought, literature, and art available to Benjamin. Hardly systematic or programmatic, this kind of agency restlessly searches for means of expression and modes of thought that resist the conditions that lead to the kind of destruction through which he was living.

But the uncanny images of the angel of history, the wolves, and the creature in Woolf's mirror move away from specific catastrophic events and experiences to a broader, more generalized sense of catastrophe. In place of Žižek's and Sontag's concern with images of particular horrific and catastrophic events, a general account of images and catastrophe avoids the question of what makes an image catastrophic and how the viewer responds or should respond to it. If the claim of photographs and images on the viewer can be generalized, at least in part, then the question of agency can also be generalized.

How do images contribute to the agency of those who see them? Photographs of people, particularly of their faces, make a paradoxical claim on the viewer: the image of the person evokes a person, but as an image, it forces recognition of the absence and distance of the person depicted. This confusion of presence and absence, I suggest, is precisely what Benjamin means by aura as a "strange weave of space and time: the unique appearance or semblance of distance, no matter how close it may be" (*SW* 4:518). In the "Short History of Photography" and the artwork essay,

Benjamin describes the modern decline of aura in terms of changes in perception: "The peeling away of the object's shell, the destruction of the aura, is the signature of a perception whose sense for the sameness of things has grown to the point where even the singular, the unique, is divested of its uniqueness—by means of its reproduction" (*SW* 4:519). In spite of the modern destruction of aura, Benjamin's work with old photographs shows how auratic experience can continue. What animates the essay on photography is a pedagogical impulse to encourage careful viewing, even of modern images. In one politically charged passage, Benjamin recommends the study of August Sander's portraits as a "training manual" for looking: "Sudden shifts of power such as are now overdue in our society can make the ability to read facial types a matter of vital importance. Whether one is of the Left or the Right, one will have to get used to being looked at in terms of one's provenance" (*SW* 4:520). Photographs can train the viewer in reading faces, a matter not of idle aesthetic enjoyment but of "vital importance" in unstable political times. More than a diverting survey of photography, Benjamin's essay articulates a notion of agency—keen observation and viewing of images—in the context of a tradition characterized by such portraits as the one of Kafka as a boy, whose "immensely sad eyes" gaze out from the image of a boy in a "humiliatingly tight child's suit overloaded with trimming, in a sort of greenhouse landscape" (*SW* 4:515).

In fact, Benjamin regarded images as crucial to political agency. Citing Benjamin's essay on surrealism, which identifies the collective as a body that can "be produced only in that image space to which profane illumination initiates it" (*SW* 2:217–18), Eli Friedlander links image to revolution:

> By way of the image (and ultimately, though not in the surrealist artistic practice, in the dialectical image), the forms of the embodied mind are brought together, held together, not so as to produce a collective corporeal substance but rather to make manifest a force: Image space allows for collective innervation to result in revolutionary discharge, in the manifestation of a force that transforms reality. In image space, the vitality of nature in the bodily configuration of the modern world is recognized.[38]

This is agency and transformation through images, and, in a detail Friedlaender does not highlight, through "profane illumination," an oxymoron that exemplifies Benjamin's refusal to embrace simple notions of secularism or tradition.

Conclusion: Beyond Modernism and Montage

After Benjamin and the Holocaust, the question of representation remains: can an image possibly represent horrible suffering and injustice? For Jean-Luc Nancy, the Shoah destroys the very concept of representation, and yet "any potential criticism of a particular work—indeed, any condemnation as well—must resist adopting the stance of an idolatrous mysticism of the 'ineffable.'"[39] This idolatry of the ban on images can be found in many discussions of art after the Holocaust, from Adorno's famous dictum about poetry to present-day debates on photographs of September 11, 2001 (e.g., the "falling man") and Abu Ghraib. The ban on images runs from the Bible and Jewish tradition to the artistic sublime, which Nancy describes as "the fainting away of the sensible . . . on the limit where the outside of presentation offers itself."[40] The dilemma for scholars of religion and the arts, certainly, is how to respect the danger if not scandal of such images without giving up our scholarly practice. After all, "the image is always sacred," as Nancy says, because it is always "set aside, removed, cut off."[41] To work for rigorous analysis against both the idolatry of images and the ban on images is already a tall order. It is even more challenging to frame this analysis in ethical and political terms as agency, but this is what Benjamin attempted to do.

What I have sketched here is a notion of agency that begins with the very trope associated with its failure in the work of Baudrillard, Žižek, and sometimes Sontag—mimesis—as it develops in Benjamin's work. Sontag's humanistic appeal to a critical kind of aesthetics more closely approaches the kind of agency sketched by Benjamin, but it takes the form of an untheorized appeal largely severed from tradition. Baudrillard's uncanny meditation on the World Trade Center may illustrate the triumph of monopoly capitalism, but it assuredly does not herald the end of reference, an irony that could be developed and theorized to recuperate a conception of agency from his own work. Žižek's application of Baudrillard's work to the attacks of September 11, 2001, which strikingly omits Baudrillard's reference to the towers, likewise falls short of its attempt to link images to the destruction of agency. By contrast, Žižek's more recent book, *First as Tragedy, Then as Farce*, endorses the kind of negative political agency he sees in Benjamin: "The task is 'merely' to stop the train of history which, left to its own course, leads to a precipice . . . This is what a proper political act would be today: not so much to unleash a new movement, as to *interrupt* the present predominant movement."[42] Such an interruption, through new forms and combinations of aesthetic, religious, and political discourses, was a goal of Benjamin's late writings.

Benjamin never fully articulated a pedagogy of the critical perception of images, and some of his thinking on the subject seems limited by his context and sensibility. The 1939 "Exposé" of his *Arcades Project* says little about this question, but the final paragraph of the earlier, 1935 "Exposé" is instructive. It calls for an awakening from the "dream world" of nineteenth-century bourgeois culture and argues that "dialectical thinking is the organ of historical awakening" (*Arcades* 13). This kind of thinking allows us to "recognize the monuments of the bourgeoisie as ruins even before they have crumbled" (*Arcades* 13). In the *Arcades Project*, Benjamin wanted to connect particular forms of experience, through writing and aesthetics, to particular kinds of thought and awareness, and through all of this to envision the sort of revolutionary-messianic sorts of ends (overcoming "mythic" law and violence) he analyzed in the "Critique of Violence." For this project alternative forms of conceptualizing and writing history would be needed, and toward this end Benjamin resorts to a series of formal experiments that make up, I think, a large part of his work. Two of his experiments are montage and the idea of "dialectics at a standstill." Both experiments are central to the *Arcades Project*, but they have roots in Benjamin's earlier work on allegory and modernist aesthetics.

Experimentation with form, particularly narrative form, has come a long way since Benjamin wrote about modern art, literature, and mass culture. There is no reason to restrict Benjamin's thinking to the details of these forms, however; at worst, this approach can lead to a kind of rigid formalism that identifies historically particular artistic genres and methods with particular political or affective outcomes in the audience. Far more interesting, and faithful to Benjamin's interests, would be an engagement with his attempt to disrupt historical progress by aesthetic means. While the *specific* aesthetic forms and methods of critical reception adduced by Benjamin can and should be contested, the importance of aesthetics to political thought remains.[43] In his defense of photographic montage as a form of political engagement with Auschwitz, Georges Didi-Huberman insists that "imagination is not a withdrawal to the mirages of a single reflection, as it too often thought. It is instead a construction and a montage of various forms placed in correspondence with one another . . . it is an integral art of knowledge in its most fertile, albeit most daring, movement."[44] Didi-Huberman criticizes a dogmatic opposition to images, a *Bilderverbot*, running through discussions of atrocity, against which he argues for a disciplined aesthetics of images "in spite of all." He describes Benjamin's aesthetics of "redemption" as a "last-gasp resistance—but a long-term lesson for us—to consolation in the face of history."[45] Didi-Huberman's claim may overreach, but Benjamin's integration of images with history and religious tradition moves reflection on human agency beyond the impasses of contemporary debates.

Chapter 7

✦

Identity and Survival in *German Men and Women* (*Deutsche Menschen*)

The flourishing of literature and thought during the age of Goethe may have inspired German nationalism in the 1930s, but Walter Benjamin identified other values in this lost era worth defending. *Deutsche Menschen* is a short collection of edited letters by well-known German authors which Benjamin published in 1936 under the pseudonym Detlef Holz in order to hide his Jewish identity. In his inscription to Scholem's copy of the book, Benjamin wrote, "May you, Gerhard, find a chamber in this ark—which I built when the Fascist flood started to rise—for the memories of your youth," and in his sister's copy Benjamin wrote, "This ark, built after a Jewish model, for Dora—From Walter."[1]

This chapter considers what Benjamin may have meant by those inscriptions. Looking beyond discussions of "German," "Jewish," and even "German-Jewish" identity, this chapter explores Benjamin's descriptions of his letter collection, asking how he conceptualized and framed it at first and how it may have changed between 1931 and 1936. The categories of tradition and agency are my focus, which I develop in the context of Benjamin's other writings and his particular interests in quotation and materialism. The formation and reception of *Deutsche Menschen* reveal a complex, ambitious project that combines many of Benjamin's ideas and goals.

Benjamin's collection began as an occasional series of letters he collected and published in the *Frankfurter Zeitung* in 1931–32, the end of the Weimar Republic. In its final, book form, *Deutsche Menschen* includes twenty-five letters by, to, and about famous German writers and scientists on topics of death, friendship, love, and other realities of life, including personal finances. Kant, Goethe, Hegel, Schleiermacher, Nietzsche, and Grimm are among the authors and subjects of the letters, which Benjamin introduced with short commentaries that contextualize and appraise the letters in the moralizing terms of the book's dedication: "From Honor without Fame / From Greatness without Glamor / From Dignity without Pay" ("Ehre ohne Ruhm, Größe ohne Glanz, Würde ohne Sold," *GS* 4:150).

The stated purpose of the collection is to depict a lost cultural age (1783–1883): "It was the age when the German bourgeoisie had to place its weightiest and most sharply etched words on the scales of history. And it had little to place there except those words." Benjamin marks the transitions of this period by Goethe's 1825 lament over the rise of modern technology and mediocrity: "We may be the last representatives—with a few others perhaps—of an era that will not easily come again" (*SW* 3:167). This passage could be construed as a straightforward expression of nostalgia, but in light of the complexity of *Deutsche Menschen* and Benjamin's use of the quotation here and elsewhere (in a playful radio play and a leftist encyclopedia article), I believe the quotation serves rather to criticize contemporary Germany in ways that have little to do with Goethe's text.[2]

Benjamin had great ambitions for his book. In his letters and manuscripts he says he seeks to reach a large audience in Germany with "a kind of golden library of classics *in nuce*" (*GS* 4:949). He envisions a book with wide appeal to school children, professors, journalists, and others that combines the elements of popular anthology, scholarly edition, and a classic edition (*GS* 4:950). This would be a large (double-sized) volume, like what people now call a coffee-table book (*GS* 4:948–49). Whatever Benjamin intended with *Deutsche Menschen*, he wanted it to reach a large public.

At first *Deutsche Menschen* looks more like a veneration of German letters written out of nostalgia or economic necessity than a major theoretical statement, but a closer look reveals a project that began with newspaper articles and became a book that reflects Benjamin's thinking about cultural traditions and practices of quotation. It is unlikely that Benjamin set out in 1931 to write a personal manifesto on the legacy of German letters, much less to build a Jewish ark against the fascist flood, but by 1936 he had achieved something that strikingly draws a number of his interests together. What I pose as a question here is how *Deutsche Menschen* balances some of these interests, particularly one that will be familiar to many readers of Benjamin, the commitment to the power of words, literature, and literary culture on the one hand, and a rather different commitment to a materialist critique of fascism on the other.

Benjamin's description of the book as an "Ark" (*Arche*), notes Erdmut Wizisla, appears only in his handwritten dedications to Jewish recipients:

his sister, Siegfried Kracauer, and Scholem.[3] So what did Benjamin mean by the Noah's Ark reference? How does he understand the biblical story? Is *Deutsche Menschen* an esoteric Jewish text? The question, of course, has sectarian implications—if Benjamin's text has a secret meaning reserved only for Scholem, his sister, and Kracauer, it stands to be lost even on Adorno, whom Benjamin still addresses as "Sie" in letters from this time. I raise the question partly to note the frisson of esotericism that runs not only through some of Benjamin's writings but also through much of Benjamin's scholarship as well.

There can be no simple resolution to the question of Jewish-German identity in Benjamin's thought, though some boundaries around the problem can be delineated. It is safe to say, for example, that Judaism and Jewish identity are not limited for Benjamin to halakhic observance; in fact, Benjamin had little direct knowledge or experience of traditional Jewish life or Hebrew texts, and his main source of knowledge about Judaism, Gershom Scholem, famously pursued the study of esoteric texts and traditions rather than traditional Jewish practices. As for German literary culture, one can also say with confidence that Benjamin was keenly sensitive to the ethnic and nationalistic politics associated with German letters. It would be just as difficult to mark Benjamin as a "melting-pot" pluralist who believed that Kantian principles of human dignity and equality could somehow be trusted to protect against the kinds of danger that he recognized in the language and culture around him even before the rise of National Socialism. Benjamin's clarity about the limitations of these three positions does not, unfortunately, add up to a systematic or compelling resolution to the question of identity. Instead, a crucial if modest gesture of Benjamin's work on this problem is a sustained commitment to attentiveness, disciplined perception, and self-awareness.

What is more, Benjamin's text was public from the beginning, and while it implies more than it says about politics, its distance from fascism and even modern nationalism is clear. And for all the evidence of esoteric intent, there is just as much to be said for Benjamin's public ambitions for the book and its development from newspaper articles. But the dedications reveal an interpretive frame for the project that likely became clearer to Benjamin between 1931 and 1936. This chapter sketches a reading of *Deutsche Menschen* with these dedications as a kind of guide. There is a tendency to read and even sentimentalize Benjamin's text as a forceful repudiation of Nazi ideology.[4] The main problem with this view is that it overlooks the scope of this project, which began well before 1931 and relates to several other writing projects, some of which are discussed here. My claim is that we can discern many of Benjamin's abiding commitments in *Deutsche Menschen*—humanism, romanticism, critique of progress, materialism (though he never mentions Judaism)—and that its "text-and-commentary" structure reflects traditional literary scholarship and anticipates the quotation-based method he devised and implemented later in his *Arcades Project.*

Structure and Design

Several separate texts on this project appear in Benjamin's *Gesammelte Schriften*, including one from 1931–32 when the letters appeared in the *Frankfurter Zeitung*, a possible radio address called "On the Trail of Old Letters." Here Benjamin adopts a genial, scholarly voice and places emphasis on the "humanity" and "living tradition" (*lebendiger Überlieferung*) conveyed by the letters. He presents the letters as neglected and overlooked classics that deserve a place in the literary canon, along with a way of reading these letters not "to underpin a cult of the writer as hero" but to credit the humanity of the writers as "noble, creditable, and rich in substance" through "something that facilitates communication with his lesser contemporaries" (*SW* 2:556–57). In this retrieval of overlooked, non-canonical, and ordinary documents of life, with its challenge to conventional literary scholars about the value and meaning of letters and the canon, *Deutsche Menschen* resembles the materialist aesthetic of Benjamin's later essay on the collector Eduard Fuchs (1937). Such a materialist reading of the text would be an alternative to the emphasis on Jewish identity suggested by Scholem and Wizisla.

A second, probably later, text called "German Letters" takes a more political tone, suggesting that these letters respond to a "civic duty in an emergency" ("*Aufruf der bürgerlichen Not*") and reveal a "secret Germany" (*ein geheimes Deutschland*). This text includes three letters on political subjects by Forster, Hölderlin, and Seume, of political nature, including the French and American revolutions (*GS* 4:946–47). This theme of emergency is echoed in a letter from 1932 in which Benjamin cites the project as one of several that deal with sites of rubble or catastrophe ("die die eigentliche Trümmer- oder Katastrophenstätte bezeichnen," *GS* 4:947).

An undated typescript collected with Benjamin's notes for the project includes headings for grouping the letters: "Schule und Leben," "Neue Gesichtspunkte," "Der Verfall und die Reichsgründung," "Publikationsfehler," "Forbildliche Editionen," "Briefe, die Klüfte erhellen wie Blitze," and "Falsche Klassizität."[8] Although this list does not appear to govern the final version of *Deutsche Menschen*, it reveals Benjamin's diverse literary and social-historical goals for the project.

Benjamin originally ended *Deutsche Menschen* with an angry farewell letter from Schlegel to Schleiermacher, but just as the book was about to be published he decided to remove it because of its "negative content" and "lesser weightiness, " making the number of letters twenty-five instead of twenty-six.[5] It is not clear why the letter was reintroduced in the 1962 edition of *Deutsche Menschen*, but it was apparently Adorno's idea. He wrote to the editor of the 1962 edition suggesting that the letter be added, saying that he found this letter in the *Frankfurter Zeitung* and that it was missing from the book for some reason, "perhaps only for the sake of an even 25" ("vielleicht nur der glatten Zahl 25 zuliebe").[6] Later, the editors of Benjamin's *Gesammelte Schriften* included this letter as an appendix. The final letter now became the letter from Overbeck to Nietzsche; Benjamin's introduction to this letter mentions theology and Christianity frequently, and it tellingly ends as follows:

> True Christianity, for him, meant an absolute, eschatologically founded denial of the world. Acceptance of the world and its culture was a repudiation of Christianity's essence, and all theology from the patristic period onward was a Satan among religions. Overbeck was aware that he had "written himself out of Germany as a theology teacher." Here is the letter, whose writer and recipient had voluntarily exiled themselves from the Germany of the *Gründerzeit*. (*SW* 3:217)[7]

Commentary, Quotation, and Agency

Commentary and quotation constitute the two main elements of *Deutsche Menschen*, and by themselves their purpose seems fairly straightforward: to inform the public about interesting letters by well-known German authors of the past. But commentary and quotation are important categories in Benjamin's thought, linked to his understandings of aesthetic and political agency.[9] For Benjamin, commentary gives life to works, and along with translation, constitutes their afterlives. He considers commentary, which "takes for granted the classical status of the work under discussion," to be as constitutive of a work as the "seasonally falling fruits" on a tree.[10] Given his shift from traditional texts to the material culture of modernity in the *Arcades Project*, *Deutsche Menschen* can easily be seen as a relic of an earlier intellectual paradigm. But in the methodological notes to the *Arcades Project*, Benjamin explicitly relates the two kinds of work: “The expression ‘the book of nature’ indicates that one can read the real like a text. And that is how the reality of the nineteenth century will be treated here. We open the book of what happened” (*Arcades* 464). Nevertheless, the “commentary on a reality” will differ from textual commentary: “In the one case, the scientific mainstay is theology; in the other case, philology” (*Arcades* 460). No explanation of this distinction follows, but the place of theology in the ostensibly materialist study of nineteenth-century culture echoes other affirmations in Benjamin’s late work of religious tradition as a companion to materialist analysis.

Of course, the opposition between theology and philology is artificial and alien to Benjamin’s work, just like the distinction between tradition and modernity or religion and secularity. What is crucial here is to see how *Deutsche Menschen* mixes Benjamin’s interests just as richly as the *Arcades Project*. Its appearance as a traditional celebration of belles lettres accompanies decidedly political and materialist interests. The letters in *Deutsche Menschen* concern ordinary life, personal finances, friendship, and death, and they are presented in a conversational tone that extols the values of a bygone era marked by Goethe and the Biedermeyer, but Benjamin’s commentaries challenge nationalistic and triumphalist canons of German literature and thought.

The idea that quotation by itself can be a powerful form of critical expression has been noted and discussed by a wide range of scholars.[11] In this vein, I suggest that Benjamin’s methods of quotation have modern sources like montage and the essays of Karl Kraus along with roots in biblical and Jewish tradition. Based on how Benjamin talks about quotation in the *Arcades Project*, it was a technique to serve materialist critical ends (though Adorno doubted its potential). The question I find most interesting about Benjamin’s description of *Deutsche Menschen* as a Jewish ark is thus not the familiar debate on German versus Jewish identity, for in Benjamin’s case I doubt we can ever get beyond the hyphen in “German-Jewish.” What interests me more is whether and how the kind of quotation and commentary he performs here can signify a kind of political agency.

The question whether a work like *Deutsche Menschen* matters politically resonates with contemporary political and cultural theory. The issue, very bluntly, is what beyond bare life is worth living and fighting for. For Benjamin, the question was pressing (not just in a personal way); he had already sharply dismissed neo-Kantian ideals of human rights based on mere life in his “Critique of Violence,” and his distance from orthodox Marxism likewise shows he cares about more than economic justice. Now he faced a crisis, one that unfolded during the years this project progressed: could the ideals of German culture be salvaged under German nationalism and fascism? *Deutsche Menschen*, which begins with a letter mourning the death of Goethe and includes four more on death and mourning, does not tell us directly, and the inscriptions only complicate matters by speaking of a *Jewish* ark. A second, related question is: if these ideals are worth fighting for, how does one do so without resorting to nostalgia, outdated literary standards, or nationalism?

In order to overcome the risks of esoteric politics and sentimental nostalgia, Benjamin's project needed not only to reach the German public, which was his great wish; but it also had somehow to convey the meaning he intended for it during a time of danger. What Benjamin offers is a strong reading of the romantic era as a rejection of its later nationalistic appropriations. He openly cites Lukacs;[12] honors the values of labor, cosmopolitanism, and humanism; and criticizes political, economic, and jingoistic tendencies of the past and present.[13] A second, more fundamental risk is the tension between materialist and linguistic-aesthetic commitments in the essay. Attention to material life, privation, and decoration (Biedermeyer) contrast the elevation of language and linguistic art as intrinsically valuable, even transcendent. The analogy between the aesthetics of Schiller and the middle-class interior (including a bust of the poet) as an asylum for those values is about as close as Benjamin comes to reconciling his materialist and aesthetic-idealist perspectives. From the standpoint of the literary frame, where catastrophe looms behind the image of the ark built to withstand the rising fascist flood, the gesture seems more noble but just as fragile. But is there any alternative?

Scholem certainly thought Benjamin's inscription indicated an affirmation of the power of writing in Jewish tradition; he comments: "Just as the Jews took refuge from the persecutions in the Writ, the canonical book, Benjamin's own book constitutes a saving element fashioned after the Jewish prototype."[14] The paradox of this example is that Benjamin's text, a celebration of the "secular," gentile tradition of German letters, elicits one of the most explicitly biblical passages in Scholem's book on Benjamin. It is also important not to forget the gentile pseudonymous author of the text, Detlef Holz, whose name is signed in a different copy of the book—inscribed in a dedication to his friend, the drug researcher Fritz Fränkel—with the flamboyantly crossed "t" and "f."[15] The book's appeal to human agency may be feeble, but it appeals to the kind of paradoxical synthesis—a "secular," gentile work helping to preserve biblical, Jewish tradition—that history was unable to achieve.

The pseudonym points to a further problem with Benjamin's Jewish reading and its affirmation by Scholem: Christianity. There are several very Christian obstacles to those who want to read *Deutsche Menschen* simply as an affirmation of Jewish identity. Benjamin introduces the final letter (Overbeck to Nietzsche) by invoking "true Christianity" (*SW* 3:217). The letter from Johann Heinrich Voss to Jean Paul celebrates the coincidence of Christmas and reading Shakespeare in the author's childhood, while Strauss's letter describes Hegel as Christlike (*SW* 3:190, 204).

Discussion of the underlying meaning of *Deutsche Menschen* has dominated the book's reception, beginning with the inscriptions Benjamin wrote on copies to Scholem and others.[16] In an essay on the handwritten dedications to *Deutsche Menschen*, Benjamin archivist Erdmut Wizisla argues that Benjamin hid messages in this text as he did in *One-Way Street*: "The collection betrays the handwriting of the editor . . . It is a 'Plaquette für Freunde.' "[17] Erich Auerbach recognized the political implications of the book, wondering in a letter to Benjamin whether it could be ordered or sent to Germany.[18] Scholem worried that it would be banned by Hitler because his commentary was "unmistakably corrupting."[19]

Mourning and/or Melancholia

Deutsche Menschen is preoccupied with mourning and presents several ways of relating the lost past to the present: intimacy, afterlife, nostalgia, and eternal recurrence. The collection begins with a letter from composer Karl Friedrich Zelter suggesting the death of his friend Goethe will somehow bring them closer: "Now that he has passed on before me, I draw closer to him daily" (*SW* 3:168). A later letter from Goethe expresses condolences to the son of a scientist with whom he had profound disagreements. Benjamin dedicates several pages of close exegetical analysis to that letter, something he does nowhere else, and rarely in any of his work. Quoting short phrases from the letter, Benjamin attaches historical and biographical significance to its language and diction: "Like him, his language stood at a frontier" (*SW* 3:205). Of the phrases "out life as it rushes past" and "turbulent and crowded," Benjamin says that Goethe "makes it abundantly clear that the writer has withdrawn contemplatively to [life's] shore" (*SW* 3:206). Mourning is the focus of two other letters, including an effusive letter by David Friedrich Strauss on the death of Hegel, the introduction of which points to "a revolutionary and unforeseen kind of afterlife [*Art des Fortlebens*]" at the funeral (*SW* 3:202). Benjamin's earlier citation of Goethe in the "Foreword" mourns the loss of an era he typified, "an era that will not easily come again [*wiederkerht*]" (*SW* 3:167). But nostalgia is not the only way *Deutsche Menschen* relates past to present. Benjamin's introduction to Metternich's letter about the Crimean War speaks of the "eternal recurrence" (*ewigen Wiederkunft*) of contradictions between political words and actions (*SW* 3:222).

Echoing Goethe's sentiments about a lost age, Adorno's "Afterword" to a 1962 edition associates the entire collection with mourning, describing it as a memorial (*Denkmal*) to the lost world and values destroyed by the Nazis.[20] For Adorno as for Benjamin (and Goethe), the loss of a past era provides critical perspective on the present, despite a sense of nostalgia. Like the use of melancholy in his study of the *Trauerspiel* (see chapter 1), the focus on mourning in *Deutsche Menschen* activates critical possibilities for reflection not only on who is lost but on what is lost, namely, the principles of honor, greatness, and dignity named in the epigraph.

Text as Ark: Asylum, Detlef Holz, Miniatures, the Biedermeier, and the Challenge of Materialism

Benjamin's designation of his book as a Jewish ark poses not just the question of what is Jewish about this very German, Christian-looking work; it also suggests associations between the catastrophe of Nazism and the biblical story of the Flood, particularly the purpose and effect of the book as an ark. Beginning with Scholem, some readers have accordingly categorized the book as a thoroughly Jewish work of commentary in the tradition of midrash and Talmud.[21] The purpose of this commentary, for Scholem at least, is no less than the performance of rescue or redemption (*retten*) through scripture (cited in Schmitt). The ark, suggests Schmitt in a clever turn of phrase, thus becomes "Arche-*écriture*" which gestures toward a restored, messianic language and scripture. If the book is an ark, then it can be seen as a mobile space for cultural memory, one that evokes continuity as well as rupture (Schmitt).

The ark, of course, is made of "cypress wood" (*Tannenholz*, Genesis 6:14), which echoes Benjamin's pseudonym Holz (wood).[22] But it would be a mistake to claim that Benjamin attempts anything like a close reading of the biblical story. His dedication uses the term "Arche" instead of the biblical "Kasten," and the only commentary in *Deutsche Menschen* applies to the letters themselves. Yet there is clearly something significant in Benjamin's reference to the Flood story. The paired letters, for instance, can be compared to the pairs of animals in the ark. Detlef Schöttker, who makes this point, notes Benjamin's view that commentary emerges from the classic status of the text and suggests the goal of the ark is "to secure the long-term survival of the types through the rescue of pairs."[23]

The importance of material culture to Benjamin—toys, art, books, and cityscapes—is no secret. But how to understand these preoccupations is not as clear. Like his interest in religion, these concerns for minute details of material reality can easily be dismissed as peccadillos or obsessions of a sentimentalist. They can also be magnified in a melodramatic fashion to mean more than they do. Benjamin's "Biedermeier" letter (from Clodius to von der Recke) appeared in 1931 and contains a number of key terms and topics that link it to the "Arche." My main point here is that the domain of miniatures—the puppet, doll house, children's toy—is crucial to Benjamin, as others have shown.[24] For Benjamin as for many people today, Noah's ark evokes childhood and childhood toys. The term "Arche" appears only rarely in Benjamin's writings, but its most frequent association is with toys and wooden figures (*GS* 3:113, 4:126, and 4:422). The ark Benjamin describes having built in his text thus carries the associations of a toy, a miniature. That doesn't diminish its seriousness, but it does place a high premium on a particular aesthetic one can find throughout Benjamin's work and that biographers might link to his childhood growing up around the collectibles of his family business.

Like "ark" (*Arche*), the term "Biedermeier" in Benjamin also evokes toys, but it has another association as well: the period of the emergence of the German middle class in the early nineteenth century, in this case particularly with respect to miniature versions of furnished interiors. Benjamin's remarkable commentary compares the Biedermeyer toy exhibit in the Louvre, which included decorative busts of Shakespeare, Tiedge, and Schiller, to Schiller's aesthetics: "However brutally the aesthetic play—the play through which the *Briefe über die äesthetische Erziehung des Menschen* sought to educate free citizens—was interrupted on the historical stage, it found a safe refuge [*Asyl*] in those middle-class rooms which could so closely resemble dollhouses" (*SW* 3:188). In other words, the domain of aesthetics (in Schiller's letters) gained refuge against danger in the dollhouse-like middle-class rooms depicted in the Louvre (188).

The inversion here is fascinating: dollhouses in France resemble German middle-class interiors, and the interiors in turn resemble dollhouses, making them a refuge (*Asyl*) for aesthetic freedom. Benjamin's interest in miniatures, suggests Friedlander in reference to the *Trauerspiel* study, deploys his theory of monads to "concentrate a dimension of infinity and produce a sense of its realization."[25] The spatial monad, such as the Paris Arcade, represents the entire nineteenth-century universe, and the temporal monad summarizes all of history. What is more, the monad reveals the potential for change and thus a kind of agency: "If the object of history is to be blasted out of the continuum of historical succession, that is because its monadological structure demands it. . . . It is owing to this monadological structure that the historical object finds represented in its interior its own fore-history and after-history" (*Arcades*, 475). Through a dialectical process, therefore, the miniature and monad uncover what may be called the power of fragility, even in the case of toy furniture.

The flood against which the ark is built appears not only in the dedications but also in a passage of *Deutsche Menschen* that extols the values and material conditions of the lives it represents: "They [spiritual sources] live not only on the great passions from which spring seed and blood, and still less on the 'influences' so often invoked, but also on the seat of daily toil and the tears which flow from enthusiasm: drops soon lost in the flood" ("*Strom*," not the biblical "*Sintflut*" of the dedications) (*SW* 3:190).

Camouflage Text

Benjamin clarified the purpose of *Deutsche Menschen* in a letter to Scholem, October 18, 1936, as follows: "Only from an interest to explain how the collection might serve to conceal some usefulness in Germany." [26] The same notion of "camouflage" (*Tarnung*) describes *Deutsche Menschen* in an unpublished letter from Adorno to Susanne Thieme (widow of Karl) upon learning that her husband had not suggested the title *Deutsche Menschen*: "The title 'Deutsche Menschen' was chosen at that time by Benjamin for a political reason, namely to allow the book of letters to be imported into Germany in order to serve an oppositional purpose there, thus as a kind of camouflage and in no way out of a profit motive."[27] (Adorno also described the tone of the book as "oppositional.")[28] Benjamin rarely uses the term "Tarnung," but it sometimes serves to indicate deceptions of capitalism (*GS* 1: 1168, *GS* 5:121). He also uses the term to describe the danger of open expression in a 1933 letter to Scholem (*Briefe* 2:566). In a passage close to the theme of *Deutsche Menschen*, namely, the decline of "das alte Bürgertum," Benjamin describes how the bourgeoisie used the Jugendstil to conceal their own decline: "It was the Jugendstil . . . in which the early bourgeoisie concealed the presentiment of a certain weakness while it rhapsodized cosmically in all spheres and, drunk on the future, abused 'youth' as a swear word."[29]

The debate whether *Deutsche Menschen* is a *Tarntext* (camouflaged text) continues. Many continue to regard the text as a coded political statement against the Nazi regime, while others have begun to question this view. One of the strongest cases for the camouflage reading is

Michael Diers's study of the graphic design, publication, and context of *Deutsche Menschen*. Noting the resemblance of the book's typeface and title to contemporary pro-fascist books, Diers cites the importance of *dissimulatio* as a figure of the baroque rhetoric studied by Benjamin in the *Trauerspiel* study, along with his publisher's expertise in espionage.[30] A skeptical rejoinder to this view is Peter Villwock's study of *Deutsche Menschen*, which attributes the text's recovery as a *Tarntext* to Adorno. This idea that *Deutsche Menschen* was a "Trojan horse," a camouflaged text, says Villwock, quickly became part of the German collective unconscious.[31] Through a survey of the book's development and publication, Villwock identifies Benjamin's humanist interests in the original newspaper versions of the letters, particularly the emphasis on Goethe and the commemoration of the Hambach Festival, which celebrated the roots of popular democracy in Germany.[32]

Given its many sources, valences, and gradual development, Villwock aptly describes *Deutsche Menschen* as a kaleidoscope or constellation: it can be seen from many angles and variously interpreted, yet its many pieces remain distinct. Citing the reference to the Orion constellation in the letter from Wilhelm Grimm to Jenny von Droste-Hülshoff and the "weak messianic power" of "On the Concept of History," Villwock goes further to claim that Benjamin uses the means of constellation and quotation to rescue splinters of German humanism from their catastrophic history. In the context of 1930s Germany, this appeal to German humanism was critical.[33]

German Culture and the Jewish Question

In order to clarify the purpose of *Deutsche Menschen* it is not only necessary to consider its origins and internal contexts. There are several related texts that resemble this text but differ in important ways from it; three I wish to discuss here are "Jews in German Culture," "What the Germans Read While Their Classical Authors Wrote," and "From Cosmopolitans to Bourgeoisie" ("Vom Weltbürger zum Grossbürger"). All three, like *Deutsche Menschen*, are purportedly designed for the education of general readers in cultural and literary traditions. These texts shed light on how Benjamin viewed the legacy of Goethe and the roles Jews played in German culture.

"Jews in German Culture" (Juden in der deutschen Kultur") is an article published in the 1930 edition of the *Encyclopedia Judaica: Das Judentum in Geschiche und Gegenwart*.[34] The article appears there with two other authors' initials: Nachum Goldmann and Benno Jacob, and Benjamin complained that the draft he submitted, now lost, was greatly shortened, and "in some places the text is neither written nor corrected by me" (*GS* 2:1521). This article appears only in facsimile form in Benjamin's *Gesammelte Schriften* (2:807–13) because, as the editors note, it is unclear how much of this text was Benjamin's.

The fact that we do not have Benjamin's notes or manuscripts for this encyclopedia article, and that he complained about how it was revised by the editors, does limit how certain we can be that any given section is his. But I argue that we can distinguish at least two levels of confidence about his authorship: first, the overall design of the article, which stages different kinds of encounters between Jewish tradition and German modernity with Mendelssohn at its beginning, is certainly consistent with Benjamin's interests. The next phase of this process, in which romanticism and nationalism enter the scene, is also a familiar concern of Benjamin's; the citation of Ludwig Strauss, with whom Benjamin corresponded, is suggestive of his hand (*GS* 2:808). Particular authors and schools also point to Benjamin, including Cohen and his students Cassirer and Rosenzweig, Georg Simmel, Rahel Varnhagen (about whom Benjamin wrote to Scholem years later),[35] and a whole list of literary figures—including Heinrich Heine, Karl Kraus, Martin Buber, Ernst Bloch, the George circle, and Hugo von Hofmannsthal—in whom Benjamin was particularly interested (*GS* 2:811–13). At this level of design and focus, and even in the case of particular names, I think it is safe to assume Benjamin's authorial role.

A second level, of particular formulations and expressions, permits less confidence about Benjamin's authorship. Two examples bear this out: the first is a characterization of Simmel's work in relation to Jewish tradition. Here Simmel's work is described as an unsystematic (*systemfeindlich*) psychological impressionism that can be compared to halakhic biblical exegesis.[36] It is unclear whether this passage is Benjamin's or the editors', but the general design of the entry and the discussion of Simmel are consistent with Benjamin's work.[37] Though he knew the term "halakhah" from his conversations with Scholem years earlier, Benjamin used it mainly in his 1938 writings on Kafka and based his use on an essay by Bialik he asked Scholem to send him in 1934, four years after the encyclopedia article appeared. On the other hand, "halakhah" does appear in the Kraus essay, written around the same time as the encyclopedia entry, where Benjamin describes Kraus's work as the "most extraordinary breakthrough of halakhic writing through the mass of the German language."[38] A second passage, crediting Heinrich Heine and Ludwig Börne with the creation of German "feuilletonism," credits their style with a focus on subjectivity and a critique of academic professionalism.[39] If this passage reflects many of Benjamin's own interests, the discussion that follows, in which Heine's relation to romanticism is discussed in detail, certainly does as well.

At first clearly distinct from *Deutsche Menschen*, Benjamin's "Jews in German Culture" shares much in common with the book on which he worked soon after. Both texts concern themselves with German literary and intellectual culture from the eighteenth century onward. The idealism and literary culture of this epoch formed the background of Benjamin's modernism, one in which Jewish and German identity were distinct but deeply intertwined. Benjamin's self-understanding as a Jewish and German writer, especially as a critic, permeates both writings. This critical perspective is consistent with the "cultural Zionism" he claims for himself in his 1912 letter to Ludwig Strauss. Even without the "Jewish ark" dedications, we could find plenty of support in *Deutsche Menschen* for this kind of Jewish-German self-understanding: the values of literary and cultural criticism ascribed to Heine, for example, run through Benjamin's entire corpus, and the "secret" and "misappropriated" Germany of the manuscripts indicates something of Benjamin's intention to offer a critical and even esoteric perspective on German intellectual tradition.[40] Finally, the "living tradition" (*lebendiger Überlieferung*) Benjamin finds in these texts resonates with Benjamin's understanding not only of scriptural tradition (text and commentary) but also with the values represented by the letters.[41]

What these two texts share is an unwillingness to separate German from Jewish identity in any absolute way; this inseparability is something Benjamin experienced from childhood and later consciously theorized in many different ways. Readers familiar with Benjamin's *Berlin Childhood Around 1900* will recognize this pattern from Benjamin's fond description of Christmas decorations. The inscriptions on copies of *Deutsche Menschen* calling it a Jewish ark thus reveal not so much a hidden meaning behind the text as an abiding expression of Benjamin's self-understanding as a critic and thinker. By 1936 he may indeed have conceived of his project as a gesture of cultural and political defiance, but the fact that he adopted much of it unchanged from drafts and newspaper versions going back at least to 1931 suggests a longer view. Likewise, the "German culture" of his encyclopedia article includes contributions from Jewish writers and thinkers. In short, both texts hold "German" and "Jewish" in tension without permitting any easy separation or subordinating one to the other. Likewise, both texts insist on the robustness of cultural traditions in the face of political pressure; the politics and the aesthetics of these texts are thus inseparable.

The Question of Tone: "What the Germans Read While Their Classical Writers Wrote"

The second text is a radio play, "What the Germans Read While Their Classical Writers Wrote," published in 1932, the same time Benjamin was publishing the serialized letters that would become *Deutsche Menschen*. As Sabine Schiller-Lerg notes, this text appeared against the background of the anniversary of Goethe's death.[42] It also reflects Benjamin's specific interest in popular (*Kolportage*) literature. In a short essay about this radio play, Benjamin notes the convergence of popular literature of the past and popularization through radio in the present. He playfully juxtaposes popular and classical forms and flaunts the divide between ordinary life and the formal study of literature. In a way that confirms contemporary scholars who view him as an early exponent of what would become cultural studies, Benjamin offers his radio play as a contribution to the sociology of the public. Such was Benjamin's stated goal for the publication of *Deutsche Menschen*: it was to be a popular and widely circulated book.

Though its topic overlaps with *Deutsche Menschen*, the genre and tone of "What the Germans Read" are completely different. The Enlightenment brought "justice and equity" (*Recht und Billigkeit*), but, jokes the narrator (playing on the meaning of *Billigkeit* as "inexpensiveness"), "the books of your friends are pretty expensive" (*GS* 4:643). The characters in the play include a pastor, literary figures, a publisher, and voices of the Enlightenment, romanticism, and the nineteenth century, and they playfully discuss popular literature, newspapers, the Bible, and many authors, including Rousseau, Jean Paul, Lavater, and Kant (*GS* 4:659–62). When the pastor laments the commercial trivialization of the Bible, the author Karl Philipp Moritz laments that the "better public" and the "simple people" both read low-quality works (*GS* 4:647). Yet the discussion also warns that knowledge without humor risks obscurantism, dogmatism, and despotism (*GS* 4:655).

Benjamin's point is not only that the Germans read popular literature while their classical authors wrote; he also paints a picture of Germany at the time as relatively quiet and absorbed in local culture. While industrial and political changes swept other countries, this was a time when Germany slept a "healthy, refreshing" sleep (*GS* 4:658). Ordinary life and letters from this period reinforce the image of Biedermeier Germany as a place of modesty and decency.

How this ordinary life relates to the classics themselves is a critical issue. One character, a pastor, mentions how wide distribution of newspapers and other print media has led to the availability of Schiller and

Goethe even to a "Bürgerstochter, die in die Küche gehört" ("middle-class woman who belongs in the kitchen"), while a bookseller notes that the public doesn't read authors like Schiller and Goethe from a lending library (*GS* 4:652, 667). At the same time, texts later considered to be definitive of the era, like Kant's book on religion, were censored, and one of the characters recommends *Indianer in England* by the popular dramatist Kotzebue as a way to understand Kant's categorical imperative (*GS* 4:651, 666).

Goethe emerges here as the rare great author whose work appealed to a wide public. References to Goethe run through the play, which ends by vindicating his work in terms of popularity as well as quality. The speaker and the voice of the nineteenth century conclude by celebrating Goethe's legacy, vying humorously with each other to explain his greatness. The play concludes with the same quotation from Goethe's letter, about the speed of modern life and the decline of the past epoch, that begins *Deutsche Menschen* (*GS* 4:669–70). If this quotation expresses a melancholic or nostalgic tone in *Deutsche Menschen*, here it concludes a playful entertainment and serves mainly as a tribute to Goethe's lasting appeal for a radio audience observing the centenary of his death.

In his essay on this radio play, Benjamin relates the popularization of literature to new times and technologies, including radio. He describes his goal as raising "scientific questions" about how literature was understood rather than to affirm great works—("nicht die Literatur, sondern das Literatur*gespräch* jener Tage," *GS* 4:673). As with *Deutsche Menschen*, this discussion has close ties to Benjamin's interest in literary scholarship, including the "so-called sociology of the public" (*GS* 4:673). No classic can or should be read in isolation from its popular context, suggests Benjamin. In the radio play and *Deutsche Menschen* alike, the values and practices of ordinary people provide the sort of context that dignifies the work of genuinely great writers like Goethe.

Benjamin also compared the mass medium of newspapers to literature. In a 1934 fragment titled "The Newspaper," Benjamin observes that newspapers are the showplace of the day's cultural confusion and antinomies (*GS* 2:628). Through the impatience of readers and the constant production of news, a dialectical moment emerges, and the difference between author and public begins to disappear: the readers become coworkers with the writers and editors. The newspaper thus performs the "literarization of life relationships" as it displays unresolved antinomies and the depreciation of language (*GS* 2:629). Written around the time of similar observations about modern culture made in *One-Way Street*, this fragment reveals Benjamin's fascination with the potential of mass culture to engage audiences. The reversal of agency between author and reader made possible by the newspaper raises the possibility that other media, including the radio play and the popular collection of letters, can engage the public in meaningful reflection on life and literature.

Like the fragment on newspapers and *Deutsche Menschen*, Benjamin's radio play demonstrates Benjamin's interest in Goethe and the "classic" period around him in relationship to his own time. With a very different genre and tone, and often the very same quotations, Benjamin displays his abiding interest not just in German letters as such but in reading them against the grain of classicizing, canonical approaches, in broader cultural and historical contexts. The lightness and humor of Benjamin's radio text, which can also be seen in parts of *Deutsche Menschen*, should help to dismantle any tendency toward a "lachrymose" reading of the Holz text, for the values it avows are always qualified: "From Honor *without* Fame / From Greatness *without* Glamor / From Dignity *without* Pay" (emphasis added). These values suggest an aesthetic not of grandiosity and fame but of modesty, good humor, and ordinary life, not to mention a love for detail and whimsy—hence the Biedermeyer and the jokes in "What the Germans Read."

"From Cosmopolitians to Bourgeoisie"

Like the radio play "What the Germans Read" and *Deutsche Menschen*, this text, which appeared in the journal *Die Literarische Welt* in 1932 and was coauthored by editor Willy Haas, gives Goethe pride of place and quotes the familiar passage, cited above, on the acceleration of time and the end of the era (*GS* 4:859).[43] Here as in the other texts the topic is literary history in relation to the middle class and contemporary culture. Like *Deutsche Menschen*, the text cites Lukacs's observation that the German middle class had not yet overcome feudalism when the proletariat arose (*GS* 4:851, 221). While much more concerned with political, economic, and social history than the other texts, this essay deals directly with the theme of cosmopolitanism and its lack in "What the Germans Read." It is unclear how much of the design and aim of this text is Benjamin's, but the following statement about the design and approach taken in the text reflects ideas familiar from *Deutsche Menschen*. Noting the tendency of "so-called historians" to present arbitrary interpretations or even to falsify history, the text goes on to insist on the importance of reading original documents, especially literature, in order to understand how ideals and material realities coincided in the past (*GS* 4:817). With its primary interest in economic class history and culture, the text reads in some ways like later Frankfurt school texts, as a critique of Enlightenment promises of universal reason and equality as it passed into market capitalism, from *Weltbürgertum* (cosmopolitans) to *Grossbürgertum* (upper classes).

The text poses an interpretive challenge because of its explicit political and cultural aims. One could read the text as a key to the political and economic subtext of *Deutsche Menschen*, suggesting that the latter really was a *Tarntext* with a hidden Marxian attack on fascism. On the other hand, the text's context in a leftist magazine and its coauthorship with that magazine's editor may suggest just the opposite: a compromise between Benjamin's cultural and literary interests and the more political agenda of *Die literarische Welt*. Finally, a more complex but more accurate reading would indicate a kind of spectrum of texts and contexts, from the playful radio play and the series of letters in the *Frankfurter Zeitung* to the explicitly anti-fascist "From Cosmopolitans to Bourgeoisie" and the implicitly anti-fascist *Deutsche Menschen*. Differences of genre, audience, publication, and distribution allowed and compelled Benjamin to frame his ideas about Goethe and the emergence of German middle-class culture and political economy in several different ways. What holds them together, initially, is the insistence that literary and political analysis belong together, and together these texts form a body of work less miscellaneous that it first appears to be, offering a sustained reflection on German political culture at a time of violent transformation.

Conclusion: Farewell, Return, and the Question of Canon

The letter Benjamin withdrew from the collection at the last minute comes from a dispute between Friedrich Schlegel and Schleiermacher. Benjamin's introduction to the letter echoes the book's epigraphical affirmation of "greatness without glory" (*von Größe ohne Glanz*): "It would give a superficial picture of the attitude which this series of letters is intended to evoke if they presented only the lustrous side [*Glanze*] of friendship" (*SW* 3:219). Schlegel's angry letter responds to Schleiermacher's critical response to Schlegel's *Ideen* and accuses his friend of lacking "understanding and love in individual matters" (219). Benjamin's decision to cut the letter for its negative tone and lack of weightiness remains unclear, but it placed added emphasis on the letter from Overbeck to Nietzsche that took its place at the end.

Overbeck's letter illustrates his character, theology, and emphatic (even financial) support for the author of *Thus Spoke Zarathustra*. Benjamin points out that Overbeck's uncompromising views of Christianity cost him a position as a theologian in Germany. The letter demonstrates the surprisingly close relationship between a devout Christian theologian and Nietzsche, but it also emphasizes how the "writer and recipient had voluntarily exiled themselves from the Germany of the Gründerzeit [late nineteenth century]" (*SW* 3:217).

The excised letter from Schlegel to Schleiermacher concludes with a personal, angry farewell, while Overbeck's letter to Nietzsche represents a friendship that survives exile from Germany. Writing just over fifty years later from his own exile, Benjamin may have preferred this ending to the Schlegel letter for its testimony to this "representative of an insightful posterity [*Nachwelt*]" (*SW* 3:228). The angry tone of Schlegel's letter is replaced by an exemplar of mutual respect between deeply different friends, both of whom have no place in the Germany of their day. If Benjamin's placement of Overbeck's letter makes it more emphatic, it may represent a "secret Germany" as a kind of Germany not so much lost, as Goethe's quotation suggests, as forced into exile.

To celebrate German values without German territory should have struck German nationalists, particularly in the 1930s, as strange. Such survival in exile sounds much more like Jewish tradition! My point here is not that Benjamin has transposed German into Jewish values but rather that *Deutsche Menschen* imagines a Germany where values vastly different from National Socialism survive. Neither esoteric nor widely read, *Deutsche Menschen* affirmed tradition by reappropriating it and may represent Benjamin's most masterful achievement in the method of quotation he attempted in the *Arcades Project*. Built of text and commentary, Benjamin's Jewish ark provided a refuge for German values designed to withstand the flood of fascism. The decency, integrity, and modesty of these German letter writers provide a necessary recognition of conflict but also extend hope for its resolution. Writing in 1936, Benjamin could hardly conceptualize political resolution, much less forgiveness, for the German perpetrators of murder, but the book clearly affirms the possibility and hope for the survival of German values beyond their day.

The same pattern, of course, appears in the Flood story of Genesis: the flood destroys nearly everything, but the ark and its inhabitants, and more importantly, the divine-human bond, survive. The design of Benjamin's literary ark and its biblical prototype is thus crucial—even the laconic biblical account accords it a high level of detail. Though he knew that books were not safe from the danger of Nazi destruction, Benjamin, the self-described "last European," presented his book as such an ark. What it was that he thought could survive the flood was not clear. To return to the analogy with the last letter, the flood removes the tradition from its land and preserves it in a moveable technology: the "ark" of the book. What is remarkable for Benjamin, writing in 1936, is that his analogy to the flood story implies not only destruction but restoration, a restoration that he would neither describe nor live to see.

Though its publication and distribution did not live up to Benjamin's grandiose hopes, *Deutsche Menschen* convinced readers as diverse as Scholem and Adorno that it succeeded. Comparing the volume to Benjamin's childhood memoir, *Berlin Childhood Around 1900*, Adorno applauds the text's attention to the issue of class and observes that the decline of the bourgeoisie matches the decline of letter-writing.[44] Scholem took the personal dedication as a key to read the book as a Jewish refuge, while Adorno read the book's bold epigraph as a statement of materialist commitment. The book does succeed in naming values worth fighting for, values illustrated but not limited by the German men and women it presents. Whether it succeeds in showing how to fight for those values is still an open question.

There is no need to choose between reading *Deutsche Menschen* in German or Jewish terms. If Benjamin's dedications to *Deutsche Menschen* reveal a secret affirmation of Jewish identity, that identity has much in common with the German humanism the collection affirms. What these Jewish and German literary identities share is a model of tradition constituted largely by text and commentary, which is exactly what Benjamin offers. From their initial design to their publication in the *Frankfurter Zeitung* and later as a pseudonymous book in 1936, Benjamin left a long trail of texts and commentaries, including the dedications to his friends, that would guide the reception of *Deutsche Menschen*.

But while the letters and their accompanying commentaries appear at first to valorize classic writers and their texts, they are in fact guided affirmations of threatened cultural values. In the end, Benjamin's collection of letters engages multiple contemporary discussions and contexts—literary studies, journalism, politics, social identities, and aesthetics. Far from an esoteric, sectarian affirmation of Jewish identity and tradition, *Deutsche Menschen* encompasses Jewish and German (or German-Jewish) values through a skillful engagement with traditional texts. The paradox of a Jewish ark rescuing German values is less sentimental than scandalously funny, a disarming celebration of the fact that both "identities" share a biblical tradition filled with stories of exile, power reversal, and writing as a tool for survival.

CONCLUSION

Benjamin provides no systematic theory of agency or tradition. Instead, by attending to overlooked texts and phenomena, he pursues nagging questions of modernity's inheritance. Postsecular before the term was coined, Benjamin resisted the cultural and intellectual currents in which he immersed himself. Unsystematic and little-known beyond a small circle until long after his death, Benjamin's work accommodates multiple perspectives, topics, and interpretations. Those who sought to define his legacy—Scholem, Adorno, and Arendt—revealed Benjamin's originality when they minimized or disagreed with parts of his work.[1]

Benjamin's interests in politics and religion cannot be disentangled as easily as many of his readers have attempted to do. Jürgen Habermas, for instance, insists that "in the face of the rise of fascism, political insight forced Benjamin to break with that esotericism of the true for which the young Benjamin had reserved the dogmatic concept of doctrine."[2] While this account only demonstrates the enduring myth of secularism, other shifts in Benjamin's work, such as efforts to conceptualize collective political agency, can be identified. In the "Work of Art" essay, *Deutsche Menschen*, and other late works, Benjamin sought more overtly than ever to imagine and activate broad political awareness.

But to an intellectual trained in the practices and dispositions of aesthetic discernment and idealist thought, the turn to collective agency did not come easily. The "Work of Art" essay draws upon encyclopedic knowledge of premodern art and a brilliant grasp of modern forms and their means of production in an attempt to theorize the collective reception of these forms. *Deutsche Menschen* applies a similar mastery of German letters to the ambitious goal of reaching thousands of German households with a progressive reframing of cultural values.

The two works balance tradition and agency differently. While the artwork essay grounds film in early photography and ancient architecture, it subordinates tradition to the potential of new media to generate political awareness. Technically reproduced works lose their aura, but aura returns in displaced forms, like the cult of the actor and the allure of fascism. The essay strains too hard to harness new artistic forms to the cause of collective political agency: the potential of new forms to bring mass transformation through shock and "heightened attention" approaches a kind of simplistic formalism (*SW* 4:267). *Deutsche Menschen* strikes a different but equally unsuccessful balance of agency and tradition. Its Goethean values of "honor," "greatness," and "dignity" surely affirm tradition, but one can hardly detect the text's political purpose. In fact, the book was well reviewed in Nazi Germany.[3]

These failures to design effective political transformation place Benjamin in company with almost every other radical and progressive thinker of the twentieth century, but he stands apart in his abiding, even stubborn, concern with tradition. This engagement leads Benjamin to resist modern, secularist conceptions of human agency shaped by the idealism of the Enlightenment and romanticism: the ideology of "progress" propelled by the actions of individuals and groups in the absence of cultural, social contexts. In his pursuit of conceptions of agency informed by tradition, Benjamin can be compared to such contemporary critics of secularist agency as Mahmood, Asad, and Abeysakara. Like these postsecular thinkers, Benjamin's engagement with religious tradition always recognizes the impossibility of traditionalism, the idea that there is a pure form of religion to which one could return.

By resisting secularist ideas of human agency, Benjamin avoids the nihilism of Nietzsche, the abstraction and nationalism of Heidegger, and the skepticism of Freud. He also challenges ideas of group identity based on religion and nationality. The allusion to Martin Luther's legendary defiance of papal authority in his 1912 letter on Zionism is more ironic than heroic; it links him with the Christian Reformer and against Zionist Jews: "I am bound here . . . Here I will stand and, as I must believe, will you also stand" (*GS* 2:838). Benjamin consistently affirmed his Jewishness, but he also saw himself as a European, just as his references to Turkish and Oriental subjects blur rather than affirm the distinctions of East and West, Orient and Occident, premodern and modern. These articulations of identity align Benjamin with feminist and postcolonial thinkers who challenge not only essentialist categories but also the unquestioned power they so often exercise.

Benjamin's broad, dynamic conception of tradition extends from commentary, translation, and quotation of texts to the reception of modern art, film, and modern cities.[4] He never doubts the survival of religious tradition, finding its traces in capitalism, fascism, and many other purportedly secular discourses. Yet he resists the tendency of thinkers like Schmitt and Nietzsche to reduce such modern formations to simple religious terms. Like Asad and other postsecular thinkers, Benjamin rejects the sharp division of history and culture into secular and religious categories.

Grand narratives of progress, decline, secularization, eternal recurrence, or religious revival all fail to capture the dynamics of tradition as Benjamin conceives it (*Arcades*, 119, 460). A better description of change within tradition is displacement, which notes how anything new takes the place of something that was there before.[5] Displacements of tradition involve practices, beliefs, and conditions of which we may not be fully aware; they may hold promise or danger, but they always call for the kind of attentive study and perception Benjamin practices and promotes.

The tropes of paradox and inversion that animate Benjamin's writings open up critical perspectives on what John McCole calls the "antinomies of tradition," to which I would add the antinomies of agency.[6] Theological paradox structures the essay on violence: human activity can generate historic transformation, but only in tandem with the divine. There can even be an inverse relationship between human and divine action. The "Theological-Political Fragment," likely written around the same time, posits the "secular order" as contributing to the "Messianic kingdom" by working in the opposite direction, "just as a force, by virtue of the path it is moving along, can augment another force on the opposite path" (*SW* 3: 305). Human agency is real, even efficacious, but only by virtue of an inscrutable divine power.

These paradoxes multiply, mixing politics and religion, direct action with practices of reading and perception: secular readers fixate on Schreber's religious mental illness; radical art and politics exclude religion but carry messianic potential; German cultural values represent Jewish survival under Nazi oppression. The angel of history illustrated by Klee's *Angelus Novus* appears completely powerless, but its gaze toward the spectator indicates the possibility of recognition necessary to any political engagement.

Benjamin's work demonstrates the value of literary, philological, and aesthetic methods to postsecular thought.[7] These concerns, tailored to a vast range of genres, explain his work better than any ideology or school of thought. The early essay "Two Poems by Hölderlin" ponders agency in an entirely literary context, favoring a model of courage defined as "submission to the danger that threatens the world" (*SW* 1:33). Failed action preoccupies the *Trauerspiel* study, in political and literary terms alike; the dramas typically feature indecisive and disempowered rulers, yet Benjamin proposes an "ascetic apprenticeship" for those who face the collapse of meaning and order in early modern culture. Benjamin's fascination with Daniel Paul Schreber's memoir is equally literary, moving from the paradox of Schreber's lucid, poetic, and theologically rich mental illness to the broader implications of how such books are published and received. Surrealism affords a "profane illumination" with genuine revolutionary potential: "Since Bakunin, Europe has lacked a radical concept of freedom. The Surrealists have one" (*SW* 2:215).[8]

The variety of Benjamin's writings reveals an intellectual temperament more disposed to challenge received understandings than to construct systematic theories. By his characteristic rhetorical inversions, juxtapositions, and paradoxes, Benjamin subverts the binaries of religion and secularity, tradition and modernity, agency and powerlessness. His "tradition" thus differs markedly from Buber's and Scholem's, since it finds religiosity and values far from institutional religion and ancient sources. Likewise, his "agency" bears little resemblance to the kind of force and power that characterize political thinkers from Marx to Schmitt. Instead, Benjamin's experiments in reading and observation, rooted in religious and scholarly traditions, seek to enable the kinds of awareness necessary to meaningful action.

NOTES

Introduction

1. I have attempted to explicate Benjamin's understanding of biblical tradition in *Walter Benjamin and the Bible* (New York: Continuum, 1996) and to develop a general conception of biblical tradition in *Biblical Curses and the Displacement of Tradition* (Sheffield, Eng.: Sheffield Phoenix, 2011).

2. Manfred Voigts, "'Die Mater der Gerechtigkeit': Zur Kritik der Zitat-Begriffes bei Walter Benjamin," in *Antike und Moderne: Zu Walter Benjamins "Passagen,"* ed. N. Bolz and R. Faber (Würzburg: Königshausen und Neumann, 1986), 97–115.

3. Anthony Giddens, *Central Problems in Social Theory: Action, Structure and Contradiction in Social Analysis* (Berkeley: University of California Press), 55–56.

4. Saba Mahmood, *Politics of Piety: The Islamic Revival and the Feminist Subject* (Princeton, N.J.: Princeton University Press, 2004), 157.

5. Ibid., 174.

6. Ibid., 188.

7. Ananda Abeysekara, "Sri Lanka, Postcolonial 'Locations of Buddhism,' Secular Peace," *Interventions: International Journal of Postcolonial Studies* 14, no. 2 (2012): 215 [211–37].

8. Talal Asad, *Genealogies of Religion: Discipline and Reasons of Power in Christianity and Islam* (Baltimore: Johns Hopkins University Press, 1993), 167. See also Asad, "Comments on Conversion," in *Conversion to Modernities: The Globalization of Christianity,* ed. Peter van der Veer (New York: Routledge, 1996), 263–73.

9. Gustav Landauer, "Puppen," in *Der Werdende Mensch: Aufsätze über Leben und Schrifttum* (Potsdam: Gustav Kiepenheuer, 1921), 98 [89–99].

10. See my review of literature on secularism and secularization in *Biblical Curses and the Displacement of Tradition*, 15–22, 109–113.

11. Peter Fenves, *The Messianic Reduction: Walter Benjamin and the Shape of Time* (Stanford, Calif.: Stanford University Press, 2011), 18–43.

12. Walter Benjamin, *Gesammelte Schriften,* vol. 1, ed. Rolf Tiedemann and Hermann Schweppenhäuser (Frankfurt: Suhrkamp, 1991), 227.

13. The text was influenced by Ernst Bloch; see *GS* 6:688–89.

14. Roland H. Bainton, *Here I Stand: A Life of Martin Luther* (Peabody, Mass.: Hendrickson, 2009), 180. Though these words may not be the words Luther spoke, they have been widely quoted since his time.

15. See, e.g., Benjamin's letter of June 25, 1936, where he comments in detail on conflict in the Middle East: "And if you, actually being there yourself, can't see a way out, then it's all the more impossible for me to do so" (*The Correspondence of Walter Benjamin and Gershom Scholem 1932–1940*, trans. Gary Smith and Andre Lefevere [New York: Schocken, 1989], 182).

16. Hannah Arendt, "Walter Benjamin," in Walter Benjamin, *Illuminations*, trans. Harry Zohn (New York: Schocken, 1969), 18.

Chapter 1

1. Multiple other examples can be found. Another paradigmatic American case is Walter Russell (1871–1963), whose writings on science and religion and artistic works earned him significant fame during his lifetime. His 1926 *The Universal One* (Waynesboro, Va.: University of Science and Philosophy), for example, places scientific diagrams alongside religious and philosophical reflections—its attempt to unite all knowledge is typically modern, and its failure to do so (at least in the eyes of scientists and thinkers) is also typical of the melancholy condition Benjamin finds in modernity.

2. Walter Benjamin, *The Origin of German Tragic Drama*, trans. John Osborne (London: New Left Books, 1977), 56.

3. National Center for Science Education, "A New Poll on Evolution and Climate Change," online at http://ncse.com/news/2011/09/new-poll-evolution-climate-change-006884. According to *Harper's*, 98 percent of Canadians "believe in global warming" while only 70 percent of Americans and 48 percent of Republicans do (*Harper's,* January 2013, 15). See also the polls by Gallup, which reflect a partisan divide over climate change but a gradual shift toward acceptance of climate change data. Online at http://www.gallup.com/tag/Climate%2BChange.aspx. I want to thank Lucy Britt, Matthew Goodrum, and Gary Downey for helping me to think through this chapter.

4. See Erving Goffman, *The Presentation of Self in Everyday Life* (New York: Anchor, 1959).

5. Jane O. Newman, *Benjamin's Library: Modernity, Nation, and the Baroque* (Cornell, Ithaca, N.Y.: Cornell University Press, 2011), 140–45.

6. Ibid., 144–45.

7. Ibid., 155–69.

8. Hannah Arendt, *The Human Condition* (Chicago: University of Chicago Press, 1958), 204.

9. See the discussion of melancholy and redemption (*Rettung*) in Heinrich Kaulen, "Rettung," in *Benjamins Begriffe,* vol. 2, ed. Michael Opitz and Erdmut Wizisla (Frankfurt: Suhrkamp, 2000), 640–41 [619–64].

10. See the Fox News report that record snowfalls challenge Gore's account of climate change, online at https://www.youtube.com/watch?v=fJe_K17EcpE. See also the recent series of debates between science educator Bill Nye and various climate change and evolutionary science skeptics. (Thanks to Lucy Britt for these references.)

11. "AAAS Board: Attacks on Climate Researchers Inhibit Free Exchange of Scientific Ideas," online at http://www.aaas.org/news/aaas-board-attacks-climate-researchers-inhibit-free-exchange-scientific-ideas.

12. The category of displacement refers to contingent changes within a tradition; it draws from Freud as well as Asad and Benjamin and forms the theoretical focus of my recent *Biblical Curses and the Displacement of Tradition.*

13. Mario Biagioli, "From Relativism to Contingentism," in *The Disunity of Science: Boundaries, Contexts, and Power,* ed. Peter Galison and David J. Stimp (Stanford, Calif.: Stanford University Press, 1996), 189–206.

14. Bruno Latour, *We Have Never Been Modern*, trans. Catherine Porter (Cambridge, Mass.: Harvard University Press, 1993) and Latour, *Politics of Nature:*

How to Bring the Sciences into Democracy, trans. Catherine Porter (Cambridge, Mass.: Harvard Univ. Press, 2004).

15. Lorraine Daston and Peter Galison, *Objectivity* (New York: Zone Books, 2007), 371.

16. Daston and Galison, *Objectivity*, 250. See also Galison, "Objectivity Is Romantic," in Jerome Friedman, Galison, and Susan Haack, *The Humanities and the Sciences* ACLS Occasional Paper No. 47 (Philadelphia: American Council of Learned Societies, 1999): 15–43.

17. Steven Shapin, "How to Be Antiscientific," in *Never Pure* (Baltimore: John Hopkins University Press, 2010), 44 [32–46].

18. Latour, *Politics of Nature.*

19. Aby Warburg, *The Renewal of Pagan Antiquity: Contributions to the Cultural History of the European Renaissance*, trans. David Britt (Los Angeles: Getty Research Institute, 1999), 597–697.

20. Ibid., 647.

21. Ibid., 650.

22. Erwin Panofsky, "What Is Baroque?" in *Three Essays on Style* (Cambridge, Mass.: MIT Press, 1995), 19–20, 51 [19–88].

23. Ibid., 80–88.

24. Georges Didi-Huberman, *Confronting Images: Questioning the Ends of a Certain History of Art* (University Park: Pennsylvania State University Press, 2005), xxi–xxii.

25. Ibid., xxii.

26. Newman, *Benjamin's Library*, 163–69.

27. An illustration of the negativity of melancholy in Benjamin is the following aphorism from the *Arcades Project*: "The awareness of time's empty passage and the *taedium vitae* are the two weights that keep the wheels of melancholy going" (Benjamin, *The Arcades Project*, trans. Howard Eiland and Kevin McLaughlin [Cambridge, Mass.: Harvard University Press, 1999], 351).

28. The problem of experience, characterized both as lived experience, the *Erlebnis* associated with the *Lebensphilosophie* of his day, as well as the more long-term *Erfahrung*, would continue to preoccupy Benjamin.

29. An echo of the Genius of Melancholy appears in a passage about hashish in the *Arcades Project*: comparing allegory and hashish, he writes: "At work in the latter are different sorts of powers: a genius of melancholy gravity, another of Ariel-like spirituality" (*Arcades,* 348–9).

30. Walter Benjamin, "Lichtenberg: A Cross Section," trans. Gerhard Schulte, *Performing Arts Journal* 14 (1992): 39–40 [37–56].

31. See Erich Ebstein, "Heinrich Julius Rütgerodt in seinen Beziehungen zu Goethe, Lavater und Lichtenberg," *Archiv für Kriminal-Anthropologie und Kriminalistik* 38, ed. Hans Gross (Leipzig: Vogel, 1910): 68–88.

32. Irving Wohlfarth, "Walter Benjamin and the Idea of a Technological Eros: A Tentative Reading of *Zum Planetarium,*" in *Benjamin Studien 1: Perception and Experience in Modernity* (Amsterdam: Rodipi, 2002), 80 [65–109].

33. "L'homme est, à l'égal de l'univers, l'énigme de l'infini et de l'éternité, et le grain de sable l'est à l'égal de l'homme" (Auguste Blanqui, *L'Éternité par les astres* [Paris: Librairie Germer Baillière, 1872], 56, 72).

34. "Au fond, elle est mélancolique cette éternité de l'homme par les astres, et plus triste encore cette séquestration des mondes-frères par l'inexorable barrière de l'espace" (Blanqui, *L'Éternité par les astres*, 58, 75).

35. Benjamin's awareness of Freud's *Beyond the Pleasure Principle* is clear from his quotation of a psychoanalytic text on gambling by Edmund Bergler that cites Freud (*Arcades* 510).

36. "Der Spleen ist das Gefühl, das der Katastrophe in Permanenz entspricht" (*GS* 5:437).

37. Benjamin describes Baudelaire as a "witness" but Blanqui as an "expert witness" before the "tribunal of history" (*Arcades* 363).

38. Letter to Horkheimer, January 6, 1938, *Corr WB*, 549; *Briefe* vol. 2, ed. Gershom Scholem and Theodor Adorno (2 vols; Frankfurt: Suhrkamp, 1966), 742.

39. Max Pensky names Benjamin as the "quintessential modern heroic melancholic" (Pensky, *Melancholy Dialectics* [Amherst: University of Massachusetts Press, 1993], 246; see also 1). Pensky is insightful on the paradoxes of passivity and agency in the tradition of melancholia and in Benjamin's use of it, but in addition to the biographical impulse, I disagree with his conceptual analysis at a number of points, particularly the distinction between melancholy criticism of allegory, which Pensky describes as a kind of political dead end, and the supposedly more potent domains of surrealism and the dialectical image (see especially pp. 183, 210).

40. My argument thus challenges Beatrice Hanssen's understanding of melancholy as a failure of political agency. In "Portrait of Melancholy (Benjamin, Warburg, Panofsky)," she writes, "Casting now a downward gaze, now a melancholic glance at the distanced spectator, Benjamin seems frozen, not unlike Klee's *Angelus Novus* or Dürer's fallen angel, or even his poetic double, Baudelaire, furiously parrying the shocks of modernity coming from outside." *MLN* 114, no. 5 (1999): 1009 [991–1013].

41. See Ilit Ferber, *Philosophy and Melancholy: Benjamin's Early Reflections on Theater and Language* (Redwood City, Calif.: Stanford University Press, 2013), 59–65.

42. Michel de Certeau, "Surin's Melancholy," in *Heterologies: Discourse on the Other*, trans. Brian Massumi (Minneapolis: University of Minnesota Press, 1986), 103.

43. Robert Burton, *The Anatomy of Melancholy* (London, 1800), 185–212, accessed through *Eighteenth Century Collections Online* (Gale Cengage).

44. Arendt, *Human Condition*, 7–17, 204.

45. Gillian Rose uses this term in her essay, "Walter Benjamin—Out of the Sources of Modern Judaism," *New Formations* 20 (1993): 77 [59–81].

Chapter 2

1. See, for example: Charles Taylor, *A Secular Age* (Cambridge, Mass.: Harvard University Press, 2007); Vincent Pecora, *Secularism and Cultural Criticism: Religion, Nation, and Modernity* (Chicago: University of Chicago Press, 2006); Jeffrey Stout, *Democracy and Tradition* (Princeton, N.J.: Princeton University Press, 2004); Talal Asad, *Formations of the Secular: Christianity, Islam, Modernity* (Stanford, Calif.: Stanford University Press, 2003); Bruce Lincoln, *Holy*

Terrors: Thinking about Religion after September 11 (Chicago: University of Chicago Press, 2003); William Connolly, *Why I Am Not a Secularist* (Minneapolis: University of Minnesota Press, 2000); and José Casanova, *Public Religions in the Modern World* (Chicago: University of Chicago Press, 1994).

2. My interest in this chapter is not to disentangle Scholem's thought from Benjamin's; in fact, my assumptions will be that their thinking was intertwined, that their correspondence and documentation capture only a part of their exchanges, and that their well-known differences are marked by shared interests and mutual influence. These assumptions draw cogency from the extensive correspondence between the friends as well as Scholem's continued interest in Benjamin's work (1940–1981, just before his own death). See Scholem, *Walter Benjamin und sein Engel*, ed. Rolf Tiedemann (Frankfurt: Suhrkamp, 1983), which includes a very detailed essay on Benjamin's family tree published in 1981.

3. Gershom Scholem, Muki Tsur and Abraham Shapira, "With Gershom Scholem: An Interview," trans. Moshe Kohn, in Scholem, *On Jews and Judaism in Crisis: Selected Essays*, ed. Werner J. Dannhauser (New York: Schocken, 1976), 1–48.

4. The claim about a counter-narrative is indebted to David Biale's *Gershom Scholem: Kabbalah and Counter-History*, 2nd ed. (Cambridge, Mass.: Harvard University Press, 1982), 6–8, 149–53, though I believe Biale exaggerates Scholem's interest in recovering tradition.

5. Scholem et al., "An Interview," 46.

6. Gershom Scholem, "Education for Judaism" (1971), in *On the Possibility of Jewish Mysticism in Our Time and Other Essays*, ed. Avraham Shapira, trans. Jonathan Chipman (Philadelphia: Jewish Publication Society, 1997), 85 [80–92]; Alasdair MacIntyre, *After Virtue: A Study in Moral Theory* (Notre Dame, Ind.: University of Notre Dame Press, 1981), 222.

7. Scholem, "Education for Judaism," 89. See Weidner's discussion of Scholem's notion of tradition, *Gershom Scholem: Politisches, esoterisches und historiographisches Schreiben* (Paderborn: Wilhelm Fink, 2003), 152–62.

8. Gershom Scholem, "Memory and Utopia," in *Possibility*, 163.

9. See notes 43 and 44, below.

10. Gershom Scholem, "Thoughts about Our Language," in Scholem, *Possibility*, 27–29.

11. Ibid., 27.

12. Gershom Scholem, *Tagebücher* vol. 2, ed. Karlfried Gründer et al (Frankfurt: Jüdischer Verlag, 2000), 612, cited in Weidner, *Gershom Scholem*, 133, my translation. Benjamin uses the term "geistige Wesen" in his writings on language (*GS* 2:141).

13. Gershom Scholem, *Major Trends in Jewish Mysticism* (New York: Schocken, 1969), 7–8.

14. Ibid., 35.

15. Scholem, "Possibility," 11–13.

16. Scholem, *Major Trends*, 249.

17. Thanks to Daniel Weidner for this suggestion.

18. Scholem, "Possibility," 16–18.

19. "I liked Graetz very much as a historian, but I was extremely critical of his attitude to the *kabbalah*. It was very clear to me that the kabbalists could

not possibly have been the kind of scoundrels, swindlers, or idiots he described." Scholem et al., "An Interview," 17.

20. See also how Benjamin relates Nietzsche's idea of "eternal recurrence" to progress as "complementary" (*Arcades* 119).

21. Letter of Benjamin to Scholem, June 12, 1938, in *The Correspondence of Walter Benjamin and Gershom Scholem 1932–1940*, 224.

22. Letter of Benjamin to Scholem, June 12, 1938, *The Correspondence of Walter Benjamin and Gershom Scholem 1932–1940*, 225 (*Briefe* 2:763).

23. Scholem, "Education for Judaism," 85.

24. Scholem et al., "An Interview," 33. Scholem's anarchism may be linked to the work of an acquaintance of his youth, the socialist Gustav Landauer. Landauer was very close to Martin Buber, despite their frequent disagreements. See Paul Mendes-Flohr, *From Mysticism to Dialogue: Martin Buber's Transformation of German Social Thought* (Detroit: Wayne State University Press, 1989), 108–10; and Biale, *Gershom Scholem*, 21–22.

25. Gershom Scholem, *Tagebücher* 2 (Frankfurt: Jüdischer Verlag, 2000), 424, cited in Jacobson, *Metaphysics of the Profane: The Political Theology of Walter Benjamin and Gershom Scholem* (New York: Columbia University Press, 2003), 194.

26. Gershom Scholem, "With Gershom Scholem: An Interview," in Scholem, *Jews and Judaism in Crisis*, 36; see Biale, *Gershom Scholem*.

27. Yossef Schwartz, "From Broken Speculation to Accords of Eternity: Adorno, Benjamin, and Scholem," in *Theodor W. Adorno: Philosoph des beschädigten Lebens*, ed. Moshe Zuckermann (Göttingen: Wallsten, 2004), 137–38 [131–39].

28. Shaul Magid, "Mysticism, History, and a 'New' Kabbalah: Gershom Scholem and the Contemporary Scene," *The Jewish Quarterly Review* 101 (Fall 2011): 519 [511–25].

29. Scholem, "Education for Judaism," 86. He also denies any ability to predict the future on the basis of his anarchism: "Today [1971] we have entered an anarchical situation. I cannot prophesy what will remain of all that has been crystallized from the battles of the past and down the generations" (86).

30. Scholem, "Possibility," in *Possibility*, 16–17.

31. Ibid., 17.

32. Ibid., 17.

33. Ibid., 18. Scholem repeats the point in "An Interview," 48. A possible source for Scholem's high regard for Whitman may be the Jewish anarchist socialist Gustav Landauer, an influential figure in the first decades of the twentieth century and a friend of Martin Buber. Landauer translated many of Whitman's poems into German, and in his 1907 essay on Whitman, he describes the poet as a priest, prophet, and creator, as well as a forerunner of an "amerikanisch-perikleischen" age. Whitman's poetry, he continues, is a "new form of the eternal teachings of the philosophers and mystics." Gustav Landauer, "Walt Whitman," in *Zwang und Befreiung: Ein Auswahl aus seinem Werk*, ed. Heinz-Joachim Heydorn (Cologne: Hegner, 1968), 116, 118 [115–26]. There is little mention of Landauer in Benjamin's work, though Landauer is listed among those whom Benjamin read (*GS* 6:690).

34. Scholem, "Possibility," 18. See Richard M. Bucke, *Cosmic Consciousness: A Study in the Evolution of the Human Mind* (New York: E. P. Dutton, 1901). There is a note in Scholem's copy of this book citing an 1816 letter by Baader on the idea of cosmic consciousness: "Ich nenne dieses Bewusstsein das kosmische" (Franz von Baader, *Sämmtliche Werke*, ed. Franz Hoffmann, vol. 15 [Leipzig: Bethmann, 1857], 302) (Scholem archive, Jerusalem). Scholem clearly read this contemporary work, perhaps uncritically, in continuity with earlier thought on mysticism.

35. Gershom Scholem, *Kabbalah* (New York: New American Library Penguin, 1974), 152.

36. Ibid., 153.

37. Scholem, *Major Trends*, 233.

38. Compare the esotericism of Leo Strauss; Strauss was a member of Scholem and Benjamin's larger intellectual circle; his name appears several times in their correspondence; Benjamin speaks favorably of him twice, in letters from 1932 and 1935. Scholem, ed., *The Correspondence of Walter Benjamin and Gershom Scholem*, 24, 160. See also Steven B. Smith, "Leo Strauss: Between Athens and Jerusalem," *The Review of Politics* 53 (1991): 75–99.

39. Scholem, *Major Trends*, p. 350 (1941). Note the more pessimistic tone in the 1963 essay "On the Possibility of Jewish Mysticism," where Scholem doubts the possible revival of mysticism in Judaism because of disbelief in Torah and revelation: "This conclusion leads us necessarily to anarchistic forms of religion" ("Possibility," 16). Note also resonances with Benjamin's "Storyteller" (1934), particularly the ideas that words can be powerful and that life and story are intertwined. Other Benjamin texts that allude to the problem of agency are *German Men and Women* (*Deutsche Menschen*) and his late work, "On the Concept of History" (see chapters 6 and 7).

40. Scholem writes, "Notwithstanding the fact that everything he said about history was utterly groundless, he nevertheless did note a place in which the hidden life of Judaism had once dwelled, to which I attached myself in my meditations." Gershom Scholem, "A Candid Letter about My True Intentions in Studying Kabbalah" (1937), in *Possibility*, 4.

41. David Biale, "Gershom Scholem's Ten Unhistorical Aphorisms on Kabbalah: Text and Commentary," *Modern Judaism* 5 (1985): 70 [67–93], my translation.

42. Daniel Weidner argues that Scholem wrote not just about tradition but texts that "*perform* and *imitate* 'tradition' and its paradoxes in modernity." Weidner, "Reading Gershom Scholem," *Jewish Quarterly Review* 96 (2006): 203 [203–31].

43. Jonathan Z. Smith, "Manna, Mana Everywhere and /u/u/," in *Relating Religion: Essays in the Study of Religion* (Chicago: University of Chicago Press, 2004), 133–34 [117–44].

44. One influential study is Karen McCarthy Brown's *Mama Lola: A Vodou Priestess in Brooklyn* (Berkeley: University of California Press, 1991).

45. Biale, "Scholem's Ten Unhistorical Aphorisms," 73.

46. Ibid., 73, 87.

47. Ibid., 86.

48. Ibid., 87–88.

49. "Etwas von dem strengen Glanze des Kanonischen—des Volkommenen, das zerbricht." Biale, "Scholem's Ten Unhistorical Aphorisms," 88.

50. Moshe Idel notes Scholem's key role in promoting the view of Jewish mysticism as Gnosticism in general and the Kabbalah in particular as a set of responses to expulsion (Idel, *Kabbalah: New Perspectives* [New Haven, Conn.: Yale University Press, 1988], 30, 266). Despite his iconoclasm toward Scholem, Idel preserves the canonical status of Kafka, as a sign of the loss of faith in the law in modernity, "the last remnants of Jewish mysticism operating in a world in which the confidence in man's acts has disintegrated" (Idel, *Kabbalah,* 271).

51. Moshe Idel, *Old Worlds, New Mirrors: On Jewish Mysticism and Twentieth-Century Thought* (Philadelphia: University of Pennsylvania Press, 2010), 118–19.

52. Ibid., 174–75. Idel also credits Reuchlin and Goethe as sources for Scholem's ideas of language and symbol (87, 115).

53. Ibid., 108.

54. Letter of August 11, 1934, *Correspondence of Walter Benjamin and Gershom Scholem, 1932–1940,* 135.

55. Letter of September 20, 1934, *Correspondence of Walter Benjamin and Gershom Scholem,* 142.

56. Robert Alter, *Necessary Angels: Tradition and Modernity in Kafka, Benjamin, and Scholem* (Cambridge, Mass.: Harvard University Press, 1991), 109.

57. Ibid., 110.

58. Ibid., 111.

59. Gershom Scholem, "The People of the Book," in *Possibility,* 171.

60. Gershom Scholem, "Reflections on Modern Jewish Studies," in *Possibility,* 54–55 [51–71].

61. See, e.g., Charles Manekin, "Steinschneider's 'Decent Burial': A Reassessment," in *Study and Knowledge in Jewish Thought Vol. I,* ed. Howard Kreisel (Jerusalem: Mossad Bialik, 2006), 239–51.

62. Scholem, "Reflections on Modern Jewish Studies," 68.

63. Ibid., 66, 69.

64. Gershom Scholem, "The Science of Judaism—Then and Now," in *The Messianic Idea in Judaism and Other Essays on Jewish Spirituality* (1959; New York: Schocken, 1971), 310.

65. Scholem, "Reflections on Modern Jewish Studies," 70.

66. Jacqueline Rose, *The Question of Zion* (Princeton, N.J.: Princeton University Press, 2005), 54–57.

67. Stéphane Mosès, *The Angel of History: Rosenzweig, Benjamin, Scholem,* trans. Barbara Harshav (Stanford, Calif.: Stanford University Press, 2009), 179.

68. Ibid., 181; Scholem et al., "An Interview," 22.

69. Piterberg also criticizes Biale for comparing Benjamin and Scholem: "I think, moreover, that the political and ethical world views that guided Benjamin and Scholem and to which they were committed—unorthodox Marxist humanism (strewn with Jewish messianism and romanticism) and Zionism, respectively—were and have remained not only incompatible, but also mutually exclusive" (179). Gabriel Piterberg, *The Returns of Zionism: Myths, Politics, and Scholarship in Israel* (London: Verso, 2008), 173.

70. Scholem, *Walter Benjamin: The Story of a Friendship*, trans. Harry Zohn (New York: Schocken, 1981), 214–15. 1938 is also the year that Adorno inscribed a copy of his *Kierkegaard* book to Scholem (Scholem archive). Scholem wrote extensive notes, some approving and some critical, in his copies of Adorno's writings, including a copy of *Negative Dialectics* (1966). Adorno's view of Scholem could be equally gracious; see his "Gruss an Gershom G. Scholem," written for the occasion of Scholem's 70th birthday, *Neue Zürcher Zeitung*, March 12, 1967, p. 5.

71. Scholem, "Candid Letter," 4.

72. See Benjamin, letter to Scholem, June 2, 1934, in *Correspondence of Walter Benjamin and Gershom Scholem*, 114.

73. See Biale, *Gershom Scholem*, 32.

74. See Jacobson, *Metaphysics of the Profane*, 114ff., 173ff. See Gershom Scholem, "Walter Benjamin" (1964), in *Walter Benjamin und sein Engel*, 28 (9–34). See also Scholem's comment on Benjamin's reading of Baader in Scholem, "Benjamin and Baader: Ein Brief an Walter Boehlich" (1981), in *Walter Benjamin und sein Engel*, 201–3.

75. Scholem, letter to Hannah Arendt, June 23, 1963, in Scholem, *On Jews and Judaism in Crisis*, 302 (301–6).

76. Arendt, letter to Gershom Scholem, in *The Jewish Writings*, ed. Jerome Kohn and Ron H. Feldman (New York: Schocken, 2007), 466–67 (465–71). See Gabriel Piterberg, "Zion's Rebel Daughter: Hannah Arendt on Palestine and Jewish Politics," *New Left Review* 48 (2007): 39–57.

77. Scholem, letter to Hannah Arendt, in *On Jews and Judaism in Crisis*, 302–3.

78. Arendt, letter to Scholem, July 24, 1963, in Hannah Arendt, *The Jewish Writings*, ed. Jerome Kohn and Ron H. Feldman (New York: Schocken, 2007), 467.

79. Hannah Arendt, *Between Past and Future: Eight Exercises in Political Thought* (New York: Viking, 1968), 70.

80. Ibid., 70.

81. Arendt, *The Human Condition*, 74, 77.

82. Gershom Scholem, "Who Is a Jew?" in *On the Possibility of Jewish Mysticism in Our Time*, 98 [93–99].

83. One example of Scholem's likely influence on Arendt is her worry in 1946 that "the utopian and ideological elements with which he [Herzl] injected the new Jewish will to political action are only too likely to lead the Jews out of reality once more. . . . [and] the parallels with the Shabbetai Tzevi episode have become terribly close." "The Jewish State: Fifty Years After, Where Have Herzl's Politics Led?" in Arendt, *The Jewish Writings*, ed. J. Kohn and R. Feldman (New York: Schocken, 2007), 387 [375–87].

84. Gershom Scholem, "Jews and Germans," in *On Jews and Judaism in Crisis*, 87, 89 [71–92].

85. Ibid., 89.

86. Scholem et al., "An Interview," 12.

87. Scholem, "Reflections on the Possibility of Jewish Mysticism in Our Time," 17–18.

88. Hannah Arendt, *Life of the Mind* (New York: Harcourt Brace Jovanovich, 1978), 202.

89. Ibid., 210.
90. Scholem et al., "An Interview," 6.
91. Ibid., 15.
92. Daniel Weidner, *Gershom*, 38, my translation.
93. Scholem et al., "An Interview," 11.
94. Biale, *Gershom Scholem*, 99.
95. Scholem, *The Messianic Idea in Judaism*, 334.
96. The point is made emphatically in the 1975 "Interview," 43–44. Earlier in that interview Scholem describes some forms of Zionism as fascism (12). See Nathan Rotnstreich, "Gershom Scholem's Conception of Jewish Nationalism," in *Gershom Scholem: The Man and His Work* (Albany: State University of New York Press, 1994), 104–19. A humorous example of Scholem's criticism of Israel comes from his account of a conversation with the poet Allen Ginsberg. When Scholem's wife asks Ginsberg to consider moving to Israel, Ginsberg replies: "Your great ideal is to build a new Bronx here. All my life I've been running away from the Bronx, and here I come to the Jewish State and find that the whole big ideal of the Zionists is to build a giant Bronx here." Scholem comments tersely, "But there is something to what he said" ("Interview," 40).
97. Gershom Scholem, "A Lecture about Israel," in *Possibility*, 35–39.
98. See especially the articles and essays about the destruction of Europe's Jews published in the 1940s in Arendt, *The Jewish Writings.*
99. See, e.g., the discussion of religion and secularization in Arendt, *Between Past and Present*, 69–70, and 187–90.
100. Scholem persisted in his criticism of Arendt, as a blistering letter on the subject to the *Frankfurter Allgemeine Zeitung* of April 7, 1977 attests (p. 11). For a contemporary revisiting of these discussions, see Judith Butler, *Parting Ways: Jewishness and the Critique of Zionism* (New York: Columbia University Press, 2012).
101. Scholem, *Major Trends*, 34–35.
102. See Gershom Scholem, *Origins of the Kabbalah*, ed. R. J. Zwi Werblowsky and trans. Allan Arkush (New York: Jewish Publication Society, 1987); and Scholem, *Kabbalah* (New York: Meridian, 1978). The project of linking rabbinic and mystical literature to the Bible continues today, for example, in Michael Fishbane's *Biblical Myth and Rabbinic Mythmaking* (Oxford: Oxford University Press, 2003).
103. Scholem, "Education for Judaism," *Possibility*, 86.
104. Gershom Scholem, "Zionism—Dialectic of Continuity and Rebellion," a 1970 interview in *Unease in Zion*, ed. Ehud ben Ezer (New York: Quadrangle, 1974), 278 [263–96]. Scholem's unease about Zionist uses of the Bible appears also in the 1975 essay "People of the Book": "And they are still the people of the book, so that even in the secularization of the holy book and its transformation into a kind of epic of the Jewish nation, their claim is preserved and there still echoes something of the call that emerges from it. Whether this people will continue to exist after the undoing of this knot—which still exists and is reflected even in the cult of archaeology, which so many people in Israel today follow in their quest for themselves . . . remains a profound and fateful question. . . . Today, when the unethical seems so self-evident, does the Bible still address us with its

call? And is the people of the book still able to do something with its book? Is it possible that a time will come when it will fall silent? I am convinced that the existence of this nation depends upon the answer to this question far more deciseively than it does upon the ups and downs of politics" ("The People of the Book" [1975], in *Possibility*, 174-175).

105. Scholem et al., "An Interview," 19.

106. Gershom Scholem, "Über Klage und Klagelied," in *Tagebücher* vol. 2, 128 (translation mine).

107. Ibid., 128.

108. Ibid., 130.

109. Ibid., 131–32.

110. Ibid., 133.

111. Benjamin, letter to Scholem, March 30, 1918, in *Briefe* 1:182.

112. Gershom Scholem, "On Jonah and the Concept of Justice," trans. Eric J. Schwab, *Critical Inquiry* 25 (1999): 354 [353–61].

113. Ibid., 359.

114. Ibid., 358.

115. Scholem, *Walter Benjamin: The Story of a Friendship*, 72.

116. Ibid., 209. The same point is made in his 1975 "Interview": "I submit that to a certain extent even he confused the two (religion and politics), for toward the end of his life he did, in fact, too much identify the two spheres with each other" (27).

117. Benjamin's articulation of theoretical problems frequently involves the category of task (*Aufgabe*), a pattern I have called the "rhetoric of the task." Britt, *Walter Benjamin and the Bible*, 63–66.

118. See Scholem's essays on Benjamin's life and work in *Walter Benjamin und Sein Engel*, written as late as 1981, the year before Scholem's death. Of the fourteen selections about Benjamin in this book, nine were written or published in the last four years of Scholem's life, including a fastidious reconstruction of Benjamin's family tree published in 1981 ("Ahnen und Verwandte Walter Benjamins," 128–57).

119. Scholem, *Walter Benjamin*, 202.

120. Scholem, Ibid., 203.

121. Gershom Scholem, *Lamentations of Youth: The Diaries of Gershom Scholem*, ed. and trans. Anthony David Skinner (Cambridge, Mass.: Harvard University Press, 2007), 249.

122. See, for example, the essays collected in the *Journal for the American Academy of Religion* 74, no. 1 (2006).

123. Giorgio Agamben, "Bartleby, or On Contingency," in *Potentialities: Collected Essays in Philosophy*, trans. Daniel Heller-Roazen (Stanford, Calif.: Stanford University Press, 1999), 269 [243–71].

124. Scholem, *Lamentations of Youth*, 181.

125. See Scholem's sardonic comments on popular yoga in "An Interview" (39) and a similar critical perspective in Adorno's "Stars Down to Earth: The Los Angeles Times Astrology Column," *Jahrbuch für Amerikastudien* 2 (1957). If Scholem's work too easily makes space for popularizations, no such danger exists for the less accessible writings of Adorno.

Chapter 3

1. Other interpretations include Elias Canetti's comparison of Schreber and fascist thought and Eric Santner's suggestion that Schreber's breakdown related to his investiture as a judge. See Canetti, *Crowds and Power*, trans. Carol Stewart (New York: Viking, 1962); and Santner, *My Own Private Germany: Daniel Paul Schreber's Secret History of Modernity* (Princeton, N.J.: Princeton University Press, 1996).

2. Michel Foucault, *Madness and Civilization: A History of Insanity in the Age of Reason*, trans. Richard Howard (New York: Vintage, 1988), 79.

3. Ibid., 79–80.

4. Daniel Schreber, *Memoirs of My Nervous Illness*, trans. Ida Macalpine and Richard A Hunter (New York: New York Review Books, 2000), 7. Hereinafter cited as *Memoirs*. The German edition, also cited parenthetically in the text, is *Denkwirdigkeiten eines Nervenkranken nebst Nachtragen und Einem Anhang Über die Frage* (Leipzig: Oswald Mutze, 1903).

5. Michel de Certeau, *The Posession at Loudun*, trans. Michael B. Smith (Chicago: University of Chicago Press, 1996), 227–28.

6. Britt, *Biblical Curses and the Displacement of Tradition*.

7. Robert J. Sternberg, "Four Alternative Futures for Education in the United States: It's Our Choice," *School Psychology Review* 33 (2004): 66 [66–77].

8. See Brian Britt, "Psalm Recitation and Post-Secular Time: Augustine, the iPod, and Psalm 90," *Journal for Cultural and Religious Theory* 12 (Fall 2012): 122–47.

9. Asad, *Genealogies*, 125, 143.

10. Ibid., 144.

11. Ibid., 125.

12. Ibid., 167.

13. Zwi Lothane, *In Defense of Schreber: Soul Murder and Psychiatry* (Hillsdale, N.J.: Analytic, 1992), 393.

14. Schreber, *Memoirs*, 82.

15. Certeau, *The Possession at Loudun*, 51.

16. Certeau, "The Institution of Rot," in *Psychosis and Sexual Identity*, ed. D. Allison et al. (Albany: State University of New York Press, 1988), 96 [88–100].

17. Ibid., 98.

18. See Sigmund Freud, "Psychoanalytic Notes upon an Autobiograhical Account of a Case of Paranoia," in *Three Case Histories*, ed. Philip Rieff (New York: Simon and Schuster, 1996), 131.

19. In a direct challenge to medical authority, Schreber notes that his father's *Medical Indoor Gymnastics* fails to grasp important differences beween men and women (155). To prove that his knowledge of leprosy must be supernatural, Schreber describes himself as a "layman in medicine" with no prior knowledge of the disease; medical causes are thus challenged by a combination of logical argumentation (as in law) and supernatural, religious causes (94).

20. Against Sander Gilman and others who read images of gender and Jewishness to be decisive for Schreber, Eric Santner considers his conflict to be a "crisis of investiture, a breakdown in the *transfer* of symbolic capital that would have allowed him to assume his mandate within the institution of the courts. It was *this breakdown and its hallucinatory repair* that Freud misread as Schreber's

homosexual longings for paternal substitutes" (Santner, *My Own Private Germany*, 37, 139). Another alternative to the sexual-cultural reading of Schreber is Alexander van der Haven, "The Other Zarathustra: Madness, Schreber and the Making of Religion in 19th Century Germany" (dissertation: University of Chicago, 2009), which argues that Schreber "was as much a Luther as a *Luder*," and that Schreber's text represents a "new monist cosmology" that placed emphasis on immanence and practices of the body (188–89). One of these practices, notes van der Haven, is the use of "language as noise to drown out other sense impressions" (243).

21. Judgment of the Royal Superior Country Court, Dresden, in *Memoirs*, 422, 425.

22. "Neben den Schreber und jenes Tabellenbuch das wir in München erstanden, tritt dieser Tage in meine Bibliothek ein neues paranoisches Welt- und Staatssystem: Ganz-Erden-Universal-Staat. Eine Schrift, die sich sehen lassen kann." Benjamin, letter to Scholem, July 21, 1925, in *Briefe* 1:397. The mention of Schreber comes immediately after a statement extolling Kafka's "Vor dem Gesetz" and a mention of Poe's writings.

23. Laurence Rickels argues that the manuscript is Benjamin's own *Trauerspiel* study, but that cannot be the case, since it was published earlier in the same year (1928) (Laurence A. Rickels, "Endopsychic Allegories," *Postmodern Culture* 18 [2007], online at http://pmc.iath.virginia.edu/text-only/issue.907/18.1rickels.txt). Another possibility is Benjamin's embryonic Arcades Project, for which he was already seeking editorial interest and support; see his letter to Hugo von Hofmannsthal of March 17, 1928, which refers to the latter's suggestions on Benjamin's "Projekt der 'Pariser Passagen'" (Walter Benjamin, *Gesammelte Briefe*, vol. 3, ed. Christoph Gödde and Henri Lonitz [Frankfurt: Suhrkamp, 1995–2000], 353). But this too is only speculation.

24. "He also induced me to read Schreber's book which contained very impressive and pregnant formulations. From a salient passage in this book Benjamin derived the designation 'flüchtig hingemachte Männer.'" Gershom Scholem, *Walter Benjamin: The Story of a Friendship*, trans. Harry Zorn (Philadelphia: The Jewish Publication Society of America, 1975), 57.

25. Freud, "Psychoanalytic Notes," 126.

26. Ibid., 131.

27. Ibid., 135–36.

28. Ibid., 159.

29. Ibid., 154.

30. Schreber's text has had a way of eliciting revealing introspection from his readers; Freud, for instance, linked paranoia and homosexuality in Schreber to his own relationship with Wilhelm Fliess. See Roberto Calasso, *The Forty-Nine Steps*, trans. John Shepley (Minneapolis: University of Minnesota Press, 2001), 126–28; Calasso's survey of readings is detailed and revealing: see 122–43.

31. Freud, "Psychoanalytic Notes," 99.

32. Ibid., 107.

33. Ibid., 127.

34. Ibid., 192.

35. Schreber, *Memoirs*, 19ff.; Freud, "Psychoanalytic Notes," 126–31; and Lothane, *In Defense of Schreber*, 398–99.

36. Schreber, *Memoirs*, 158, 126.

37. Boris Böhm, personal communication, November 23, 2012.

38. The topic of quotaton, along with the analogous notion of visual montage, is also taken up in later chapters, especially chapter 6.

Chapter 4

1. Voltaire, *Candide, or Optimism*, trans. John Butt (New York: Penguin, 1988), 141–42.

2. Edward Said, "Erich Auerbach, Critic of the Earthly World," *boundary* 2 31 (2004): 11–34.

3. Sources on Said and Auerbach include Kader Konuk, *East West Mimesis: Auerbach in Turkey* (Stanford, Calif.: Stanford University Press, 2010); Aamir R. Mufti, "Auerbach in Istanbul: Edward Said, Secular Criticism, and the Question of Minority Culture," *Critical Inquiry* 25 (1998): 95–125; and Siraj Ahmed, "Notes from Babel: Toward a Colonial History of Comparative Literature," *Critical Inquiry* 39 (Winter 2013): 296–326.

4. The correspondents' shared identity as German-Jewish intellectuals is certainly not accidental to their interests in the Orient and secularism, but it is important not to oversimplify the role of identity in the letters or their reception, which is in part what I argue Said did by making Auerbach's exile central to his reading of *Mimesis*. A more subtle treatment of this topic is Galili Shahar, "Auerbach's Scars: Judaism and the Question of Literature," *Jewish Quarterly Review* 101 (Fall 2011): 604–30.

5. Orhan Pamuk, *Istanbul*, trans. Maureen Freely (London: Faber and Faber, 2005), 216.

6. Ibid., 232.

7. Ibid., 261.

8. Ibid., 230.

9. Ibid., 82, 160–79.

10. The migration of several million people from Turkey to Germany since the 1960s has led to dramatic changes in German culture. Examples include literary contributions by such authors as Yadé Kara (*Selam Berlin* [Zürich: Diogenes, 2003]) and films by Fatih Akın and many others. (See Sabine Hake and Barbara Mennel, eds., *Turkish German Cinema in the New Millennium: Sites, Sounds, and Screens* [New York: Berghahn, 2012] and Diana Schäffer, *Deutscher Film mit türkischer Seele: Entwicklungen und Tendenzen der deutsch-türkischen Filme von den 70er Jahren bis zur Gegenwart* [Saarbrücken: VDM Verlag, 2007].) The University of Michigan now offers a graduate program in Turkish-German studies; faculty include scholar of comparative literature and culture Kader Konuk, whose work contexualizes the current situation in the twentieth century (see, e.g., "Germans and Jews in Turkey: Ethnic Anxiety and Mimicry in the Making of the European Turk," in *Ethnicity in Today's Europe*, ed. Roland Hsu [Stanford, Calif.: Stanford University Press, 2010], 157–90).

11. Martin Elsky, M. Vialon, and R. Stein, "Scholarship in Times of Extremes: Letters of Erich Auerbach (1933–46), on the Fiftieth Anniversary of His Death," *PMLA* 122 (2007): 749 [742–62]. The German reads: "Die Lage hier is nicht ganz einfach, aber auch nicht ohne Reiz. Man hat hier alle Tradition über Bord geworfen und will auf europäische Art einen—extrem

türkisch-nationalistischen—durch-rationalisierten Staat aufbauen. Es geht phantastisch und gespenstisch schnell, schon kann kaum noch wer arabisch oder persisch, und selbst türkische Texte des letztvergangenen Jahrhunderts werden schnell unverständlich, seit die Sprache zugleich modernisiert und am Urtürkischen neuorientiert ist und mit lateinischen Buchstaben geschrieben wird" (Karlheinz Barck, "5 Briefe Erich Auerbachs an Walter Benjamin in Paris," *Zeitschrift für Germanistik* 6 [1988]: 691 [688–94]).

12. Elsky, Vialon, and Stein, "Scholarship in Times of Extremes," 750. The German reads: "Die Wohnung am Bosporus ist herrlich, die Arbeit wissenschaftlich ganz primitiv, aber menschlich, politisch und organisatorisch überaus interessant" (Barck, "5 Briefe," 691).

13. Elsky, Vialon, and Stein, "Scholarship in Times of Extremes," 750. The German reads: "Wir lehren hier alle europäischen Philologien, Romanistik, Anglistik, alte Philologie, Germanistik, wir versuchen das Unterrichts- und Bibliotheks-wesen zu beeinflussen und die wissenschaftliche Betriebstechnik, vom Stundenplan bis zum Zettelkasten, zu europäisieren. Das ist natürlich absurd, aber die Türken wollen es . . ." (Barck, "5 Briefe," 692).

14. Elsky, Vialon, and Stein, "Scholarship in Times of Extremes," 751. The German reads: ". . . eine wunderbar gelegene aber doch unliebenswürdige und unverbindliche Stadt aus zwei verschiedenen Teilen . . . Vom 19. J(ahrhundert) sieht man auch am Bosporus überall verfallenen oder verfallende oder museumshaft erhaltene Sultans- und Paschapaläste, in einem halb orientalischen, halb rokokohaften Geschmack. . . . Im übrigen aber wird das Land konsequent und vollständig beherrscht vom Atatürk und seinen anatolischen Türken, einem naiven, mißtrauischen, ehrlichen, etwas unbeholfenen und bäurischen, dabei sehr emotiven Menschenschlag . . . aber doch wohl gut zu leiden und mit viel Lebenskräften, gewohnt an Sklaverei und harte, aber langsame Arbeit. Der grand chef ist ein sympathischer Autokrat, klug, großzügig und witzig, vollkommen verschieden von seinen europäischen Kollegen . . . das Resultat ist ein fanatischer antitraditioneller Nationalismus: Ablehnung aller bestehenden mohammedanischen Kulturüberlieferung, Anknüpfung an ein phantastisches Urtürkentum, technische Modernisierung im europäischen Verstande, um das verhaßte und bewunderte Europa mit den eigenen Waffen zu schlagen . . . Resultat: Nationalismus im Superlativ bei gleichzeitiger Zerstörung des geschichtlichen Nationalcharakters. Dieses Bild, das in anderen Ländern, wie Deutschland und Italien und wohl auch Rußland (?), noch nicht für jederman sichtbar ist, bietet sich hier in völliger Nacktheit. Die Sprachreform, zugleich phantastisch urtürkisch (Befreiung vom arabischen und persischen Einschlag) und modern-technisch, hat es fertiggebracht, daß kein Mensch under 25 Jahren mehr irgendeinen religiösen, literarischen oder philosophischen Text verstehen kann, der alter ist als 10 Jahre, und daß die eigentümlichkeit der Sprache unter dem Zwang der lateinischen Schrift, die vor einigen Jahren zwangsweise eingeführt wurde, rapide verfällt . . . Immer deutlicher wird mir, daß die gegenwärtige Weltlage nichts ist als eine List der Versehung, um uns auf einem blutigen und qualvollen Wege zur Internationale der Trivialität und zur Esperanto-kultur zu führen. Ich habe das schon in Deutschland und in Italien, angesichts der grauenvollen Unechtheit der Blubopropaganda (Blut-und-Boden-Propaganda) vermutet, aber hier erst wird es mir fast zur Gewißheit" (Barck, "5 Briefe," 692).

15. Carlo Ginzburg, "Toleranza e Commercio: Auerbach legge Voltaire," *Quaderni Storici* 109 (2002): 268–69 [259–83].

16. Geoffrey Green, *Literary Criticism and the Structures of History: Erich Auerbach and Leo Spitzer* (Lincoln: University of Nebraska Press, 1983), 50.

17. Elsky, Vialon, and Stein, "Scholarship in Times of Extremes," 751.

18. Scholem, cited in Stephane Moses, *The Angel of History: Rosenzweig, Benjamin, Scholem*, trans. Barbara Harshav (Stanford, Calif.: Stanford University Press, 2009), 168–69. The German reads: "Das gespenstische Volupük, das wir hier auf der Gasse sprechen, bezeichnet genau jene ausdruckslose Sprachwelt, in der die 'Säkularisierung' der Sprache allein möglich werden konnte. . . . Denn kein Sehender hätte den dämonischen Mut aufgebracht, eine Sprache da zu beleben, wo nur ein Esperanto entstehen konnte" (Scholem, "Une lettre inédite de Gerschom Scholem a Franz Rosenzweig: A propos de notre langue une confession," *Archives de Sciences Sociales des Religions* 30 [1985]: 83–84).

19. Thomas R. Hart, "Literature as Language: Auerbach, Spitzer, Jakobson," in *Literary History and the Challenge of Philology: The Legacy of Erich Auerbach*, ed. Seth Lerer (Stanford, 1996), 231 [227–39].

20. Perry Anderson, "After Kemal," *London Review of Books*, September 11, 2008: 8 [3–12].

21. See the extensive discussion of this object at the following: http://www.karlonline.org/402_5.htm.

22. A striking reverse image of this Turkish-attired puppet is the late Ottoman satirical image of the Europeanized individual, the *kukla* (puppet). See Konuk, *East West Mimesis*, 101. The hybridity of this figure also resembles the "half-Europeanized" Turkish merchant of *One-Way Street*; see below.

23. Scholem, "Walter Benjamin and His Angel," in *Jews and Judaism in Crisis*, 211.

24. Fenves, *The Messianic Reduction*, 263, n. 13.

25. Thanks to Irving Wohlfarth for this suggestion.

26. Martin Buber, "The Spirit of the Orient and Judaism," in *On Judaism*, ed. N. Glatzer (New York: Schocken, 1967), 57 [56–78].

27. Ibid., 68.

28. Ibid., 78.

29. Ibid., 77.

30. See Mufti, "Auerbach in Istanbul," 102–3.

31. Edward Said, *Orientalism* (New York: Vintage, 1979), 259.

32. Edward Said, "Secular Criticism," in *The World, the Text, and the Critic* (Cambridge, Mass.: Harvard University Press, 1983), 6.

33. Ibid.

34. Ibid., 12.

35. Ibid., 16. Said's Columbia colleague David Damrosch understood Auerbach's exile in more historical terms: "Writing his great book in Istanbul, Auerbach both responded to his exile and refused to submit to it. But he was wrong as to the nature of this exile: his problem was not that he was cut off from earthly life like Alcofrybas, Farinata, Quixote, the Proustian narrator, all of whom in varying ways recover this loss through memory, stories, interpretations. Auerbach's exile is the reverse: far more irrevocably wedded to his present age than he would wish to be, he lives in exile from the past, from the worlds of his

beloved texts, which cannot finally provide an Olympian refuge from the dual tyrannies of time and of political pressures." Damrosch, "Auerbach in Exile," *Comparative Literature* 47 (1995): 114 [97–117].

36. Mufti, "Auerbach in Istanbul," 107. See also Mufti, "Critical Secularism: A Reintroduction for Perilous Times," *boundary* 2 31 (2004): 2–3 [1–9].

37. Mufti, "Auerbach in Istanbul," 107.

38. Gil Anidjar, *Semites* (Stanford, Calif.: Stanford University Press, 2008), 48. Thanks to Ananda Abeysekara for calling this passage, and its attendant implications, to my attention.

39. Said, *Orientalism*, 122.

40. A similar but more developed and theoretically rigorous case for the pervasiveness of Christianity is Jean-Luc Nancy, *Dis-Enclosure: The Deconstruction of Christianity*, trans. Bettina Bergo et al. (New York: Fordham University Press, 2008).

41. Aamir Mufti, "Orientalism and the Institution of World Literatures," *Critical Inquiry* 36 (2010): 464 (458–93).

42. Emily Apter, "Saidian Humanism," *boundary 2* 31 (2004): 47 [35–53]. See also W. J. T. Mitchell, "Secular Divination: Edward Said's Humanism," *Critical Inquiry* 31 (2005): 462–71.

43. Emily Apter, "Global *Translatio*: The 'Invention' of Comparative Literature, Istanbul, 1933," in *Debating World Literature*, ed. Christopher Prendergast (London: Verso, 2004), 76–109.

44. Ibid., 82.

45. Ibid., 102.

46. Kader Konuk, "Deutsch-jüdische Philologen im türkischen Exil: Leo Spitzer und Erich Auerbach," in *Erich Auerbach: Geschichte und Aktualität eines europäischen Philologen*, ed. K. Barck and M. Treml (Berlin: Kadmos, 2007), 229 [215–29].

47. Konuk, *East West Mimesis*, 14–16.

48. See Andrea Polaschegg, *Der Andere Orientalismus: Regeln Deutsch-Morgenländischer Imagination im 19.Jahrhundert* (Berlin: Walter de Gruyter, 2005).

Chapter 5

1. Walter Benjamin, "Critique of Violence," *SW* 1:250, *GS* 2:200 [179–203]. Further references appear in the text.

2. Giorgio Agamben, *Homo Sacer: Sovereign Power and Bare Life*, trans. Daniel Heller-Roazen (Stanford, Calif.: Stanford University Press, 1998), 64.

3. Jacques Derrida, "Force of Law: The 'Mystical Foundation of Authority,'" in *Acts of Religion*, ed. Gil Anidjar (New York: Routledge, 2002), 259–60, 298 [228–98]. Judith Butler challenges Derrida's use of Schmitt and the implication that Benjamin's essay approaches fascism: "Critique, Coercion, and Sacred Life in Benjamin's 'Critique of Violence,'" in *Political Theologies: Public Religions in a Post-Secular World*, ed. Hent de Vries and Lawrence E. Sullivan (New York: Fordham University Press, 2006), 206–7, 214–15 [201–19].

4. Agamben, *Homo Sacer*, 64.

5. Beatrice Hanssen, *Critique of Violence: Between Poststructuralism and Critical Theory* (New York: Routledge, 2000), 23.

6. See Benjamin's letter to Martin Buber, in *Briefe* 1:126, ed. Gershom Scholem and Theodor Adorno, vol. 1 (Frankfurt: Suhrkamp, 1966), 126; and the description of the Benjamin-Scholem discussions of the period in Eric Jacobson, *Metaphysics of the Profane: The Political Theology of Walter Benjamin and Gershom Scholem* (New York: Columbia University Press, 2003), 161–72.

7. Hanssen describes it as a kind of "theological foundationalism" (*Critique of Violence*, 23), and Derrida speaks of divine violence as a kind of secret and silent form of divine sovereignty: "Nothing resonates, then, but the name, the pure nomination of the name before the name," ("Force of Law," 293).

8. Hanssen, *Critique of Violence*, 23.

9. Judith Butler makes such a point about the essay's conclusion: "That Benjamin's essay ends so abruptly might be understood as a kind of sudden ending, the very operation of critique on the model of a destruction and upheaval that contravenes teleological time," (Butler, "Critique, Coercion, and Sacred Life," 219).

10. Britt, *Walter Benjamin and the Bible*, 63–64.

11. Immanuel Kant, *Foundations of the Metaphysics of Morals*, trans. Lewis White Black (New York: Macmillan, 1985), 51.

12. See Anson Rabinbach, "Between Enlightenment and Apocalypse: Benjamin, Bloch and Modern German Jewish Messianism," *New German Critique* 34 (1985): 119–21.

13. See, for example, the passage on commentary and translation in *One-Way Street*: "Commentary and translation stand in the same relation to the text as style and mimesis to nature . . . On the tree of the sacred text both are only the eternally rustling leaves; on that of the profane, the seasonally falling fruits" (*SW* 1:449).

14. Baruch A. Levine, *Numbers 1–20*, The Anchor Bible, vol. 4A (New York: Doubleday, 1993), 405; see also 89, 101–4.

15. Momme Brodersen, *Walter Benjamin: A Biography*, trans. Malcolm R. Green and Ingrida Ligers (London: Verso, 1996), 33. I thank Terry Papillon for pointing out the likelihood of Ovid as Benjamin's source. Several editions of Ovid's works were published for *Gymnasium* students. One edition was part of a series of Latin and Greek texts published in the nineteenth and twentieth centuries by Teubner. Another version was *Metamorphoses: Auswahl für den Schulgebrauch mit sachlicher Einleitung, erläuternden Anmerkungen und einem Register der Eigennamen*, ed. J. Meuser and Alfons Egen (Paderborn : Druck und Verlag von Ferdinand Schöningh, 1889).

16. Ovid, *Metamorphoses*, trans. A. D. Melville (Oxford: Oxford University Press, 1986), 126.

17. Ibid., 125, 130.

18. Hermann Bahr, *Die Rotte Korahs* (Berlin: Fischer, 1919). A detailed summary and analysis of the novel appears in John Ward, *Jews in Business and Their Representation 1827–1934* (Frankfurt: Peter Lang, 2010).

19. Walter Benjamin, "Theologische Kritik," *GS* 3:276.

20. Bahr, *Die Rotte Korahs*, 290; Num. 16:5, 6, 11, 16, 40 / 17:5, 26:9–10 and 27:3.

21. Walter Benjamin, letter to Gershom Scholem, July 23, 1920, in *Corr WB* 166. In German: *Briefe*, 1:243. I thank Christian Nilsson for pointing me to this letter.

22. Karl Bernhard Stark, *Niobe und die Niobiden in ihrer literarischen, künstlerischen und mythologischen Bedeutung* (Leipzig, 1863).

23. Butler, "Critique, Coercion, and Sacred Life," 208.

24. Ibid., 209.

25. Ibid., 210.

26. It may be for this reason that Butler's analysis places undue emphasis on the role of personal agency in divine violence: "As a form of ethical address, the commandment is that which which each individual must wrestle without the model of any other" ("Critique, Coercion, and Sacred Life," 212); and "Imagine, if you can, that Apollo and Artemis tell their mother to get a grip and refuse to obey her command" (219).

27. Butler, "Critique, Coercion, and Sacred Life," 214.

28. See Brian Britt, "Romantic Roots of the Debate on the Buber-Rosenzweig Bible," *Prooftexts* 20 (2000): 262–89.

29. Georges Sorel, *Reflections on Violence*, trans. T. E. Hulme and J. Roth (New York: Collier, 1972), 165.

30. Beatrice Hanssen, *Walter Benjamin's Other History: Of Stones, Animals, Human Beings, and Angels* (Berkeley: University of California Press, 1998), 135.

31. Ibid., 132.

32. Ibid., 135–36.

33. The works of Derrida, Heidegger, and the late Wittgenstein are among the most influential sources for this line of thinking. See also J. Hillis Miller, *Speech Acts in Literature* (Stanford, Calif.: Stanford University Press, 2001).

34. William Connolly, *Why I Am Not a Secularist* (Minneapolis: University of Minnesota Press, 1999); Slavoj Žižek, *The Puppet and the Dwarf: The Perverse Core of Christianity* (Cambridge, Mass.: MIT Press, 2003); Asad, *Formations of the Secular*.

35. Derrida, "Force of Law," 287–93.

36. Jacques Derrida, *On Cosmopolitanism and Forgiveness*, trans. Mark Dooley and Michael Hughes (New York: Routledge, 2003), 59. A similar point is made by J. Hillis Miller in "Derrida, Benjamin, the Internet, and the New International," *Parallax* 7 (2001): 6–8.

37. Agamben, *Homo Sacer*, 64–65.

38. Giorgio Agamben, *Means Without End: Notes on Politics*, trans. Vincenzo Binetti and Cesare Casarino (Minneapolis: University of Minnesota Press, 2000), 113.

39. Derrida, *On Cosmopolitanism and Forgiveness*, 55, 57.

40. Ibid., 44. 59.

41. Giorgio Agamben, "The Messiah and the Sovereign," in *Potentialities: Collected Essays in Philosophy*, ed. and trans. D. Heller-Roazen (Stanford, Calif.: Stanford University Press), 163.

42. Ibid., 174.

43. Derrida, "The Force of Law," 228.

Chapter 6

1. Jean Baudrillard, *The Gulf War Did Not Take Place*, trans. Paul Patton (Bloomington: Indiana University Press, 1995).

2. Jean Baudrillard, *Simulations*, trans. Paul Foss et al. (New York: Semiotexte, 1983), 28.

3. Ibid., 135–36.
4. Ibid., 152.
5. Ibid., 27–28.
6. Ibid., 29.
7. Ibid., 151.
8. Walter Benjamin, "On the Mimetic Faculty," *SW* 2:720.
9. Slavoj Žižek, "Welcome to the Desert of the Real," online at http://www.egs.edu/faculty/slavoj-Žižek/articles/welcome-to-the-desert-of-the-real/.
10. Susan Sontag, *Regarding the Pain of Others* (New York: Farrar, Straus, and Giroux, 1983), 99.
11. Ibid., 106–7.
12. Ibid., 109–10.
13. Ibid., 102–3. Compare Megan Boler on the problem of sympathy in *Feeling Power: Emotions and Education* (New York: Routledge, 1999), 159–61. Thanks to Jane Lehr for this observation.
14. Judith Butler, *Frames of War: When Is Life Grievable?* (London: Verso, 2009), 63–100.
15. See Asad, *Formations of the Secular*, 80–81.
16. "Alles Mimetische der Sprache ist vielmehr eine fundierte Intention, die überhaupt nur an etwas Fremdem, eben dem Semiotischen, Mitteilenden der Sprache als ihrem Fundus in Erscheinung treten kann. So ist der buchstäbliche Text der Schrift der Fundus, in dem einzig und allein sich das Vexierbild formen kann" (*SW* 2:697; *GS* 2:1, 208–9).
17. ". . . das vollkommenste Archiv unsinnlicher Ähnlichkeit . . . in dem sich die Dinge nicht mehr direct wie früher in dem Geist des Sehers oder Priesters sondern in ihren Essenzen, flüchtigsten und feinsten Substanzen, ja Aromen begegnen und zu einander in Beziehung treten" (*SW* 2:697–98; *GS* 2:209).
18. Michael Taussig, *Mimesis and Alterity: A Particular History of the Senses* (New York: Routledge, 1993), 251.
19. See Samuel Weber, "Exception to Decision: Walter Benjmain and Carl Schmitt," *Diacritics* 22 (Autumn–Winter 1992): 18 [5–18]; and Brian Britt, "The Schmittian Messiah in Agamben's *The Time That Remains,*" *Critical Inquiry* 36 (2010): 277 [262–87].
20. See Luce Irigaray, *This Sex Which Is Not One*, trans. Catherine Porter (Ithaca, N.Y.: Cornell University Press, 1985); and Judith Butler, *Excitable Speech: A Politics of the Performative* (New York: Routledge, 1997).
21. Roland Barthes, *Camera Lucida*, trans. Richard Howard (London: Vintage, 2000), 26. Barthes goes on to designate *studium* as the domain of liking, civility, and education, while *punctum* "is that accident which pricks me (but also bruises me, is poignant to me)" (27–28).
22. Ibid., 95.
23. Ibid., 96.
24. Ibid., 116–19.
25. Jessica Nitsche, *Walter Benjamins Gebrauch der Fotografie* (Berlin: Kulturvorlag Kadmos), 163–70.
26. The question raises the larger issue of how aura relates to religion. For an interesting contemporary engagement with the question, see S. Brent Plate, *Walter Benjamin, Religion, and Aesthetics* (New York: Routledge, 2005).

27. The echo motif appears in Benjamin's "On the Concept of History" ("Begriff der Geschichte"): "Streift denn nicht uns selber ein Hauch der Luft, die um die Frueheren gewesen its? Ist nicht in Stimmen, denen wir under Ohr schenken, ein Echo non nun verstummten?" (*GS* 1:693).

28. Sigrid Weigel, *Die Kreatur, das Heilige, die Bilder* (Frankfurt: S. Fischer, 2008), 36 (English translation: *Walter Benjamin: Images, the Creaturely, and the Holy,* trans. Chadwick T. Smith [Stanford, Calif.: Stanford University Press, 2013]).

29. Weigel, *Die Kreatur*, 49.

30. Sigrid Weigel, "Uneinholbare Maßstäbe," in *Die Kreatur*, 56.

31. The basis for my reflections is the juxtaposition of Freud's Wolf-man case and Virginia Woolf in Maud Ellmann, *The Nets of Modernism: Henry James, Virginia Woolf, James Joyce, and Sigmund Freud* (Cambridge: Cambridge University Press, 2010), 11ff.

32. Virginia Woolf, *Moments of Being*, ed. Jeanne Schulkind (San Diego: Harcourt, 1985), 69. Compare Benjamin's description of the creature as a concave mirror that displays and distorts the moral world of the baroque (*GS* 1:270).

33. It is remarkable that later references to Duckworth in Woolf's text make little reference to this incident.

34. Sigmund Freud, 'From the History of an Infantile Neurosis," in *The Wolf-Man by the Wolf-Man: The Double Story of Freud's Most Famous Case,* ed. Muriel Gardiner (New York: Basic Books, 1971), 204 [153–262]. German edition: Freud, "Aus der Geschichte einer infantilen Neurose," in *Gesammelte Werke* 12 (Frankfurt: S. Fischer, 1966), 27–157; Peter Brooks, "Fictions of the Wolfman: Freud and Narrative," *Diacritics* 9 (1979): 71–81; Marcus Klammer, "Visual Images in Freud's Concept of Paranoia," paper presented at Schreber Centenary Conference, April 2011, Pirna, Germany.

35. In a 1940 letter to Gretel Adorno (*GS* 1:1226), Benjamin directs her to Thesis 17 of "On the Concept of History," which contrasts the empty time of historicism to the shock and messianic stoppage of time available to historical materialism, as a key to his thinking about progress and history.

36. Horst Bredekamp, *Theorie des Bildakts* (Frankfurt: Suhrkamp, 2010). Like most speech act theory, Bredekamp's theory of "picture acts" notices the religious associations and roots of many image-making traditions, especially when they are truly efficacious in some way, but he neglects to theorize or discuss them at length.

37. Here I differ from Josef Fürnkäs, who distinguishes sharply between the aura of the photography and Baudelaire essays; see his "Aura" in *Benjamins Begriffe,* vol. 1, 141–42 [95–146].

38. Eli Friedlander, *Walter Benjamin: A Philosophical Portrait* (Cambridge, Mass.: Harvard University Press, 2012), 89.

39. Jean-Luc Nancy, *The Ground of the Image*, trans. Jeff Fort (New York: Fordham University Press, 2005), 49; see also Didi-Huberman, *Confronting Images.*

40. Jean-Luc Nancy, *The Inoperative Community*, trans. Peter Connor, et al. (Minneapolis: University of Minnesota Press, 1991).

41. Nancy, *The Ground of the Image*, 1.

42. Slavoj Žižek, *First as Tragedy, Then as Farce* (London: Verso, 2009), 140.

43. See Lutz Koepnick, *Walter Benjamin and the Aesthetics of Power* (Lincoln: University of Nebraska Press, 1999), especially 5–19 and 213–37.

44. Georges Didi-Huberman, *Images in Spite of All: Four Photographs from Auschwitz,* trans. Shane B. Lillis (Chicago: University of Chicago Press, 2012), 120.

45. Ibid., 171.

Chapter 7

1. Scholem, *Walter Benjamin: The Story of a Friendship*, 202.

2. The stakes for interpreting Goethe, widely considered the most important German writer of any period, were high. See W. Daniel Wilson, "Goethe and the Nazis," *Times Literary Supplement,* March 14, 2014, 14–15.

3. Erdmut Wizisla, "Plaquette für Freunde: Widmungen für die ersten Leser," in *Walter Benjamins Deutsche Menschen*, ed. Barbara Hahn and E. Wizisla (Göttingen: Wallstein, 2008), 61 [45–67].

4. This is something on which Scholem and Adorno agree. See Adorno's "Nachwort" in *Noten zur Literatur* (Frankfurt: Suhrkamp, 2003), where he describes the motto of the book as "oppositionell" (686), a defense of the values destroyed by Nazis (687), and the book as "Denkmal" of this lost world that shows how far it is ("lehrt die Distanz von ihnen," 692) [686–92]. Scholem, *Walter Benjamin: The Story of a Friendship*, 203. Recent versions of this view can be found in Axel Schmitt, "Schiffbruch," *literaturkritik.de* 6 (June 2004), online at http://www.literaturkritik.de/public/rezension/php?rez_id=7151; and Albrecht Schöne, "'Diese nach jüdischem Vorbild erbaute Arche': Walter Benjamins *Deutsche Menschen,*" in *Juden in der deutschen Literatur: Ein deutsch-israelisches Symposion*, ed. S. Moses and A. Schöne (Frankfurt: Suhrkamp, 1986), 350–65.

5. "Ich könnte mir denken, daß Sie mit mir der Meinung sind, dies sei keine ansprechende Zahl. Zu dieser Überlegung würde sich dann meine Wahrnehmung fügen, daß der Brief von Schlegel an Schleiermacher sowohl seinem negativen Gehalt wie seinem minderen Gewicht nach keine ganz glückliche Figur macht" (*Gesammelte Briefe* 5:377). Compare Michael Diers, "Einbandlektüre, fortgesetzt. Zur politischen Physiognomie der Briefanthologie," in *Walter Benjamins "Deutsche Menschen,"* ed. Hahn and Wizisla, 24–29, which makes the best argument for the political aims of the book, even down to lettering, title, and design. Brodersen goes on to note that the letter was added back to the posthumous 1962 edition (in the middle, after Hölderlin's letter) with an afterword by Adorno, noting that it was left out of a later edition and added as an "Anhang," in the *Gesammelte Schriften* (Walter Benjamin, *Deutsche Menschen,* ed. Momme Brodersen [Frankfurt: Suhrkamp, 2008], 313).

6. Adorno to Siegfried Unseld, January 11, 1962, in *"So müßte ich ein Engel und kein Autor sein": Adorno und seine Frankfurter Verleger,* ed. Wolfgang Schopf (Frankfurt: Suhrkamp, 2003), 399. Unseld agreed with Adorno wholeheartedly, noting that it was a "very beautiful letter" and that Benjamin's commentary "develops a good image" (Unseld to Adorno, January 12, 1962, 401).

7. See the first published edition: Walter Benjamin, *Deutsche Menschen* (Lucerne: Vita Nova, 1936), 112.

8. Walter Benjamin, *Deutsche Menschen*, ed. Brodersen, 123–24.

9. See Benjamin Sax, "Walter Benjamin's Karl Kraus: Negation, Quotation, and Jewish Identity," *Shofar* 32, no. 3 (2014): 1–29.

10. Walter Benjamin, "Commentary on Poems by Brecht," in *SW* 4:215 [215–50]; and Benjamin, *One-Way Street*, in *SW* 3:449 [443–88]; Harold Bloom, *The Anxiety of Influence: A Theory of Poetry* (London: Oxford University Press, 1973).

11. See, for example, Manfred Voigts, "'Die Mater der Gerechtigkeit': Zur Kritik des Zitat-Begriffes bei Walter Benjamin," in *Antike und Moderne: Zu Walter Benjamins "Passagen,"* ed. Norbert W. Bolz and R. Faber (Würzburg: Könighausen & Neuman, 1986), 97–115; and Friedlander, *Walter Benjamin*.

12. "Georg Lukacs made the far-sighted observation that the German bourgeoisie had not yet wrested its first opponent—feudalism—to the ground by the time its last opponent—the proletariat—already stood before it" (*SW* 3:212, in introduction to Metternich letter).

13. See, for example, the introduction to the letter by Forster (*SW* 3:173), the introduction to the Clodius letter (*SW* 3:188), and the introduction to Liebig (*SW* 3:195–96).

14. Scholem, *Walter Benjamin: The Story of a Friendship*, 203.

15. Wizisla, "Plaquette für Freunde," 55.

16. Ibid., 52.

17. Ibid., 61.

18. Letter from Auerbach to Benjamin, January 28, 1937, in Karlheinz Barck, "5 Briefe Erich Auerbachs an Walter Benjamin in Paris," *Zeitschrift für Germanistik* 6 (1988): 691, 694 (688–94), cited in Wizisla, "Plaquette für Freunde," 64.

19. Letter from Scholem to Benjamin of March 1, 1937, in *The Correspondence of Walter Benjamin and Gershom Scholem*, 192, cited in Wizisla, "Plaquette für Freunde," 64.

20. Theodor Adorno, *Noten zur Literatur* (Suhrkamp, 2003), 687, 692 [686–92].

21. See Schmitt, "Schiffbruch."

22. Note also that "Detlev" and "Deutsch" are etymologically related to an Indo-European root meaning "people" (thanks to Stephen Britt for this observation.) The title *Deutsche Menschen*, along with the pseudonym "Detlev," thus emphasizes the humanity, not the particular ethnic identity, of the "Germans."

23. Detlev Schöttker, *Konstruktiver Fragmentarismus* (Frankfurt: Suhrkamp, 1999), 98 (Ilit Ferber made a similar comment [personal communication, January 2012]). Compare Jacques Derrida, *Fichus: Frankfurter Rede*, trans. F. Lorenzer (Vienna: Passagen, 2003), where Derrida plays with the "D" of his dream, described in a letter to Gretel Adorno (signed Detlef), about a scarf in the shape of this letter (29–31).

24. Friedlander, *Walter Benjamin*, 5, 260, n. 23.

25. Friedlander, *Walter Benjamin*, 260, n. 23; a discussion of the idea as monad appears in the *Trauerspiel* study: *GS* 1:228.

26. "Nur aus dem Interesse, die Sammlung die vielleicht in Deutschland einigen Nutzen stiften könnte, zu tarnen, zu erklären ist" (*Gesammelte Briefe* 5:402).

27. "Der Titel 'Deutsche Menschen' war seinerzeit von Benjamin gewählt worden aus einem politischen Grund, nämlich um zu ermöglichen, daß das Briefbuch nach Deutschland importiert wurde, um dort oppositionell zu wirken, also al seine Art Tarnung, keineswegs aus Profitinteresse," September 20, 1965, Adorno Archive Document (TWAA, Br 1534/6).

28. Adorno, *Noten zur Literatur,* 686.

29. "Es ist der Jugendstil . . . in dem das alte Bürgertum das Vorgefühl der eignen Schwäche tarnt, indem es kosmisch in alle Sphären schwärmt und zukunftstrunken die 'Jugend' als Beschwörungswort mißbraucht" (*GS* 3:394).

30. Michael Diers, "Einbandlektüre, fortgesetzt: Zur politischen Physiognomie der Briefanthologie," in Hahn and Wizisla, *Deutsche Menschen*, 24–29 [23–44].

31. Peter Villwock, "Walter Benjamins Brief-Projekt," *Auftrrag des Instituts für Textkritik* 13 (2012): 152 [151–62]. Thanks to Ursula Marx for showing me this reference.

32. Ibid., 158.

33. Ibid., 158, 161–62.

34. *Encyclopedia Judaica: Das Judentum in Geschichte und Gegenwart*, vol. 5, 1930, cols. 1022–1034.

35. Letter of Benjamin to Scholem, February 20, 1939, *Briefe* 2:804.

36. "Der halachischen, seine Virtuosität in der assoziativen Verbindung zu der Exegetik und sienen Symbolreichtum zur allegorischen Bibelauslegung in Beziehung zu setzen" (*GS* 2:810).

37. While the exact wording of this passage cannot be definitively assigned to Benjamin, the text clearly echoes Benjamin's ideas and interests. See Ubaldo Fadini, "Presentazione di un Benjamin 'Falsificato," *L'Ombra d'Argo* 1 (1983): 1 [1–2].

38. Karl Kraus, "der großartigste Durchbruch der halachischen Schriftums mitten durch das Massiv der deutschen Sprache," *GS* 2:624.

39. "Schrankenlose Betonung der Subjektivität; kritische Haltung gegen die professorale Wissenschaft; scharfe Belichtung aktueller Probleme" (*GS* 2:811).

40. Benjamin, *Deutsche Menschen*, ed. Brodersen, 136, 123.

41. Ibid., 120.

42. Sabine Schiller-Lerg, *Walter Benjamin und der Rundfunk: Programmarbeit zwischen Theorie und Praxis* (Munich: K.G. Saur, 1984), 233. See her discussion of Benjamin's reflection on time and technology (242).

43. See also the 1926 encyclopedia article on Goethe in *GS* 2:705–39, which, though it doesn't quote this letter, addresses class issues (717–18). The article was intended for a Soviet encyclopedia.

44. Letter from Adorno to Benjamin, November 7, 1936, quoted in *GS* 4:949.

Conclusion

1. Hannah Arendt, "Walter Benjamin: 1892–1940," in Benjamin, *Illuminations,* ed. Hannah Arendt, trans. Harry Zohn (New York: Schocken, 1968), 48 [1–51]; Scholem, *Walter Benjamin: The Story of a Friendship*, 207; Adorno, letter to Benjamin, November 10, 1938, in *SW* 4: 99–105.

2. Jürgen Habermas, "Walter Benjamin: Consciousness-Raising or Rescuing Critique," in *On Walter Benjamin: Critical Essays and Reflections*, ed. Gary Smith (Cambridge, Mass.: MIT Press,1988), 108 [90–128].

3. Villwock, "Walter Benjamins Briefe-Projekt," 154; Momme Brodersen, "Die Entstehung der *Deutsche Menschen,*" in *Walter Benjamins "Deutsche Menschen,"* 22 [9–22].

4. Such a broad, dynamic model of tradition exceeds Alasdair MacIntyre's notion of tradition as "historically extended, socially embodied argument" (MacIntyre, *After Virtue*, 222).

5. See Britt, *Biblical Curses and the Displacement of Tradition*, 191–98.

6. John McCole, *Walter Benjamin and the Antinomies of Tradition* (Ithaca, N.Y.: Cornell University Press, 1993).

7. Note Benjamin's defense of his work as philological to Adorno, letter to Adorno December 9, 1938 (*SW* 4:107–8 [105–12]).

8. See Erdmut Wizisla, "Revolution," in *Benjamins Begriffe*, vol. 2 (Frankfurt: Suhrkamp, 2000), 676–77 [665–94].

INDEX